CW00455408

THE ROYAL WELSH COOKBOOK

Thanks to everyone who contributed recipes to this cookbook.

Edited by Gilli Davies, planned by Dorcas Cresswell and published by Graffeg for the Friends of The Royal Welsh Regimental Museum.

The Royal Welsh Cookbook.
Published by Graffeg 2020 on behalf of the Friends of The Royal Welsh Regimental Museum. Registered Charity No: 1065098 The Royal Welsh Regimental Museum, The Watton, Brecon, Powys, LD3 7ED

Edited by Gilli Davies copyright © 2020. Designed and produced by Graffeg Limited copyright © 2020.

Graffeg Limited, 24 Stradey Park Business Centre, Mwrwg Road, Llangennech, Llanelli, Carmarthenshire, SA14 8YP, Wales, UK. Tel 01554 824000. www.graffeg.com.

Gilli Davies is hereby identified as the author of this work in accordance with section 77 of the Copyrights, Designs and Patents Act 1988.

A CIP Catalogue record for this book is available from the British Library.

All rights reserved. No part of this publication may be reproduced, stored in a retrieval system or transmitted, in any form or by any means, electronic, mechanical, photocopying, recording or otherwise, without the prior permission of the publishers.

Cover photo: Eton Mess © Huw Jones Photography.

ISBN 9781912654932

1 2 3 4 5 6 7 8 9

CONTENTS

Welcome	4
Foreword	5

SOUPS, STARTERS, SMALL MEALS & SAUCES   7

Welsh Lamb Cawl	8
Crab or Lobster Bisque	9
Leek and Sweet Potato Soup	10
Chicken Liver Paté	11
Cauliflower Rice	12
Orange Salad with Walnuts	13
Pear and Goats' Cheese Salad with Apple Vinaigrette	14
Squid and Prawn Salad	15
Granny Crewe-Reed's Game Paté	16
Marinated Kipper Fillets	17
Cheese and Potato Pie	18
Earth and Sea	19
Homemade Currywurst Sauce	20
Recipe for Onion Sauce	21
The Beano	22
Cheese Soufflé	23
Salmon Fishcakes	24
Devilled Chicken	25
Ham with Creamy Mushroom Sauce	26
Sausage Rolls	27

MAINS   29

Salmon Fillets with Chilli Sauce	30
One-Pot Mussels with Sausage, Celery and Scrumpy	31
Haddock with Tomatoes and Chives	32
Coronation Chicken	33
Kedgeree	34
Braised Lamb	36
Chicken and Mango Salad	37
Bobotie	38
Roast Glazed Gammon	39
BBQ Chicken	40
Pork Fillet with Orange Sauce	41
Hungarian Goulash	42
Homestyle Chicken Curry	43
Burgundian Beef Stew	44
Chicken and Mushroom Dairy-Free Pasta	45
Pheasant Breasts in Port	46
Pork Fillet with Apples, Rosemary and Cider	47
Quick Chicken and Leek Crumble	48
Dai 88's Texan BBQ Beans	49
Normandy Chicken	50

PUDDINGS, BAKING & DRINKS   53

Eton Mess	54
Lemon Soufflé Custard	55
Passion Fruit Mousse with Mango Coulis	56
American-Style Cheesecake	57
Christmas Fruit Salad	58
Danish Lemon Mousse	59
Black Forest Gateau Meringue	60
Rhubarb Miracle Pudding	61
Banana Bread	62
Ginger Biscuits	63
Cheat's Lemonade Scones	64
Tiffin	65
Flapjacks	66
Auntie Bill's Chocolate Cake	67
Wartime Beetroot Red Velvet Cake	68
A Good Small Loaf	70
A Rum Punch from Belize	72
A Strawberry Daiquiri from Berlin	73
A Classic White Lady	74
Chabeel	75
Orange Liqueur	76
Blackberry Brandy	77

WELCOME

As we all snuggled down into lockdown in the Spring of 2020, I decided to look for ways to continue our fundraising for the Museum. Our Friends Committee has always been active and successful in the past and I thought that we could ask colleagues from the Welsh regiments to supply recipes to contribute to this cookbook.

It has been an enjoyable task, with contributions coming from former members of the regiments and also from our far-flung friends in South Africa where, in 2019, we celebrated the 140th anniversary of the Anglo-Zulu wars, known to most people in the UK for the epic battle at Isandlwana and the defence of Rorke's Drift.

If it would interest you to join the Society of Friends of the Museum, you would:

- Receive regular newsletters
- Enjoy free entry to the museum at Brecon
- Be able to participate in our programme of talks, walks and social events
- Have the opportunity to volunteer to work with other Friends
- Benefit from a discount on selected items in the shop.

Please contact me:
Dorcas Cresswell
Phone: 01497 847262 or email: dorcascresswell@gmail.com

The Friends of the Royal Welsh Regimental Museum, Registered Charity No: 1065098. Address: The Royal Welsh Regimental Museum, The Watton, Brecon, Powys, LD3 7ED. www.royalwelsh.org.uk.

FOREWORD

Welcome to the Regimental cookbook. I hope you will enjoy flicking through the many recipes and trying some out for yourself. They are a really eclectic mix which represent our long and proud history of serving and living around the world. They have been submitted by people from across the Regimental family, in its broadest sense, and I am most grateful for all the contributions.

One of the places that we reminisce and share our stories with each other is around the dining table, so it is fitting that the proceeds from this excellent book with all its delicious recipes will go towards the new Regimental museum in Brecon, a bold and imaginative initiative that will help tell the stories of the whole Regiment to the hundreds of thousands of visitors to Mid Wales.

Thank you also to the two people who have brought this book to life: to Dorcas Cresswell for conceiving the idea, attracting such a rich variety of entries and taking the project through to completion, and to Gilli Davies, our editor, for lending us her experience and expertise as a published cookery writer.

James Swift
Colonel of the Regiment

SOUPS, STARTERS, SMALL MEALS & SAUCES

WELSH LAMB CAWL

By Tim Van Rees

Tim is the Vice Chair of the Museum Trustees.
This is a translation of a recipe that was originally in Welsh.

Ingredients

1kg shoulder or neck of Welsh lamb (on the bone)

1 onion, peeled and finely chopped

4 potatoes, peeled and finely chopped

5 carrots, peeled and finely chopped

1 small swede, peeled and finely chopped

1 or 2 parsnips, peeled and finely chopped

1 celery stick, chopped

2 tomatoes, peeled and halved

2 bay leaves

1 teaspoon paprika

1 teaspoon thyme or mixed herbs

1 tablespoon flour

2 leeks, sliced

2 tablespoons chopped parsley

salt to taste

Serves 6

❶ Place the lamb in a large saucepan, cover with 2 litres of water and bring to the boil. Turn down the heat and simmer for 2-3 hours. Leave to cool overnight. The next day, remove any fat on the surface.

❷ Cut the meat off the bone and return it to the stock, discarding the bone.

❸ Add the vegetables, herbs, paprika and salt and simmer. Add more water if needed.

❹ When the vegetables are tender, mix the flour with water to create a thin paste and add this to the cawl to thicken it.

❺ Finally, add the leeks and parsley and simmer for a few minutes.

❻ Serve the cawl with plenty of cheese and fresh bread.

This cawl will be even tastier if reheated the next day.

CRAB OR LOBSTER BISQUE

By Jim Downs (2/Lt 1957-59)

'In 1959 I found myself on the Mess committee, maybe it was with Major Thornton in Benghazi. I didn't last long because I was being too extravagant. Don't forget this is the 1950s – the mess steward had come by a turtle and we tried hopelessly to make turtle soup, which was ghastly! I have much more confidence in this one, with acknowledgements to Richard Shepherd, who was head chef of Langan's Brasserie in the early 1980s.'

Ingredients

500-900g crab or lobster with fingers removed (they are the poisonous bits inside)

450g mixed chopped onion, leek, carrot and celery

50g butter

small bunch mixed fresh herbs

1 can chopped tomatoes

1 teaspoon tomato purée

1 litre fish stock or water and 2 stock cubes

50g rice

1 good glass of white wine

1 large night cap of brandy

Garnish

chopped parsley

double cream

tiny amount of brandy

Serves 4-6

1 Sweat the vegetables in the butter in a large saucepan.

2 Add the carcasses, tomato, all liquids, rice and herbs and simmer for an hour or two.

3 Allow to cool, then remove all the carcass bits and place them in a thick-bottomed pan without any liquid. (Ideally you should now pulverise the carcase bits to extract all the flavour). Heat the shells for a minute or two then add a maximum half a pint of water, bring to the boil and simmer for 10 minutes to extract all flavour.

4 Using a sieve, return this stock to the vegetables and bring the soup to the boil.

5 Finally, liquidise the contents of the saucepan, check seasoning and serve in individual bowls garnished with the parsley, a swirl of cream and a drop of brandy.

LEEK AND SWEET POTATO SOUP

By Lt Col David A Williams

'I was very keen to offer suggestions to the wonderful idea to produce a Regimental cookbook during this period of lockdown and this recipe is my own for a truly hearty starter, particularly in the winter, of leek and sweet potato soup.'

Ingredients

450g Welsh leeks, trimmed, washed and diced

450g sweet potatoes, peeled and cut into ½ inch cubes

25g butter

1 tablespoon oil

2-3 pints vegetable stock

4 tablespoons double cream

2 measures Penderyn whisky (optional)

salt and pepper

Serves 4

❶ In a large pan sweat the leeks in butter and oil over a low heat until softened and starting to caramelise.

❷ Add the stock (the exact amount will depend on your preference of consistency for your soup) and diced sweet potato.

❸ Simmer until the potato cubes are softened, about 20 minutes, and then blend the entire mixture with a stick mixer or in a food liquidiser.

❹ Return to the heat and season to taste. A few measures of Penderyn or your favourite whisky can be added as a special touch for a really warming soup in the winter months.

❺ Serve with a tablespoon of double cream in each bowl to finish off.

CHICKEN LIVER PATÉ

By Peter Kerruish

Peter is a former Commanding Officer of 1RRW.

Ingredients

225g chicken livers

225g butter

2 tablespoons brandy

1 heaped teaspoon wholegrain mustard

½ teaspoon powdered mace

¼ teaspoon dried thyme or chopped thyme

2 cloves of garlic, crushed

salt and freshly milled black pepper

Serves 4-6

1 Melt the butter in a heavy frying pan.

2 Cook the chicken livers over a medium heat for 5 minutes, stirring well to cook through.

3 Pour them into a blender and add the remaining ingredients.

4 Blend until you have a smooth purée.

5 Pour into an earthenware pot and chill until needed or freeze in individual containers.

CAULIFLOWER RICE

By Sue Bromhead

'It's actually a salad but you don't think it is! It's really delicious. The rice bit in the title is because it looks like that, or rather couscous!'

Ingredients

½ cauliflower

2 tablespoons maple syrup

1-2 teaspoons curry powder

1 tablespoon white wine vinegar

pistachios and almonds, roughly chopped

fresh mint and coriander, chopped

Serves 4-6

❶ Chop the cauliflower into florets and then 'blitz' in a food processor or liquidiser to bread crumb size pieces but not liquid.

❷ Warm the maple syrup, vinegar and curry powder and stir until it dissolves.

❸ Pour this sauce over the cauliflower.

❹ Scatter over the nuts and herbs for garnish.

ORANGE SALAD WITH WALNUTS

By Dorcas Cresswell

Ingredients

3 oranges

½ iceberg lettuce

3 spring onions

75g chopped or halved walnuts

Dressing

4 tablespoons walnut oil

1 ½ tablespoons raspberry vinegar

1 teaspoon cream

salt and pepper

Serves 4

❶ Peel the oranges and cut into thin slices.

❷ Chop the iceberg lettuce, put the oranges neatly on top and sprinkle with chopped spring onions and walnuts.

❸ Thoroughly shake all ingredients for the dressing together and add to the salad just before serving.

PEAR AND GOATS' CHEESE SALAD WITH APPLE VINAIGRETTE

By Dan Clayton Jones

Dan served as the Intelligence Officer and as a Company Commander with 3rd Bn RRW and honed his cookery skills in the galley while sailing round the Greek Islands every year for a fifteen-year period!

Ingredients

1 fresh Williams or Bartlett pear

100g fresh frisée, lollo rosso, lettuce or watercress

55g sheep or goats' cheese

40g seedless red grapes

20g walnuts, toasted and chopped

Dressing

1 apple, peeled, cored and quartered

120ml white wine vinegar

2 tablespoons honey

½ teaspoon salt

pinch of white pepper

60ml walnut oil

Serves 4

❶ First prepare the dressing:
In a pan, simmer the apple and vinegar until they are reduced by half (about 10 minutes). Transfer to a blender and blend with the honey, salt and pepper until smooth, then slowly add the oil and blend until well mixed in.

❷ For the salad:
Cut the unpeeled pear into wedges.

❸ Toss the lettuce with the vinaigrette.

❹ Arrange the lettuce on 4 plates, placing the pear slices on the side.

❺ Sprinkle with some vinaigrette and then add the cheese, grapes and walnuts.

❻ Optional: Sprinkle the cheese with brown sugar and brown it with a kitchen torch until it caramelises

SQUID AND PRAWN SALAD

By Dorcas Cresswell

Ingredients

Marinade

2 tablespoons grapeseed oil

2 tablespoons freshly squeezed lemon juice

2-3 cloves garlic, crushed

salt and pepper

Squid/prawns mixture

200g squid, fresh or frozen

200g prawns, peeled

25g parsley, finely chopped

Serves 4

1 Mix all the ingredients for the marinade.

2 Slice the squid into neat rings. Do not slice the arms, but keep them whole. If the squid were frozen, it is easier to slice them whilst still half frozen.

3 Bring a saucepan of water to the boil. Add the squid rings and arms, then bring back to the boil (about 2 minutes).

4 Drain the sliced squid, and add it immediately to the marinade. Also add the prawns to the marinade, and leave to marinate for anything between 1 and 24 hours.

5 Just before serving check for seasoning, and add the finely chopped parsley.

6 Can be served on a bed of radicchio lettuce with wedges of fresh lemon and bread.

GRANNY CREWE-REED'S GAME PATÉ

By Granny Crewe-Reed

Ingredients

Liver and heart of 2 or more game birds

40g butter

1 small onion

1 rasher streaky bacon

1 tablespoon chopped parsley

1 tablespoon of sherry

salt and pepper

Serves 4-6

1 Chop the livers and hearts, the onion and the bacon.

2 Heat a little of the butter and add the bacon and onion. Cook until the onion is soft.

3 Add the chopped livers and hearts. Stir well.

4 Add the parsley and simmer for about 5 minutes. Season.

5 Put into a liquidiser and add the sherry.

6 Melt the remaining butter and stir in.

MARINATED KIPPER FILLETS

By Zara Elliott

This delicious recipe is from Zara Elliott, whose husband was Colonel Blethyn Elliott of the South Wales Borderers. It needs to be prepared a day in advance.

Ingredients

8 kipper fillets, skinned

1 small onion, peeled and sliced into thin rings

1 bay leaf

Marinade

1 teaspoon caster sugar

1 teaspoon prepared mustard

3 tablespoons white wine vinegar

4 tablespoons olive oil

salt and pepper

Garnish

lemon slices

watercress/lettuce

Serves 8

❶ Arrange the kipper fillets in the bottom of a dish and cover with onion rings and a bay leaf.

❷ Mix the ingredients for the marinade and pour over the fillets.

❸ Cover the dish and leave in a cool place for 24 hours.

❹ Next day, drain the fillets and arrange on a shallow dish.

❺ Garnish with lemon slices and watercress or lettuce.

❻ Serve with brown bread and butter.

CHEESE AND POTATO PIE

By Trevor Woodyatt

Ingredients

1kg potatoes

500g strong cheese, grated

3 hard-boiled eggs

½ teaspoon English mustard

butter and/or milk for mashing potatoes

salt and pepper

4 tomatoes, sliced

Serves 4-6

❶ Peel, boil and mash the potatoes with butter and/or milk.

❷ Add ¾ of the grated cheese.

❸ Add the mustard, salt and pepper to taste.

❹ Slice the eggs in half and place evenly at the bottom of a serving dish.

❺ Cover with the mashed potatoes.

❻ Arrange the tomato slices around the edge of the dish.

❼ Scatter the remaining grated cheese over the top.

❽ Pop under the grill until golden brown.

❾ Serve with vegetables.

EARTH AND SEA

By Carole Greenhalgh

'This was given to me in Osnabrück, Germany, in the early 1970s by my neighbour Vicky Hirsch.'

Ingredients

5/6 potatoes, boiled, peeled and sliced

2 onions, peeled and sliced

4/5 tomatoes, peeled

1 packet of frozen prawns, defrosted

150g mushrooms, sliced (optional)

pinch of chilli paste

salt and pepper

1 packet frozen sweetcorn

50g sliced cheese

Serves 4

❶ Preheat oven to 180°C.

❷ Line a greased casserole dish with sliced potatoes.

❸ Fry the onions until golden brown, add peeled tomatoes, prawns, mushrooms, chilli paste, salt and pepper and cook for a few minutes.

❹ Boil the sweetcorn in a little water. Using the same water, add a knob of butter and liquidize it all.

❺ Pour the prawn mixture over the sliced potatoes, then the corn mix.

❻ Cover with slices of cheese and put in a preheated oven until all the cheese melts and browns slightly.

HOMEMADE CURRYWURST SAUCE

By David Roberts

'I got this recipe from a lady who ran a small bar in Berlin. You have it over bratwurst sausages with a dusting of curry powder. Anyone who has served in Germany would have had one of these.'

Ingredients

1 cup tomato sauce

¼ teaspoon baking powder

4-5 teaspoons milk curry powder

2 teaspoons onion powder

pinch cayenne pepper

2 teaspoons Worcestershire sauce

4 tablespoons beef broth (Oxo cube)

2 or more tablespoons of water

Serves 4-6

❶ Put the tomato sauce into a small pan on a medium heat and warm for a few minutes.

❷ Add the baking powder and stir while it foams then add the remaining ingredients.

❸ Simmer for 5-10 minutes.

RECIPE FOR ONION SAUCE

By Sir Norman Lloyd-Edwards

'This sauce makes a very useful addition to spaghetti bolognese and other pasta dishes which may need some extra sauce. It keeps well in the fridge and can be reheated for other meals.'

Ingredients

drizzle of vegetable oil

1 medium large onion, peeled and chopped

2 cloves of garlic, peeled and chopped

some herbs

½ red or green pepper, deseeded and chopped

3 tablespoons pasta tomato sauce

Serves 2-4

❶ Put a drizzle of vegetable oil into a microwaveable dish and add the onion, garlic and herbs. Cover and microwave for 5 minutes.

❷ Add the pepper and cook for a further 3 minutes then add the pasta sauce and cook for another 3 minutes.

THE BEANO

By Maj Robert Ross RWF

'This is the ideal recipe for the gentleman who has been left to prepare his own dinner – but it is not for those with delicate constitutions because arteries may well become clogged!'

Ingredients

1-2 slices of white bread (depending on how hungry you are)

butter

1 tin baked beans

6 or more rashers of bacon

a handful of grated cheese

black pepper

French mustard

Serves 1

1 Grill the bacon until crisp.

2 Lightly toast the bread and lightly butter.

3 Heat the beans and pour over the buttered toast.

4 Place the bacon rashers on the beans.

5 Completely cover the beans, bacon and toasted bread in grated cheese.

6 Add black pepper to taste.

7 Place under the grill until the cheese is bubbling and turning brown.

8 **Note:** From experience if you leave corners of toasted bread peeking out while grilling there is a risk of it burning. To prevent this make sure that all the toast is well covered with cheese. This does tend to result in melted cheese accumulating in the pan. However, when scraped out it has become to be considered, by some, to be the best bit of the dish. (You will also appreciate now why this is best indulged in when the memsahib is absent).

9 Serve with mustard on the side.

10 Complement with light ale or red wine.

Heaven on a plate!

CHEESE SOUFFLÉ

By Dorcas Cresswell

Ingredients

40g butter

1 tablespoon dry white breadcrumbs

30g flour

½ teaspoon English mustard

pinch of cayenne pepper

250ml milk

85g strong Cheddar or Gruyère cheese, grated

4 eggs, separated

salt and pepper

Serves 2

❶ Melt a small knob of butter and brush out a 15cm souffle dish. Dust lightly with breadcrumbs.

❷ Melt the rest of the butter in a saucepan and stir in the flour, mustard and cayenne pepper. Cook for 45 seconds. Add the milk and cook, stirring vigorously, for 2 minutes. The mixture will get very thick and leave the sides of the pan. Take it off the heat.

❸ Stir in the cheese, egg yolks, salt and pepper (the mixture should be very well seasoned).

❹ Whisk the egg whites until stiff but not dry, and mix a spoonful into the mixture, then fold in the rest and pour into the soufflé dish, which should be about two-thirds full. Run your fingers around the top of the souffle mixture. This gives the 'top-hat' appearance to the cooked souffle.

❺ Bake in a preheated 200°C oven for 25-30 minutes and serve immediately.

SALMON FISHCAKES

By Trish Rees

Ingredients

450g floury potatoes, cut into chunks

350g salmon

2 teaspoons tomato ketchup

1 teaspoon English mustard

zest of ½ lemon plus wedges for serving

1 tablespoon chopped parsley

1 tablespoon chopped dill

3 tablespoons plain flour

1 egg, beaten

4 tablespoons oil

100g dried breadcrumbs

Serves 4

❶ Place the potatoes into a pan of water and bring to the boil, cover and cook for 15-20 minutes until tender, drain and steam dry.

❷ Season the salmon and grill or sauté for about 5-6 minutes until just cooked. Cool and then break into large flakes.

❸ Mix the potato, ketchup, mustard, lemon zest, chopped parsley, chopped dill and seasoning. Lightly mix in the salmon, taking care not to break it up too much.

❹ Shape it into 4 large fishcakes.

❺ Put the flour, beaten eggs and breadcrumbs into 3 shallow dishes, dip the cakes into the flour, then the beaten egg and finally the breadcrumbs.

❻ Heat the oil in a frying pan. Fry the cakes for about 3-4 minutes each side until golden and heated through.

❼ Serve with asparagus and lemon wedges.

DEVILLED CHICKEN

By Shân Legge Bourke

'This is quick and easy and an excellent way to use up cooked chicken and give it a real bite.'

Ingredients

cooked chicken, enough for 2

150ml double cream

1 tablespoon HP sauce

1 tablespoon Worcestershire sauce

1 teaspoon English mustard

Serves 2

❶ Heat the oven to 180°C

❷ Slice the cooked chicken and arrange in a shallow baking dish.

❸ Whisk the cream until thick but not stiff.

❹ Fold in the HP sauce, Worcestershire sauce and mustard.

❺ Pour this sauce over the chicken and bake for about 15 minutes until brown and bubbling.

HAM WITH CREAMY MUSHROOM SAUCE

By Shân Legge Bourke

'This recipe works equally well with cooked chicken. It is just about as simple as a recipe can be, and surprisingly delicious.'

Ingredients

slices of cooked ham or chicken – enough for 2

1 tin of condensed mushroom soup

Serves 2

❶ Heat the oven to 180°C.

❷ Arrange the slices of ham in a shallow baking dish.

❸ Pour over the tin of soup, just as it is, without adding any water to dilute.

❹ Bake in the oven for 15-20 minutes until bubbling.

It is just about as simple as a recipe can be, and surprisingly delicious.'

SAUSAGE ROLLS

From 's-Hertogenbosch, Netherlands

This recipe comes with best wishes from the Mayor Jack Mikkers, Nicolette Meeuwsen, Suzan van Lersel and Jan de Wit, City of 's-Hertogenbosch. You can eat them for breakfast, lunch, or with a cold beer!

Ingredients

Bread dough

250g flour

6g salt

70g butter

10g caster sugar

13g fresh yeast or some dried yeast

125m warm milk

Filling

450g minced meat

1 rusk, crushed

½ egg

pinch salt

fresh pepper

nutmeg powder

Extra:

1 egg, beaten to make egg wash

Serves 5

❶ Mix together the flour, salt, butter, sugar, yeast and milk to make a dough.

❷ Keep kneading for at least 5 minutes, then divide the dough into pieces of 90g.

❸ Make small balls and let them rest under clingfilm for about 10 minutes.

❹ Mix the meat, the egg and the rusk. Add salt, pepper and nutmeg powder. Split into pieces of 90g. Roll the pieces into sausages.

❺ Take the pieces of dough and roll them in an oval shape.

❻ Brush the edges with egg was hand put the sausage in the middle of the dough.

❼ Fold the sides over the sausage and press the seams carefully.

❽ Lay the 'worstenbroodjes' with the seam down on a baking tray which is covered with baking paper. Leave them to rise for 45 minutes under clingfilm.

❾ Heat the oven to 200°C. Brush the 'worstenbroodjes' with eggwash and bake for 30 minutes.

Enjoy your meal!
Eet smakelijk!

MAINS

SALMON FILLETS WITH CHILLI SAUCE

By Rhodri Traherne, Museum Trustee.

'The reason I like this dish is that it is very healthy and tastes surprisingly good. I also like it because I am a really awful cook but even I can manage to produce it without precipitating a major disaster in the kitchen!'

Ingredients

2 salmon fillets

1 small pot of plain yogurt

½ lemon, juice of

chilli sauce

sea salt and black pepper

vegetable or sunflower oil

Serves 2

❶ Season the fillets with sea salt and black pepper then pan fry in a little oil until 'cooked through'.

❷ Put the yogurt, lemon juice and a few dashes of chilli sauce into a small saucepan and place over a very gentle heat just to 'warm through'.

❸ Place the fillets on warm plates and pour the sauce over.

❹ Serve with new potatoes and a green salad.

ONE-POT MUSSELS WITH SAUSAGE, CELERY AND SCRUMPY

By Michael Burkham

'When I commanded 3RWF, my lovely wife, Diane, published a recipe book entitled *How to Feed a Dragon*. She sold out, and I hope this will too.
As the creator of the present RWF museum and, as a result, living on the very edge of the mussel-rich Menai Strait, I offer a recipe that I enjoy.'

Ingredients

1 teaspoon olive oil

100g pancetta, diced

½ onion, peeled and sliced

2 cloves garlic, grated or crushed

1 stick celery, sliced

150ml rough cider

500g mussels, in their cleansed shells

1 teaspoon chopped green chilli

1 Granny Smith apple, core removed, finely diced

1 tablespoon chopped parsley

50g cheddar cheese, crumble

2 tomatoes, peeled, deseeded and diced

Serves 1-2

❶ Heat the olive oil in a deep pan and cook the pancetta and onion gently until soft. Add the garlic, celery and cider with the mussels.

❷ Cover and let this simmer for at least 5 minutes before adding the green chilli, apple, parsley, cheese and tomato.

❸ When you think it is ready to serve, do so with sourdough bread and butter.

HADDOCK WITH TOMATOES AND CHIVES

By Dorcas Cresswell

Ingredients

4 x 170g fresh haddock fillets

salt and freshly ground pepper

300ml fish stock

150ml white wine

30g butter

30g flour

150ml cream

2 large tomatoes, skinned, deseeded and cut into slivers

1 tablespoon chopped parsley

1 tablespoon chopped chives

Serves 4

❶ Heat the oven to 180°C.

❷ Wash and season the fillets.

❸ Lay the fish skin-side up in an ovenproof dish. Pour over the strained fish stock and the wine. Cover with foil and bake in the oven for 15-20 minutes.

❹ Lift out the fish. Strain the cooking liquor into a small heavy saucepan and boil rapidly until reduced to 300ml.

❺ Melt the butter in another saucepan, add the flour and stir for 1 minute. Draw off the heat and strain in the reduced fish liquor. Return to the heat, bring slowly up to the boil and simmer for 2 minutes.

❻ Add the cream, salt and pepper to taste and simmer for 1 minute, then add the tomatoes and chives.

❼ Skin the fish and lay in a serving dish. Pour over the sauce.

CORONATION CHICKEN

By Jean and Paul Calderwood

'This recipe was passed to me by a mother at my son's school and it has become a family favourite. I have made a vegetarian version by merely substituting Quorn pieces for the chicken. I was told, although I cannot verify the truth of the claim, that this recipe was published so that everyone could join in the celebrations for the Queen's coronation.'

Ingredients

4 cooked chicken breasts

1 onion, finely chopped

olive oil for frying

1 tablespoon curry powder

1 teaspoon tomato purée

juice of half a lemon

150ml chicken stock

3 tablespoons apricot jam or mango chutney

300ml mayonnaise

3 tablespoons single cream (optional)

Serves 4-6

❶ Cut the chicken into pieces.

❷ Fry the onions gently in the oil until translucent.

❸ Add the curry powder and fry for a further 2 minutes.

❹ Stir in the tomato purée, chicken stock and jam or chutney and leave to cool.

❺ When cold, stir in the mayonnaise, lemon juice and single cream if desired.

❻ Add the chicken pieces and leave to stand before serving.

KEDGEREE

By Dorcas Cresswell

'During the colonial rule in India, local British officials began mixing Indian dishes with their native palates, creating the Victorian craze for Anglo-Indian cuisine such as kedgeree. The officers of the 24th Regiment of Foot possibly got a taste for the dish during the Chilianwala Campaign and we can imagine them on the dawn of the Battle of Isandhlwana tucking into a breakfast of Indian curry.'

Ingredients

600g smoked haddock fillet, skin on, undyed if available

50g butter

4 tablespoons olive oil

2 onions, chopped

450g brown basmati rice

3 dessertspoons curry powder

2 teaspoons ground turmeric

1 litre vegetable stock

300g button mushrooms, sliced

juice of 1 large lemon

300ml double cream

salt and freshly ground black pepper

Topping

2 onions, sliced thinly

1 large egg per person, duck eggs are especially good

1 bunch of coriander, chopped

Serves 4-6

❶ Heat the oven to 200°C. Cook the haddock skin side down in a covered dish with half of the butter, salt and pepper for 15-20 minutes or until the fish is cooked. Leave to cool in the dish.

❷ Heat half of the oil in a large pan and fry the onion for 2-4 minutes. Add the rice, curry powder and turmeric and stir together for about a minute.

❸ Pour in 750ml of the stock, cover with a lid and bring to the boil. Allow to boil for a couple of minutes, then reduce the heat and simmer very gently for around 30-40 minutes, adding more stock if needed, or until all of the liquid has been absorbed and the rice is just cooked but still has a bite. Remove from the heat and set aside with the lid on.

❹ **For the topping:** Pour the remaining oil into another frying pan, and frying the sliced onion over a medium heat for about 10 minutes or until soft and browned then set aside on a plate.

KEDGEREE

5 In the same pan add the remaining butter and fry the mushrooms over a high heat until browned.

6 **For the eggs:** Fill a large saucepan with water, bring to the boil and add a pinch of salt. Reduce the heat to a simmer, crack the eggs into the water and poach for 3-4 minutes (depending on size) so that the yolk remains runny.

7 Combine the mushrooms, cooked rice, lemon juice and cream. Remove the haddock from the skin and add to the rice mixture, together with any juices. Season with salt and pepper and stir gently so as not to break up the haddock too finely.

8 Divide the kedgeree onto individual plates, top with the sliced onions and chopped coriander, then finish by placing a poached egg on top of each portion.

'During the colonial rule in India, local British officials began mixing Indian dishes with their native palates, creating the Victorian craze for Anglo-Indian cuisine such as kedgeree.'

BRAISED LAMB

By Lt Col D A Williams

'This is a delightful and traditionally Welsh main course, submitted by Kevin Sines, who is the Head Chef from Sodexo, leading a wonderful team of chefs who really take care of us within Government House Officers Mess. They are worthy of special mention, throughout this period of lockdown they have continued to support us and have sustained the senior staff officers leading the Defence contribution in the fight against Coronavirus. Without them we simply could not do our jobs effectively.'

Ingredients

1kg welsh lamb shoulder, bone in if possible (alternatively, 2 lamb shanks would work well)

1 tablespoon cooking oil

2 large onions, peeled and quartered

5 carrots, cut into large chunks

4 sticks of celery, diced

1 swede, peeled and cut into chunky cubes

4 cloves of garlic, chopped

4 sprigs of rosemary, chopped

1 teaspoon fresh thyme, chopped

1 level teaspoon fennel seeds

zest of 2 small or 1 large lemon

2 heaped tablespoons tomato purée

1 litre of lamb or beef stock

½ bottle red wine

2 tablespoons honey

salt and pepper

Serves 6-8

❶ Heat the oil in a heavy-based pan and brown the lamb.

❷ Take out the lamb, add all vegetables and sauté for a few minutes.

❸ Add the garlic, rosemary, thyme, lemon zest, fennel seeds and honey, sauté for a further minute then add tomato purée and the wine.

❹ Return the lamb to the pan, add the stock and cover the pan.

❺ Cook at 180°C for 3 hours or until tender.

❻ If necessary, thicken the sauce by removing the lamb and boiling the sauce to reduce.

❼ Season with salt and pepper and serve with buttery mash potato finished with fresh mint.

CHICKEN AND MANGO SALAD

By Carole Greenhalgh

With memories of Osnabrück.

Ingredients

250ml coconut milk

1 tablespoon Thai fish sauce

1 tablespoon caster sugar or light brown sugar

4 chicken breasts

2 mangos, peeled and thinly sliced

6 spring onions, thinly sliced

small bunch coriander, coarsely chopped

45g macadamia nuts, coarsely chopped and roasted

Dressing

2 tablespoons olive oil

grated rind of 1 lime

2 tablespoons lime juice (approx. 2 limes)

Serves 4-6

1 Pre- heat the oven to 180°C.

Put the coconut milk, fish sauce and sugar in a large casserole and bring to the boil. Stir well, reduce the temperature and add the chicken breasts.

2 Cover the dish and poach the chicken in the oven for 15 minutes or until it is just cooked. (This can be done on the top of the stove).

3 Leave the chicken to cool in the coconut milk.

4 To make the dressing, pour 125ml of the coconut milk from the chicken into a measuring jug and add the lime juice, oil and rind. Whisk to combine and season to taste.

5 Cut the chicken breasts into strips and arrange on a serving dish. Place the mango strips on top, followed by the spring onions, coriander and macadamia nuts.

6 Add the dressing just before serving.

7 Serve with couscous and roasted peppers of various colours and warm ciabatta bread, plus a watercress and cucumber salad.

BOBOTIE

By Nicky Rattray

Nicky is owner of Fugitive Lodge in KZN, overlooking the famous Buffalo River. She is a great friend to the Regiment and generously hosts soldiers attending the Rorke's Drift celebrations on the famous battlefield at Isandlwana. Nicky says that this is a traditional South African favourite.

Ingredients

4 tablespoons olive oil

25g butter

1kg beef mince

6 cloves garlic, crushed

½ cup sultanas

1 cup carrot, grated

1 cup apple, grated

4 teaspoons curry powder

2 teaspoons ground coriander

1 teaspoon ground ginger

2 tablespoons thyme, parsley and coriander, chopped

2 teaspoons turmeric

1 teaspoon cinnamon

pinch of cayenne pepper

salt and pepper

4 bay leaves

2 tablespoons lemon juice

4 slices white bread, crusts removed and soaked in some milk

3 tablespoons chutney

Topping

1 cup milk

½ cup buttermilk

salt and pepper

3 eggs

Serves 6-8

❶ Heat the oil and butter in a large pan. Add the minced beef and fry briskly, stirring all the time, until it is brown all over.

❷ Add the garlic, sultanas, carrots, apple and spices and continue to cook for another 10-15 minutes before adding the lemon juice, bread and chutney.

❸ Spread the mixture in an oven proof dish and push bay leaves into the mixture.

❹ Beat all the ingredients for the topping together and pour over the top.

❺ Bake the bobotie uncovered for 35-40 minutes at 190°C until golden brown.

ROAST GLAZED GAMMON

By General James Swift, Colonel of the Regiment

'This is the dish my family ask me to cook most often; great served warm and eaten up cold.'

Ingredients

2-4kg smoked boneless gammon joint (unsmoked will do if you cannot find a smoked joint)

2 onions, halved

2 unpeeled carrots, cut into 5cm chunks

2 celery stalks, cut into 5cm chunks

4 bay leaves

12 black peppercorns

1 litre cider

For the glaze:

small handful of cloves

4 tablespoons runny honey

4 tablespoons Dijon mustard

Serves 6-12

1 Place the ham (at room temperature) in a large, lidded saucepan and cover with water. Bring it to the boil, then discard the water.

2 Add the ingredients to the pan. If the cider does not cover the ham, top up with water.

3 Bring to the boil and then reduce to a simmer for 20 minutes per 500g.

4 Remove the ham and let it cool a little so that it is safe to handle.

5 Heat the oven to 200°C. Mix the honey and mustard together to make the glaze.

6 Using a sharp knife, remove the rind, leaving as much of the fat as you can. Score the fat in a criss-cross, diamond pattern, with lines about 2cm apart. Rub the glaze all over the ham and place a clove into the junction of the scoring.

7 Line a baking tin with baking foil so that it comes about halfway up the joint. Place the joint in the tin and roast for 20 minutes or until the glaze is dark golden brown. I often add a mostly drained tin of sliced peaches at this stage, as they go really well with the gammon.

8 Let the gammon rest for 15 minutes before carving it really thin.

9 I love to serve this with peas and mashed potato. Especially if cooked in peaches, there should be some sauce captured in the foil that is much sought after, but otherwise I do not serve with gravy.

BBQ CHICKEN

By Paul Calderwood

'This recipe is a marinade for BBQ chicken and it is delicious! I normally cook this dish in the oven in all its marinade and serve it with pilau rice and salad. Any leftovers are good the next day served cold or as a sandwich filler. For a smaller dish, just halve the ingredients; I usually use diced chicken breast. A few years ago I attended a friend's lunch party and one of the dishes was BBQ chicken thighs, wings and drum sticks with a very similar marinade, but the host had added chopped chilli and coriander to the mix.'

Ingredients

8 chicken thighs or 4 chicken breasts, or a mixture of both

zest and juice of a lime

4 tablespoons olive oil

4 tablespoons dark soy sauce

4 garlic cloves, crushed

Serves 4

❶ Mix the ingredients together and pour over the chicken, leave the dish to stand for at least an hour, longer is better.

❷ Cook thoroughly either on the barbecue or in the oven (180°C for at least 1 hour).

'I normally cook this dish in the oven in all its marinade and serve it with pilau rice and salad.'

PORK FILLET WITH ORANGE SAUCE

By Dorcas Cresswell

Ingredients

2 pork fillets (about 700g)

1 tablespoon olive oil

25g butter

salt and pepper

200ml fresh orange juice

200ml cream

2 teaspoons flour

Serves 4

❶ Trim the meat and cut it into slices.

❷ Heat the oil in a frying pan, add the meat and fry for 2 minutes on each side.

❸ Add the butter and sprinkle with salt and pepper.

❹ Pour the orange juice and cream over the pork and let it cook for about 2 minutes.

❺ Pour the sauce into a saucepan and keep the meat warm in a serving dish.

❻ Reduce the sauce and thicken with flour and water.

❼ Can be served with rice and vegetables.

HUNGARIAN GOULASH

By Alun Davies

'I have been the Honorary Consul for Hungary for ten years and during that time have enjoyed a variety of Hungarian foods and wines. Perhaps the best-known Hungarian dish is goulash, which in Hungarian means "herders". This is essentially a simple meat casserole cooked by herders, or farm workers, in the fields. They traditionally use an open pot which hangs over a fire on a tripod. The special ingredient is, of course, paprika. In the 15th century, invading Ottoman Turks introduced this new spice to Hungary. While the rest of Europe remained lukewarm towards this red chili pepper from the New World, Hungary embraced it and paprika has since become a defining element of Hungarian cuisine.'

Ingredients

600g of veal, pork, or beef, diced into 2-3cm cubes

1 onion, peeled and thinly sliced

2 tablespoons olive oil

½ teaspoon sweet paprika

60ml water

2 bell peppers – red or yellow

1 tomato

300ml sour cream and 200ml for garnish

3 tablespoons plain flour

Serves 4

❶ In a heavy-based casserole or frying pan, fry the onion in the oil until golden, then remove the pan from the heat.

❷ Add the paprika and water and let it bubble up briefly.

❸ Season the meat with salt and add it to the pan then cover with a lid. Cook on a high heat and stir frequently, adding a little water if required.

❹ After 10 minutes, stir in the thinly sliced peppers and the chopped tomato.

❺ Meanwhile, combine 300ml of the sour cream with the flour and stir until a smooth paste then stir into the goulash. Leave the pan uncovered, turn the heat down to a simmer and leave for 30 minutes.

❻ Check the meat to see that it is tender and serve with a dessert spoon of sour cream as garnish.

❼ This goulash goes well with pasta, rice or dumplings.

HOMESTYLE CHICKEN CURRY

By Trish Rees, secretary to the Friends of the Museum.

Ingredients

8 chicken thighs, skinless, boneless and cut into 3cm chunks

1 onion, chopped

6 garlic cloves, roughly chopped

50g root ginger, roughly chopped

4 tablespoons vegetable oil

2 teaspoons cumin seeds

5cm cinnamon stick

1 teaspoon chilli flakes

1 teaspoon garam masala

1 teaspoon turmeric

1 teaspoon castor sugar

400g can chopped tomatoes

2 tablespoons chopped coriander

Serves 4

❶ Heat the vegetable oil in a wok or sturdy pan over a medium heat.

❷ Combine the cumin seeds, the cinnamon stick and chilli flakes and add to the pan. Swirl around for about 30 seconds until the spices release a fragrant aroma.

❸ Add the chopped onion – it will splutter at first. Fry until the onions turn a dark golden colour – this should take about 8 minutes.

❹ Add the garlic and ginger and cook for 2 minutes, stirring all the time.

❺ Stir in the garam masala, turmeric and caster sugar before adding the chopped tomatoes.

❻ Continue cooking on a medium heat for about 10 minutes without a lid until the tomatoes darken and thicken.

❼ Add the chicken chunks to the pan and cook for 5 minutes to coat the chicken with the sauce and seal in the juices, then pour over the chicken stock.

❽ Simmer for 10 minutes without a lid until the chicken is tender and the sauce slightly thickened. Add more stock or water if required.

❾ Sprinkle with the chopped coriander and serve with flat breads or basmati rice with yoghurt on the side.

BURGUNDIAN BEEF STEW

By Trish Rees

Ingredients

125g streaky bacon, diced

1½kg rump of beef – cut into 4cm cubes

30g seasoned flour

4 tablespoon olive oil

½ bottle red burgundy

300ml beef stock

a fresh bouquet garni of thyme, parsley and bay leaf

20 button onions

30g butter

225g button mushrooms

1 teaspoon sugar

Serves 6

1 Preheat the oven to 180°C.

2 Coat the beef cubes in the seasoned flour.

3 Heat half the olive oil in a flameproof casserole and brown the bacon, then remove with a slotted spoon and set aside.

4 Brown the meat a few pieces at a time in the same fat to ensure that all the pieces are evenly browned, adding a little oil if needed;

5 Return all the meat and the bacon to the pan, add the wine and bring to the boil then add enough stock to just cover the meat.

6 Add the bouquet garni, stir and season with salt and pepper, then cover and simmer in the oven for 2 hours.

7 While the meat is cooking, simmer the onions in the remaining stock for 5 minutes, then drain.

8 Heat the remaining oil and the butter in a frying pan, add the onions and mushrooms and sprinkle with the sugar, stirring until brown.

9 Stir into the casserole and cook for a few more minutes.

10 Serve with creamy, fluffy mashed potatoes.

CHICKEN AND MUSHROOM DAIRY-FREE PASTA

By David Roberts
Branch Secretary and Standard Bearer for Pembrokeshire, RWFCA.

'I have a dairy-free recipe that is made for my son because he cannot eat any dairy products as he suffers from lactose intolerance. There are many people out there who have the same condition, so here is my recipe for chicken and mushroom dairy-free pasta.'

Ingredients

3 chicken breasts, cubed

salt and pepper

olive oil

1 large shallot, finely diced

100g mushrooms, sliced

3 cloves garlic, crushed

3 tablespoons plain flour

400ml coconut milk

240ml chicken stock

1 tablespoon fresh parsley, chopped

Serves 4

❶ Season the chicken cubes with salt and pepper.

❷ Heat the olive oil in a frying pan and cook the chicken, turning frequently until golden brown. Remove and keep warm.

❸ Boil the pasta in a large pan with 3 tablespoons of olive oil.

❹ Add a little more oil to the pan and fry the shallot, mushrooms and garlic. Season well and stir in the flour, then add the coconut milk and stock and simmer until thick.

❺ Add the cooked chicken back into the sauce and serve this with the pasta, topped with fresh parsley. Lemon juice can be added if necessary to sharpen the sauce.

❻ Serve with garlic bread.

PHEASANT BREASTS IN PORT

By Judith Randell

'In our pheasant shoot, the syndicate members, guests and beaters eat whatever is shot, but on occasions this is a tall order, especially towards the end of the season, when the cry is, "Oh no, not another pheasant for supper". This is a great recipe for using just the best bits but if I am feeling enthusiastic I could make stock from the legs and bones.'

Ingredients

2 pheasant breasts

50g butter

50g smoked lardons

50g button mushrooms, finely sliced

225ml port

225ml pheasant stock

salt and pepper

Serves 2

❶ Melt 25g of the butter in a heavy casserole or frying pan and gently fry the pheasant breasts for 10 minutes, turning regularly. Remove to a serving dish and keep warm.

❷ Add the lardons and mushrooms to the pan and fry until crisp and brown then scoop out with a slotted spoon and scatter over the pheasant breasts.

❸ Pour the port into the pan and boil rapidly to reduce by half, stirring well all the time.

❹ Now add the stock and reduce again until the sauce becomes syrupy.

❺ Mix in the remaining butter, a little at a time, stirring vigorously, until the sauce looks rich and shiny.

❻ Check the seasoning and pour over the pheasant breasts.

PORK FILLET WITH APPLES, ROSEMARY AND CIDER

By Granny Crewe-Reed

Ingredients

50g butter

1 dessert apple, peeled, cored and sliced into wedges

350g trimmed pork tenderloin

1 level tablespoon chopped rosemary

150ml dry cider

salt and pepper

Serves 3-4

1. Heat the oven to 200°C.

2. Melt half the butter and gently fry the apples until golden. Set aside.

3. Slice a deep cut down the centre of the tenderloin, (be careful not to slice all the way through).

4. Mix the cooked apple, rosemary and seasoning; place in the incision and tie at intervals.

5. Brown the fillet on all sides and transfer to a roasting tin.

6. Place in the oven and cook for 20 minutes.

7. Remove the pork, add the cider to the pan and reduce by half.

8. Whisk in the remaining butter to make the sauce.

9. Slice the fillet and serve with the sauce.

QUICK CHICKEN AND LEEK CRUMBLE

By Gail Baldwin

Ingredients

2 chicken breasts, diced

1 leek, sliced

250g reduced fat soft cheese

salt and pepper

50g oats

50g chopped nuts

1 tablespoon grated Parmesan cheese

Serves 2

1 Heat the oven to 200°C.

2 Heat the oil and fry the chicken for 2 minutes, turning frequently.

3 Add the chopped leek and fry for another 3 minutes.

4 Stir in the soft cheese and cook for 1 minute.

5 Season the mixture and transfer to an ovenproof dish.

6 Mix the oats, chopped nuts and parmesan cheese and sprinkle over the chicken.

7 Bake for 20 minutes.

8 Serve with green beans.

DAI 88'S TEXAN BBQ BEANS

'This is such an easy dish to make that most people will be able to work out what to do just by looking at the ingredients without any instruction. Preparation is everything; having all the chopping and marinating done and organised beforehand makes cooking this dish totally stress free.'

Ingredients

2 or 3 chicken breasts, diced

200g smoked bacon lardons

1 tablespoon Cajun spice mix

1 tablespoon olive oil

1 large onion, peeled and sliced

2 or 3 jalapeños, deseeded and diced

2 or 3 cloves of garlic, crushed

500g carton of tomato passata or 425g of tinned plum tomatoes

425g tin baked beans in tomato sauce

425g tin kidney beans, drained

425g tin of butter beans, drained

2 green peppers, deseeded and diced

½ bottle of good quality BBQ sauce

salt

Garnish
grated Mexican cheese and sour cream

Sides
rice and pitta with chips and dips

Serves 4

❶ Mix the chicken and bacon with the Cajun spices and 2 tablespoons of BBQ sauce and leave to marinade for an hour or so.

❷ Heat the oil and cook the onion until soft.

❸ Add the marinated chicken and bacon and cook until sealed (slightly brown).

❹ Add the jalapeños and garlic for a minute or so, making sure the garlic doesn't burn.

❺ Add the tomatoes and all the beans along with the green peppers and the BBQ sauce.

❻ Cover and simmer on a low heat for around 1 hour, stirring occasionally and adding small amounts of water if needed to stop the dish from drying out.

❼ Season with salt to taste before serving.

❽ Cook the rice and warm the pittas. Tortilla chips and dips are great for sharing for the centre of the table and once served, garnish with grated Mexican cheese and a dollop of sour cream.

❾ This dish goes equally will with red or white wine or good Mexican/Spanish lagers.

NORMANDY CHICKEN

By Janet Holcroft
Janet is Education Officer at the Museum.

'This lovely creamy chicken dish has a great tarragon flavour and takes only 45 minutes to prepare.'

Ingredients

4 chicken breasts, sliced into chunks

1 tablespoon olive oil

40g butter

2 leeks, sliced

2 courgettes, sliced

1 glass of white wine

1 mug of chicken stock

tarragon to taste (fresh or dried)

salt and pepper

250ml creme fraiche

Serves 4

❶ Heat the oil and half of the butter in a large frying pan or solid-based casserole and fry the chicken chunks, turning frequently until golden brown on all sides.

❷ Remove and keep warm.

❸ Add the sliced leeks and courgettes to the pan with the remaining butter and fry gently until golden and slightly softened.

❹ Return the chicken to the pan with the wine, stock, tarragon and seasoning.

❺ Bring to the boil and simmer gently until the chicken is cooked right through and the liquid has reduced.

❻ Stir in the creme fraiche until you have a lovely, creamy consistency.

❼ Serve with mash, carrots and peas.

'This lovely creamy chicken dish has a great tarragon flavour and takes only 45 minutes to prepare.'

PUDDINGS, BAKING & DRINKS

ETON MESS

By Peter Kerruish

Ingredients

500g strawberries, hulled

4 crushed meringue nests (you can, of course, make them)

400ml double cream

fresh mint leaves

Serves 6

❶ Keep 6 strawberries for garnish and crush the rest with a fork.

❷ Mix the strawberries with the crushed meringues.

❸ Lightly whisk the cream and fold into the mixture.

❹ Fill individual deep glasses, adding the remaining chopped strawberries and mint as garnish.

❺ Cool until needed.

LEMON SOUFFLÉ CUSTARD

By David Hodges

David joined the 24th in Lydd in 1968 and enjoyed five wonderful years with them, and the RRW.

Ingredients

4 eggs

2 large lemons

225g caster sugar

25g butter

50g plain flour

475ml milk

Serves 8

❶ Separate the eggs. Put the yolks, grated rind and juice of the lemons, sugar, butter and flour into a processor and blend with the milk poured in through the funnel opening.

❷ Whisk the egg whites until firm and fold into the mixture.

❸ Pour into a 1.4 litre ovenproof dish.

❹ Place the dish in a bain marie, pour boiling water halfway up the tin and place in the oven at 180 degrees for about 35 minutes.

❺ Delicious hot or cold and can be served with cream or ice cream.

PASSION FRUIT MOUSSE WITH MANGO COULIS

By Dorcas Cresswell

Ingredients

6-8 ripe passion fruits

450ml whipping cream

65g caster sugar

3/4 sachets gelatine powder

6 tablespoons lemon juice

Mango Coulis

1 big very ripe mango, peeled and sliced off the stone

50g caster sugar

5 tablespoons lemon juice

Serves 4-6

❶ Halve the passion fruits and scoop out the flesh and juice.

❷ Whisk the cream with the sugar until it's stiff and fold the fruit in.

❸ Heat up the lemon juice and dissolve the gelatine in it.

❹ Let it cool down before folding into the whipped cream and passion fruit.

❺ Put the mousse in either individual pots or a larger dish and let it set in the fridge for 3-4 hours.

❻ Cook the mango flesh with the sugar and lemon juice for 5 minutes and leave to cool before liquidising to a purée.

❼ Serve with the mousse.

AMERICAN-STYLE CHEESECAKE

By Peter Kerruish

Ingredients

Base

250g digestive biscuits, crushed with a rolling pin

125g butter

Filling

225g caster sugar

3 tablespoons cornflour

675g cream cheese

2 eggs

1 teaspoon vanilla essence or grated zest of ½ a lemon

300ml whipping cream

75g sultanas, optional

Topping

425g canned cherries in syrup

½ tablespoon cornflour

Serves 4-6

1 Line a 23cm springform baking tin with baking paper and grease the sides.

2 To make the base, melt the butter and stir in the broken biscuits then press them over the base of the tin.

3 To make the filling, mix the sugar and cornflour and beat in the cream cheese.

4 Add the eggs and vanilla essence and beat until smooth.

5 Slowly whisk in the cream until it thickens, stir in the sultanas and pour over the base.

6 Bake for 1 hour in an oven at 180°C.

7 To make the topping, drain the cherries, reserving 120ml of the syrup.

8 Mix the cornflour with 1 tablespoon of syrup and pour the remainder into a pan.

9 Heat gently, stir in the cornflour mixture and bring to the boil, stirring until thick.

10 Cool then decorate your cheesecake with circles of cherries and pour over the sauce.

CHRISTMAS FRUIT SALAD

By Dorcas Cresswell

Ingredients

14 mandarins

200g kumquats

100g caster sugar

200ml water

100g cranberries

250g sugar

4 tablespoons rose water

Serves 4

1 Peel the mandarins and divide into segments.

2 Halve the kumquats and cook them in sugar and water until they are tender. Leave them in the sugar solution afterwards.

3 Put the cranberries with the remaining sugar in a casserole, add 2 tablespoons water and let it simmer over a very low heat for about 10 minutes (trying to keep the berries whole).

4 Mix all the ingredients just before serving (otherwise the whole salad will go red).

5 Can be served with ice cream or whipped cream.

DANISH LEMON MOUSSE

By Dorcas Cresswell

Ingredients

4 eggs, separated

100g caster sugar

1 large lemon (juice and grated rind)

1 sachet (15g) gelatine

2 egg whites

300ml whipping cream

Serves 4-5

1 Whisk the egg yolks and sugar until thick and white.

2 Heat up the lemon juice and sprinkle in the gelatine, stirring until it all dissolves. Leave to cool to room temperature.

3 Add the lemon juice/gelatine mixture to the egg/sugar mixture.

4 Whisk the egg whites and whipping cream separately until both are stiff.

5 Add the lemon rind to the lemon mixture, then carefully fold in the whisked egg whites and whipped cream.

6 Leave the mousse in a serving dish for a few hours until set.

7 Decorate with zest of lemon.

BLACK FOREST GATEAU MERINGUE

By Gilli Davies

'I have such happy memories of giving cookery classes in my kitchen in Osnabrück, Belfast, Queen Anne Square Cardiff, Aldershot, Berlin and Cyprus. Things didn't always go right, but we laughed a lot!'

Ingredients

4 egg whites

225g caster sugar

225g dark chocolate

4 tablespoons water

300ml double cream

1 tin best black cherries, stoned and drained

1 dessertspoon liqueur

chocolate flake for decoration

Serves 8-10

❶ Line 3 baking sheets with non-stick paper.

❷ Soak the drained cherries in the liqueur.

❸ Beat the egg whites till very stiff and then beat in the sugar, bit by bit.

❹ Spread the meringue into 3 equal-sized circles on the baking paper and bake in a low oven (below 100°C) for about an hour until crisp.

❺ Break the chocolate into a heatproof bowl and dissolve either in gentle heat in the microwave or over a pan of simmering water. Leave to cool.

❻ Whisk the cream until almost stiff and add the melted chocolate.

❼ Spread two meringues with chocolate cream and the cherries scattered over.

❽ Layer up the cake and cover the top and sides with chocolate cream.

❾ Shake over the broken flake to decorate.

RHUBARB MIRACLE PUDDING

By Gilli Davies

This is one of the simplest puddings to make but very delicious and you can alter the fruit to use stewed plums, apricots or greengages.

Ingredients

450g stewed rhubarb

1 orange, juice and grated rind

1 teaspoon rose water

caster sugar to taste

300ml double cream

300ml Greek yogurt

1 packet ratafia or amaretti biscuits

Serves 4-6

❶ Stew the rhubarb with the grated orange rind and juice, ideally in the microwave or baked in the oven. Leave to cool.

❷ Sweeten to taste and add the rose water then arrange in the bottom of a serving bowl. Whisk the cream and fold in the yogurt. Spread this mixture over the fruit.

❸ Decorate with the biscuits and chill.

BANANA BREAD

By Margaret Retief

The South African Army's Pretoria Armour Regiment (PAR) is a Reserve unit under command of the South African Army Armour Formation, with the headquarters and the unit both based in the capital city of South Africa – Pretoria. The regiment was previously called the Pretoria Regiment, with ties going back to the Royal Welch Fusiliers from 1927. The ladies of PAR appreciate being part of history-making by contributing towards the Royal Welsh Cookbook. 'Our contributions are South African traditional and indigenous recipes which we are proud of and we hope this one will add value to the cookbook initiative.'
Mimie Chabalala (Wife of the Commanding Officer)

Ingredients

150g caster sugar

2 large or 3 small bananas, mashed

175g vegetable oil

2 eggs

275g flour

100g sunflower seeds

1 teaspoon bicarbonate of soda

½ teaspoon baking powder

½ teaspoon salt

2 teaspoons vanilla essence

Serves 4-8

❶ Heat the oven to 180°C.

❷ Grease a loaf tin.

❸ Put the sugar, bananas, oil and eggs in a large bowl.

❹ Stir in the remaining ingredients and beat well.

❺ Pour into the prepared tin.

❻ Bake for 40 to 50 minutes or until golden brown and a wooden pick comes out clean when inserted into the cake.

❼ Remove from the oven and let stand for about 10 minutes before loosening the sides of the loaf and tipping out gently.

❽ Cool completely before slicing.

It improves a little with age.... really good after 2 or 3 days.

GINGER BISCUITS

by Julie Dawson

These delicious biscuits are from Julie Dawson, who designed the Museum website; her business is called IAF.

Ingredients

225g plain flour

4 teaspoons ground ginger

225g demerara sugar

110g butter

1 teaspoon bicarbonate of soda

1 tablespoon milk

1 large egg

blanched almond halves

Makes 12-15

1 Mix the flour, ginger and sugar together in a bowl.

2 Melt the butter in a saucepan or microwave.

3 Dissolve the bicarbonate of soda in the milk.

4 Add the beaten egg, milk mixture and butter to the flour and stir well.

5 Roll the mixture into balls, place on a paper-lined baking tray and flatten gently. They spread out, so leave plenty of room.

6 Press an almond onto the top of each biscuit and bake for 20 minutes at 160°C.

7 If you want them chewy in the middle, cook for less time; for crispy biscuits, cook for longer.

CHEAT'S LEMONADE SCONES

By Harriette Thomas

Harriette Thomas' grandfather served with the SWB and died, without trace, at Mametz Wood. This recipe works well with both cloudy and clear lemonade. Handle the dough as little as possible to keep the scones light.

Ingredients

400g self-raising flour

175ml double cream

175ml lemonade

Makes 15

❶ Put the flour in a large bowl and stir in the double cream and lemonade.

❷ Mix to a dough and turn it out onto a floured surface.

❸ Pat the dough down to a thickness of 2cm and cut the scones out.

❹ Bake on a lined baking tray at 220°C for 12-15 minutes.

TIFFIN

By Geoff and Annie Catling

'We chose the tiffin recipe because of its military links to our regimental forebears who served in India and also because bars of tiffin were a highly prized item in our 24-hour ration packs in the late 60s/early 70s.'

Ingredients

110g butter

55g castor sugar

2 tablespoons drinking chocolate powder

1 egg, beaten

230g crushed digestive biscuits

110g raisins

225g dark cooking chocolate

Makes 12-15

1 Place the butter, sugar and drinking chocolate powder into a large saucepan and melt over gentle heat.

2 Add the beaten egg and stir until the mixture thickens.

3 Remove from the heat and add the crushed digestive biscuits and raisins.

4 Stir well and then pour the mixture into a lightly greased swiss roll tin. Press down well. Melt the cooking chocolate and pour over. Gently move the tin in your hands to achieve a consistent chocolate covering. Set aside to cool.

5 When cold, cut into pieces.

FLAPJACKS

By Beth Richardson Aitken

Beth is the wife of Bob Richardson-Aitken, who served with 1 Welch 1960–1971, and daughter of Lt Gen Sir Charles Coleman, who was Colonel of the Welch Regiment 1958–1965.

Ingredients

170g Welsh butter

170g demerara or soft brown sugar

225g rolled oats

Makes 15

1 Heat the oven to 170°C.

2 Warm the butter to soften and stir in the sugar and oats.

3 Turn the mixture into a 12"x 8" baking tin and smooth the surface with a palette knife.

4 Cook in the oven for approximately 15 to 20 minutes until golden brown.

5 Remove from the oven and allow to cool for about ten minutes then cut into squares and leave in the tin until completely cold.

6 Loosen around the sides of the tin and carefully remove the flapjacks.

AUNTIE BILL'S CHOCOLATE CAKE

By Annabel Elliott

'I married Christopher Elliott in 1970 and have loved the whole adventure of our life together within the family of the Regiment and the wider life beyond. Being a rather disorganised person, I well remember watching a friend giving a demo in her army quarter and learning the valuable art of washing up as I went along! Zara Elliott, my mother in law, is now 97 – she and Colonel Blethyn Elliott lived in Cyprus and Singapore early on in their married life and although she hardly knew how to cook an egg before she married, these countries inspired her to become a wonderful cook. This cake is delicious and is best eaten while fresh.'

Ingredients

75g sugar

225g self-raising flour

pinch salt

2 heaped tablespoons cocoa

1 heaped teaspoon bicarbonate of soda

1 large tablespoon golden syrup

75g butter or margarine

300ml water

1 teaspoon vanilla essence

Milk Chocolate Icing

70g butter or margarine

225g icing sugar, sieved

3 tablespoons milk

1 teaspoon vanilla essence

Serves 6-8

❶ Grease 2 x 20cm round cake tins and line the bases. Heat the oven to 150°C.

❷ Sift together the sugar, flour, salt, cocoa and bicarbonate of soda into a bowl.

❸ In a saucepan, gently heat the syrup, butter, water and vanilla essence and pour this mixture into the dry ingredients.

❹ Mix well and divide the mixture between the two tins. Bake for 20-30 minutes, then leave to cool.

❺ **For the icing:** gently melt the butter and beat in the rest of the ingredients.

❻ Sandwich the two circles of cake together with half the icing and decorate the top with the other half.

WARTIME BEETROOT RED VELVET CAKE

By Dorcas Cresswell

'During World War II, food rationing led bakers to use boiled beetroot to add moisture and sweetness to cakes and in this case also to reduce the cocoa powder required (which, although not rationed, was in short supply during the war years). In wartime the cake would have been baked as a single layer with no frosting.'

Ingredients

250g fresh beetroot, peeled and finely chopped

75ml milk

2 teaspoons lemon juice

2 teaspoons white wine vinegar

1 teaspoon vanilla extract

125g unsalted butter (at room temperature)

2 large free-range eggs

250g self-raising flour

150g caster sugar

3 tablespoons cocoa powder

1½ teaspoons baking powder

Frosting

200g cream cheese

300g icing sugar

2 teaspoons vanilla extract

cocoa powder for dusting (optional)

Serves 8-10

1 Heat the oven to 180°C and line 2 x 15cm round sandwich tins with baking parchment.

2 In a small bowl or jug, combine the milk and the lemon juice.

3 In a food processor or blender combine the beetroot, milk and lemon mixture, white wine vinegar and vanilla and blitz to a fine purée.

4 Add the butter to the purée and blitz until combined.

5 Add the eggs and blitz again until smooth.

6 Sift the flour, sugar, cocoa powder and baking powder into the purée and mix well until everything is combined.

7 Divide the mixture evenly between the tins and bake for 30-40 minutes, until a skewer inserted into the centre of a cake comes out clean.

8 Once cooked, cool for 10 minutes before gently removing the tins and then leave the cakes to cool completely.

9 For the frosting, beat the cream cheese in a bowl, adding the icing sugar a little at a time until fully combined. Finally, add the vanilla extract.

10 To assemble the cake, spread half of the frosting across the top of one cake. Place the other cake on top so that the frosting is sandwiched in the middle and spread the rest of the frosting over the top of the cake. Dust with a little cocoa powder, if desired.

'In wartime the cake would have been baked as a single layer with no frosting.'

A GOOD SMALL LOAF

By Ian Powys

'Just thought you might like a "chuck-it-all-in" sort of recipe for a very basic staff of life food. This works very well for a small loaf, with a shelf life of a couple of days. You do need a large slow cooker and be resigned to losing a whole 284ml of good lager. Don't use a "beery" beer. Saves having to go to the local Co-op if you've run out of bread!'

Ingredients

2 coffee mugs of self-raising flour

1 heaped teaspoon salt

1 small bottle of lager

Serves 8-10

❶ Grease the inside of a small loaf tin with a little butter.

❷ In a mixing bowl, mix the flour, salt and beer slowly together until it is the consistency which allows it to be rolled into a ball (i.e. not too liquid).

❸ Turn the dough into the greased loaf tin and transfer to the slow cooker.

❹ Cook for about two hours.

DRINKS

THREE COCKTAILS

A RUM PUNCH FROM BELIZE

By Alun Davies

'When 1RRW was in Belize I enjoyed various rum punches, all of which combine fruit juices and local rums. This is a colourful one that I have made over the years with success.'

Ingredients

handful of ice cubes

60ml of light rum such as Bacardi

orange juice

pineapple juice

a dash of grenadine

Serves 1

❶ In a long glass (a highball glass), put a handful of ice cubes. Add 60ml of light rum, such as Bacardi, and top the glass up with an equal mix of good orange juice and pineapple juice. Give it all a good stir, then, using a teaspoon, slide a dash of grenadine down the inside of the glass.

❷ Serve it at once and encourage people to drink it before the grenadine hits the bottom of the glass.

A STRAWBERRY DAIQUIRI FROM BERLIN

By Alun Davies

'When stationed in Berlin we used to visit a small bar called the Rum Trader, where the patron sold only rum-based drinks; they were lethal. This was his frozen strawberry daiquiri but just as good is the banana daiquiri, which is simply made by substituting half a banana instead of the strawberries.'

Ingredients

60ml of white rum

30ml of triple sec (or Cointreau)

juice of 1 lime

1 level teaspoon of caster sugar

4-6 strawberries

a lemon slice

Serves 1

❶ In a blender, put 60ml of white rum and 30ml of triple sec (or Cointreau). Add the juice of 1 lime, a level teaspoon of caster sugar and 4-6 strawberries, depending on their size. Fill the blender with a good handful of ice cubes and blitz the lot until all the ice cubes have been broken up.

❷ Pour the cocktail into a chilled Martini glass – you may decorate the rim by rubbing it with a lemon slice and dipping it in caster sugar if you wish. Like all cocktails, it should be drunk "while it is smiling at you"!

'Like all cocktails it should be drunk "while it is smiling at you"!'

A CLASSIC WHITE LADY

By Alun Davies

'As part of the British Army in Germany many of us went skiing in the Alps, where I first came across a White Lady. The White Lady is one of the great cocktails which were developed in the late 1920s. It was being served in a couple of places in London, such as the American Bar in the Savoy, but I like the story about St Moritz. It is said that after a late breakfast in the Palace hotel, fashionable young ladies in silk skiing trousers and mink coats would spend the first half of the morning choosing jewellery at Cartier's moving to Hanselmann's coffee shop at about 11.30am where, worn out by the efforts of the morning, they would revive with White Ladies served to perfection.'

Ingredients

60ml of good gin

30ml of triple sec (or Cointreau)

20ml of lemon juice

a large amount of ice

a dash of egg white

Serves 1

❶ To make that perfect White Lady, put 60ml of good gin into a cocktail shaker with 30ml of triple sec (or Cointreau) and 20ml of lemon juice. Add a large amount of ice and a dash of egg white. Shake vigorously and pour into a chilled champagne coupe or a Martini glass and dream of being in the Alps.

CHABEEL

By Lt Col David A Williams

'When members of the Sikh faith in the British Army came to share their celebration of the martyrdom in 1606 of the 5th Sikh Guru, one of the key members of that team was Cpl Pardeep Kaur, a chef with our 1st Battalion, based in Tidworth. They introduced us to this wonderfully sweet, cooling and refreshing drink, which is superb drunk in the shade on hot, lazy summer afternoons.'

Ingredients

1 litre milk (skimmed or semi-skimmed is fine but full fat gives the best flavour)

35-40cl rose syrup (available online or in health food shops or speciality delicatessens)

ice cubes

Serves 5-10

❶ Mix the milk and rose syrup.

❷ Add sufficient ice cubes to cool the drink.

❸ Chill and serve.

❹ **Variation**
For a variation to the texture and taste, ground pistachio nuts can also be added to the drink if desired.

ORANGE LIQUEUR

By Granny Crewe-Reed

Ingredients

6 Seville oranges

1 litre of brandy (cheap variety)

450g sugar

½ teaspoon ground cinnamon

½ teaspoon ground coriander seed

Serves a good few!

❶ Thinly pare the oranges, avoiding any pith, and finely chop the peel.

❷ Put the chopped peel into a jar with the juice from the oranges, the sugar, both spices and the brandy.

❸ Stir well, cover tightly and leave for 3 months.

❹ Strain and filter the liquid into clean bottles.

❺ The peel can be frozen and used in next year's marmalade.

BLACKBERRY BRANDY

By Granny Crewe-Reed

Ingredients

900g blackberries

a pinch of cinnamon

8 cloves

a pinch of nutmeg

granulated sugar

300ml brandy

Makes about a pint

❶ Place the blackberries in a saucepan with ½ pint water and the spices. Simmer for 20 minutes, then leave to cool.

❷ Strain the fruit through a muslin or a fine sieve, then measure the juice and add 225g sugar to one pint of liquid.

❸ Pour the liquid back into the saucepan and heat gently until the sugar has dissolved.

❹ Leave to cool, then add the brandy and put into bottles.

❺ The brandy is ready to drink straight away.

NOTES

NOTES

NOTES

PLAYBOY
playmaker

INTERNATIONAL BESTSELLING AUTHOR

MAREN MOORE

Copyright © 2023 by Maren Moore/R. Holmes
All rights reserved.
No part of this book may be reproduced in any form or by any electronic
or mechanical means, including information storage and retrieval
systems, without written permission from the authors, except for the use
of brief quotations in a book review.
This is a work of fiction. Names, characters, places, businesses,
companies, organizations, locales, events and incidents either are the
product of the authors' imagination or used fictitiously. Any
resemblances to actual persons, living or dead, is unintentional and co-
incidental. The authors do not have any control over and do not assume
any responsibility for authors' or third-party websites or their content.

Cover Design: Cat with TRC Designs

For the girls who go after whatever they want with fire in their hearts and no hesitation to be seen.
This one's for you.

PLAYLIST

Play with Fire-Sam Tinnesz feat Yacht Money

Nobody Gets Me- SZA

i'm yours- Isabel LaRosa

messy in heaven- venue, goddard.

One Life- Dermot Kennedy

STARWALKIN- Lil Nas X

Very Few Friends- Saint Levant

I Guess- Saint Levant

Sure Thing- Miguel

Collide- Justine Skye, Tyga

Your Heart Or Mine- Jon Pardi

Downfall- Julian June

Wildcard- Miley Cyrus

White Roses- Casual Sex

Fast Car- Luke Combs

These Boots Are Made for Walking- Jessica Simpson

Click here to listen to the full playlist on Spotify

ONE

HUDSON

"You do realize staring at it isn't going to make her text back, right?" I say, nodding toward the phone in Chaney's hand, which he's been staring at for the past fifteen minutes while everyone around us is celebrating our hard-earned Stanley Cup win.

The win I should also be celebrating, but instead, I've been at this table with the rookie, nursing the same beer for far too long.

He hesitates before dragging his eyes to meet mine. "I believe in manifestation, okay? *Power of the mind.*" Tapping his finger along his temple, he smirks, then glances back down at his phone. "Fuck, you're right. She *is* ghosting me. How the fuck does this keep happening to me?"

"I dunno, maybe you're trying too hard? Too clingy?

You know, you really are like a younger version of Adams," I say, mentioning my best friend, Graham, who once was the rookie but is now retired and living in Tennessee. "Of course, *I* get stuck babysitting the rookie. Not once, but twice. History repeating itself," I groan, then take another pull of my lukewarm beer.

"Yeah, well, we're the last men standing, so it's me or daddy daycare. Take your pick, Rome."

Annoying as he is, and surprisingly charming too... he's also right. Even if I won't ever be admitting that to him. I glance around the crowded room and find my friends and teammates throughout the swarm of people.

Reed and Briggs are gleefully chasing the youngest kids around the room while Holland, Reed's wife, watches and sips her sparkling water with a small smirk on her red lips. Maddison, Briggs' wife, clinks her glass against Holland's, and they both laugh while watching the fiasco unfold. Asher and Auden are in deep conversation with Coach Evans while their son, Alex, has his head bent with Evan, Reed's nephew, looking at the glowing game held between them.

Man, everything has changed. Shit is so different now, and I think there's a little part of me that wishes that things stayed the same. We used to spend our nights in the bar, getting into whatever trouble we could find. Young, freshly drafted to one of the best hockey teams in the country with the world at our fingertips—Chicago was *our playground.*

Now, we spend our days at a *literal* playground, keeping their kids out of trouble instead of making our own. The guys joke all the time that when everyone retires from hockey, they'll just open a daddy daycare since these fuckers have enough kids to fill their own.

I mean, honestly, what the fuck is my life?

Reed, Briggs, and Asher are my best friends and my teammates on the Avalanches, Chicago's reigning Stanley Cup champions. But they're more than that—they're family. My *brothers.* There's nothing I wouldn't do for them, but as much as I love my nieces and nephews, I'd rather not be stuck home on a Saturday night changing diapers and spoon-feeding toddlers. I'm the cool uncle that lets them stay up way past their bedtime and then sends them back home on a sugar overload for their parents to deal with. Other than that, I'm out.

So, Chaney's right. It's just us left. The only two of our crew that don't have a ball and chain in the form of wives and children. We're the last standing bachelors.

He's the rookie of the team, the last to join our tight-knit circle, and even though I give him shit, I actually *do* like the kid. But I wasn't just saying that when I said he *is* a mini version of Adams. He might be worse, and none of us can handle not one but two of those dramatic fuckers. Not that Graham is really around anyway right now. He went and fell in love with Reed's younger sister, Emery, and they had twin girls. Now they live in his hometown, and we only see them on holidays.

"What's your deal tonight, anyway?" Chaney asks, his brows bunching together as he finally glances up from his phone again. "We're supposed to be celebrating. We won the fucking Stanley Cup, and you're being grumpy as fuck, ruining my vibe."

I narrow my eyes at him, starting to feel slightly claustrophobic in the bow tie and tux I have on. The truth is, I don't know what my deal is.

Hell, he's right.

We won the Stanley fucking Cup.

Some people wait their entire lives to be able to say that. Most never even get to hold that cup above their head. And we did it.

I played the best season of my entire career, and yet... I don't know. Something still feels off. Maybe I'm just in a mood tonight, and I don't feel like being in a room full of people, plastering on a fake smile for the cameras. But it seems like I've been in a mood for a while now, if I'm being honest.

"Just not feeling it, I guess. I think I'm going to head out." I set my beer down on the table beside us, standing straighter to adjust the button of my tux jacket.

Chaney shakes his head, "Don't be lame, Rome. I

know you're old and shit, but stay, man. Enjoy the party. You more than earned it."

"I'm only fucking thirty-three, you dick. I'm not *old*. Not my fault I've got hair on my balls older than you."

He looks offended for a moment before a smug grin spreads on his face, "Yeah, well, you've got some wrinkles right there, dude. I know this girl who specializes in Botox..."

"Fuck you."

The asshole only grins harder, then tosses back the amber liquid in his clear plastic cup, draining it in one quick gulp. "Well, since you're dipping out because you're lame and my Tinder date has *officially* ghosted me, my night's now wide open, and there are plenty of beauties right here that require my very undivided attention." He straightens his tie and winks, gesturing to the crowd of women who are staring at us from across the room.

Puck bunnies who want nothing more than one night with any of us, and any other time, I might have been game, but tonight?

I'm not feeling it.

And I don't blame the rookie for not wanting to stick around to listen to me being a grumpy asshole. Hell, I can hardly stand to be around myself right now. I should be celebrating with my friends, yet all I want to do is head home and sit on my couch with a six-pack and game highlights. *Alone.*

It's not like me, but then again, lately, I don't feel very much like myself.

It feels weird being in the very best physical shape of my life, playing better than I ever have, and mentally not being on the same page. Like my mind is at war with my body. Maybe it's because, like the rookie said, I *am* getting older. Logically, I know I'm not *old*—I'm in my thirties. But mid thirties is practically an expiration date for hockey players. Unless you're the next Gretzky or Howe, you're likely retiring before thirty-five. Most people's bodies can't handle the grueling gameplay and aggressive hits they receive on the ice, no matter how in shape they are.

I've known it since I was a kid and made hockey my dream. That if I ever did make it to the big leagues, there would always be an end date long before most men retire. I guess I just didn't realize how fast it would go. Hell, what would I even do if I wasn't playing hockey?

"Alright, catch you later," I tell him. "Be smart. No more fucking people's girlfriends."

He shrugs. "Not my fault they're not being entirely truthful."

I don't even bother with a response to that and instead make my way through the exit. I've had enough of Chaney for the night.

The moment the cool night air hits my cheeks, my shoulders dip in relief. I feel like I'm taking my first full breath of the night without my chest tightening in restlessness. I feel less caged in. I pull my phone from my pocket and unlock it, aimlessly scrolling through my notifications as I walk toward the dim, empty courtyard.

More texts from my ex that I swipe away and don't even bother opening. Definitely not in the mood to deal with that shit. A few emails from sponsors. Most of the notifications are from the family group chat between Mom, Dad, and Hailey, my little sister.

FAMJAM

Hailey: I'm bringing someone to our family dinner this month. Hudson, if you start shit, I'm going to leak your number on twitter. Again.

Mom: Hailey Elizabeth!

Dad: Haha. This is going to be GREAT.

For fuck's sake.

"Oof."

Suddenly, my phone flies from my hand and skids across the concrete of the courtyard with a dramatic crunch as I collide with something soft and pliable, taking me by surprise.

Well, fuck.

I drag my gaze up and see what... or more like who I've run into. She's short, her head barely reaching the middle of my chest, with long, golden-blonde hair that falls down her back in loose curls. Her body is wrapped in a tight red dress that has my mouth watering just at the sight. The material is molded to her figure, accentuating her toned thighs and curvy hips. *Damn.* My eyes move upward, drinking in her supple bust, lingering on how perfectly she fills out the dress clinging to her body like one very lucky glove, until I snap out of it and drag my gaze back to her face.

Her plump, glossy lips are tightened in a scowl as her gaze narrows.

"Shit, are you okay?" I ask, wincing when I realize she's rubbing the part of her head where she hit me, like it hurts.

Her bright pink nails rub at the spot, and she shakes her head slightly. "Um, yes? I guess, considering I just got plowed into by a giant."

I bite back a smirk from the innuendo. Even with the mask of frustration resting upon her face, she's still one of the most beautiful women I've ever seen. Long, dark, thick lashes frame her blue eyes. Her nose has a slender, delicate slope that makes her look even more... soft? Dainty? Feminine.

Fuck me. She's stunning. And I quite literally ran into her, nearly knocking her down like an asshole.

Even with heels on, she's so much shorter than me that I'm looking down my nose at her. She's fun-sized, but curvy where it counts.

"I'm so sorry. I was texting and not paying attention to where I was going."

"It's fine. I'm okay." Pulling her hand away, she peers up at me with wide eyes. "I think your chest might actually be made of concrete or something. Jesus."

I laugh. "I've taken a few hits in my life. My ego thanks you." I squat down and pick up my phone, and of course, the screen is fucking shattered. Pieces of glass are chipped and falling out. I groan. "Shit."

"Oh god, well, now I'm the one who feels bad," she says as she gawks at my destroyed phone. She rolls her plump, glossy lip between her teeth, and I'm not even going to pretend that my eyes aren't glued to that simple yet sexy-as-fuck motion.

"Nah, it's just a phone. It can be replaced." I tuck it into my pocket and lift my eyes back to hers, trying like fuck to ignore the fact that she's so beautiful. "I just want to make sure you're okay. Only an asshole texts and walks. Let me make it up to you."

The words are out of my mouth in a rush before I can even think about how it could sound. Because I'm obviously not. Thinking, that is.

Her eyebrows raise in question, the corner of her lips turning up slightly. "Are you... *propositioning* me?"

"What? No. Shit." I try to gauge her reaction. "I mean, maybe? If you're going to say yes, then definitely. Absolutely."

Mystery girl throws her head back and laughs, the soft, sweet sound floating around the empty courtyard around us. "That might be the best or... maybe the worst way I've ever been hit on in my life. Not sure just yet."

I shrug. "Guess I need to make it the best, then, huh? Why are you out here anyway and not inside enjoying the party?"

"Mmm... not really my kind of party," she says simply, tucking a stray piece of hair behind her ear. "Needed some fresh air."

"Hockey not your thing?"

"Not really. More of a baseball kind of girl, and it's my first time here, so I've kind of just been people-watching."

Hm. So not a puck bunny and never been to the practice arena?

"How about a grand tour, then?" I ask. I know the last thing I should be doing is picking up a stranger at the Stanley Cup party, yet there's something about her, something that I can't put my finger on, that has me desperate for even a few more minutes to get to know her. "Once-in-a-life-time kinda tour. Maybe by the end, you'll be a hockey fan."

For a second, I think she might say no as she shuffles from one foot to the other and hoists the purse higher on her shoulder, but then a wide smile spreads on her face, and she gestures toward the entrance. "Lead the way, then, Mr...."

She trails off, and that's when I realize through the entire conversation neither of us offered up our names.

Maybe she really doesn't know a thing about hockey, and if that's true, then she has no clue who I am.

And that sounds more appealing than it should.

Anonymity.

Being whoever I want to be. Not Hudson Rome the hockey player or the Playboy Playmaker, who gets plastered all over the tabloids. No pressure to be anyone but... *me.*

Maybe it's wrong, but I offer up the first thing that comes to my mind.

"You can call me... Romeo."

I see the understanding in her eyes, but she just shakes her head and laughs lightly. "Okay... then you can just call me *Juliet.*"

"CHAMPAGNE TASTES SO MUCH FUCKING BETTER when it's the good shit," I say, taking another sip from the bottle we've been sharing for the last hour. I swiped it from a server's tray before we started the behind-the-scenes tour of the arena.

I pass the bottle to her, and she takes a hefty sip, draining the rest of the bottle. I didn't realize how quickly we'd gone through it until the last drop hit her tongue. I lost track of time as we walked, exchanging random things about ourselves and her laughing at my lame jokes, or at least pretending to.

It's the first time in a long time I've felt no pressure, where I can just be exactly who I am, without worrying about what that really means.

"Not that I have a *ton* of experience in expensive champagne, but this does taste incredible. So smooth. Like velvet."

Her eyes are a little glossy, her words a little slow, and her movements match my own. The good shit always does that to you. It sneaks up when you're least expecting it and hits you right where it should.

She sets the bottle down and reaches into her purse, pulling out a small pack of gum, and pops the piece into her mouth. Her cheeks heat when she catches me staring. "What?"

I shrug. "Nothing. Didn't strike me as a Hubba Bubba kinda girl."

Her eyebrows raise. "I'll have you know that I am supporting a very long addiction to this gum. The strawberry watermelon flavor is the best thing I've ever tasted. Do you want to try?"

"I take your word for it, *Bubblegum*." My tone is laced with amusement.

Tossing her head back, she laughs, her small shoulders shaking. "I think I like that nickname. Definitely more than Juliet."

This girl is interesting, and fuck, she's *fun*.

"Good. And this..." I say, gesturing to the door at the end of the hallway, the last stop on my tour, "is... the broom closet?"

"Oh, is that included as part of this tour? The broom closet?" She laughs, stepping in a breath closer.

The sweet, fruity smell of her bubble gum surrounds me, and fuck, I don't know if it's the champagne or the dizzying effect she has on me, but I lean in, murmuring, "Of course. Had to save the best for last. I'm a grand finale kind of guy."

When she looks up at me, the corner of her lips slants upward into a teasing grin. "Are you going to kiss me or not, *Romeo*? I've been waiting all night, you know."

Fucking Christ.

I reach for the closet door and wrench it open, tugging her inside behind me. She lets out a surprised yelp, and the door closes behind us, sealing us in darkness.

Suddenly, I feel her hands along my abdomen, and I step forward, reaching for her at the very same time.

My lips hover over hers for only a single moment, the briefest second of hesitation before we collide together inside the tiny closet I've crammed us in. It smells a little musty, and it's hot as shit in here, but I can't think about anything other than the feel of her lush body pressed against mine. Her lips are soft, and every time she sucks in a breath, a tiny stuttery moan escapes, shooting straight to my dick.

I'm gonna have to admit that it's been a while since I've been with anyone who made my blood race, and right now, my heart feels like it's going to jump out of my goddamn chest. This girl, she's fucking gorgeous, and every inch of her fits perfectly in my hands. Like she was made just for me. I squeeze the fabric at her hips, dragging her even closer against me as my tongue slides against the seam of her lips, dipping into her mouth as I swallow another breathy moan.

There's nothing but chaos between us, a frenzy of hands and lips, fevered caresses, and desperate kisses. My hands drag down her body, pausing over her delicious ass, which I squeeze in my palms before I lift her off her feet. Her sharp heels dig into my back as she wraps her legs around my waist, gripping me with her shapely thighs.

"I live right up the road... with a big bed and an even bigger shower. A huge kitchen counter..." I tear my lips away and stare back at her, panting, "Let." *Kiss.* "Me." *Kiss.* "Take you." *Kiss.* "Home?"

She tugs at the short strands of my hair, bringing my mouth back to hers on a breathless moan. "As much as I am enjoying this, and I am thoroughly enjoying it... I'd rather not complicate this."

I pull back and gaze back at her. "So, that's a no?"

"It's a no. Listen, I really, really want to have sex with

you. Can we just like... fuck? Like have incredible, mind-blowing sex, then walk away like it never happened? Two strangers simply getting each other off? Sounds fun, right?"

I mean...

Before I can even respond, I feel her hand brush against my cock, and it jerks at the feel of her. The dirty bastard doesn't give a shit, and then, well, I just don't bother responding at all. I claim her lips, walking her backward until her back hits the far side of the wall so hard that cleaning supplies go clattering to the floor around us. Neither of us so much as pauses at the commotion.

She wants to get fucked and skip the small talk? Fine with me.

That just means that if this is the only time I get to blow her mind, I'm going to make every damn second count.

TWO
HUDSON

When I said I was making every second count, I meant it, and I'm going to savor every moment I get with her. However short that may be.

Darkness surrounds us completely; the only light illuminating her is the small sliver that peeks from under the opening at the bottom of the door. She somehow is able to get the belt of my slacks undone, and she slips her tiny hand into the waistband of my briefs, circling my cock as much as she can. Her fingers don't meet, and when she realizes that, she moans against my lips, then tears her mouth away completely, her legs sliding down my hips, almost bringing my pants with her as her heels hit the concrete floor beneath us.

Tonight is full of surprises, including how I went from wanting nothing more than to be home and alone, to having this curvy, fun-sized goddess drop to her knees in front of me, enthusiastically grabbing my cock and guiding it to her mouth.

The second her lips envelop my cock, sucking me into her wet, waiting mouth, my hands fly to her hair, and a deep rumble of a groan tumbles from my chest.

"Holy fuck," I pant. In the dim light, I watch as she greedily sucks me deeper, struggling with my size but not letting it deter her in the least. She sucks my cock like she was made to do it. Like it's a fucking sport, and she's after the trophy. I fist her hair, guiding her deeper until the head of my cock bumps against the back of her throat, causing her to gag slightly around my length. "Fuck yeah, just like that."

Part of me wants to slow the fuck down and take my time with her, spend the entire night exploring every inch of her sexy body, and the other part of me wants to fuck her throat hard and fast, completely unhinged and out of control, like I feel right in this moment.

I'm even more surprised when she pulls off my cock and drags her tongue along my length until she's swiping at the beads of precum seeping from the slit. She uses her hands in tandem, swiveling them around me as she sucks greedily.

Like she might suck the soul right the fuck out of me.

I fist my hands tighter in her hair at the nape of her neck, forcing her to look up at me. Her wide eyes are filled with tears as she bobs her head back down, deep-throating me even further, her lips a perfect O around my length.

I could come just like this, flexing my hips further, fucking her throat gently, with her perched on her knees, opening her throat just for me.

"Is this what you wanted?" I grind out, tightening my fingers in her hair. "To suck a stranger's cock? To let him dirty you all up before sending you on your way?"

The crass words leave my mouth on a grunt as I surge deeper into her mouth, relishing in the sound of her moan that vibrates around my cock. The dirtiness of my words only seems to encourage her, and I can feel my spine tingling, my balls tightening.

I won't last much longer, not with her perfect mouth wrapped around me.

I withdraw from her mouth, using my hand fisted in her hair to pull her off, guiding her off her knees until she's standing at full height. Her glossy lips are now red and swollen from sliding along my cock, and the sight has my cock further thickening.

"Fuck, Juliet, you tryin' to kill me? We just met," I rasp, pulling her against me as I slide my hands under the fabric of her dress along the soft, pliant skin of her hips. So fucking sweet, and now I want to know if her pussy tastes as good as her lips do.

I drop to my knees in front of her and slide my hands up the smooth skin of her thighs, inching the dress higher and higher. Torturously slow, I bunch the fabric at her waist, revealing the little square of satin that scarcely covers her pussy. There's a wet spot right in the center, her little clit pushing against the fabric, begging to be sucked.

My fingers slip under the tiny straps on her hips, brushing along the soft curve of her skin as I slowly, so goddamn slowly, drag my nose along that little wet spot, inhaling deeply. She smells so fucking good and I don't need to run my tongue along the satin to know that she'll taste even sweeter.

I want her pussy on my tongue. Right the fuck now.

I want every drop until she's panting and writhing in my arms as she begs me to fuck her. And she will beg for my cock. I won't stop until she does.

Eyes pinned to the apex of her thighs, I drag the satin down her legs, letting the panties pool at her feet before I pick them up and then shove them into my pocket, silencing her protest with one long swipe to her pretty pink cunt.

Fuck, I was right. She tastes so good that I want to stay here for hours, eating her pussy until she's trembling and dripping.

"O-h god," she whispers, her hands flying to my shoulders, fingers digging into my skin through the jacket. "Do that again, please."

That's it, baby, fucking beg for it.

Tell me exactly what you want.

I bring her leg to my shoulder, hooking it around my neck, and then wrap my arms around her thighs to lift her off the floor, standing straight with both of her legs wrapped around my shoulders like a pair of fucking earmuffs.

"W-what?" she stutters. "Put me down. I'm too heavy."

Dragging my gaze from her perfect pussy up to her eyes, I shake my head, tightening my grip on her thighs, lifting her even higher just for good measure.

"Juliet, don't insult me. I could bench-press you above my head for a fucking hour. Now, please let me devour your pussy before I fucking die of starvation. The only thing I want to hear from those pretty lips is my name when you come on my face."

And that's exactly what I do with her hoisted against the wall. I eat her swollen, wet pussy like a man who's been starved, my hips flexing as I grind my cock against a fucking wall. Because until now, I didn't realize just how long I'd gone without the decadence of a meal. That's how she should be treated—like a delicacy. Because that's what she is.

I take my time acquainting myself with her pussy, tasting her. Every time I circle her clit with my tongue, she bucks against my mouth.

"So damn responsive," I mutter, then graze the sensitive bundle with my teeth. She whimpers and tightens her grip on me. I continue my assault of her clit, switching between flicking her with my tongue and sucking the tight bud into my mouth, dragging my teeth along her.

Her hips move in tandem with my mouth, bucking against me as her orgasm builds.

"That's it, ride my face, fuck my tongue," I say as I lift her higher, circling her entrance and tonguing her tight hole. I free one hand so I can fuck her with my fingers. When I slide two into her pussy, she clamps down around them, tossing her head back against the wall as she pulls my hair.

"I'm close... I—"

I fuck her harder, my fingers slamming in and out of her drenched pussy. The sound of her wetness, combined with her labored breathing and her throaty moans, has me ready to slam into her and make her come with my cock, but I have to make sure she's ready for me.

"Come for me, Juliet."

Sucking her clit into my mouth, I brush against her G-spot with my fingers. Her entire body shudders with pleasure as an orgasm rocks through her. She clenches around my fingers like a vise, so goddamn tight, her legs trembling on my shoulders as her back arches, and she cries out. A rush of wetness hits my tongue as her pussy spasms, and I greedily lick it up. Every fucking drop.

I'm thirty-three years old and can say without a fucking doubt that this girl squirting on my face in a stuffy, musty broom closet is the best thing that has fucking happened to me in a long time. Hell, maybe ever.

She sags against me, her entire body pliant and sated as her orgasm subsides. I slowly, carefully slide her down my body until her legs wrap around my waist, and we're face-to-face, her hovering slightly above me.

Her fingers dance along my lips, which are still slick with her cum. I suck her thumb into my mouth, swirling my tongue along the pad, gently nipping until she yelps with a heavy-lidded stare.

"That was..."

"Fucking incredible. Amazing. Highlight of my goddamn week," I tell her.

"Good thing it's not over yet, then, huh?" Her eyes shine with amusement but quickly darken as I reach out and brush my thumb along the hardened peak of her nipple that is straining against the thin fabric of her dress.

And while I could touch her all damn day, what stops me in my tracks is the dainty metal barbell piercing that my finger connects with.

Goddamnit.

No bra and now, no panties because they're mine, and she can't have them back.

"Good thing," I murmur in agreement, then yank her closer to me, sealing my lips over hers. I can still taste myself on her tongue, and if anything, it makes the kiss wilder. Feral. More unhinged, a rushed tangle of hands and teeth. "I need to be inside you, right the fuck now."

She nods against my lips, fisting her hands into the rumpled fabric of my button-down and yanking. A button goes flying, causing us to both laugh. Damn, I love the sound of her laugh.

So fucking adorable. Everything about her is sweet. I almost feel guilty for defiling her so filthily in a broom closet, except I know she wants it as badly as I do. The evidence is still on my tongue.

I reach between us, palming my aching cock before guiding it to her pussy and dragging it through her slick, soaked center. She coats my cock, and fuck, it feels like heaven, and I'm not even inside of her yet.

Her arm hooks around my neck as she lifts herself and slides down onto my cock, impaling herself in one swift motion that has us both groaning.

It echoes around us, mingling with the sound of her wetness as I withdraw and slam her back down onto me. I press her against the wall and tug the front of her dress down, revealing her full, perky tits.

The piercings.

Completely unexpected, they take me by surprise, a groan rumbling from my chest as I drop my forehead to the center of her chest. "These are so goddamn sexy," I tell her before sealing my lips around her nipple, sucking the taut peak into my mouth as I begin to move my hips.

My teeth scrape the metal, earning a soft, breathy moan from her and a tight clench around my cock when I tug on it.

"God, fuck, oh god," she pants when I start fucking her into the wall, harder with each slap of my hips against her soft, creamy thighs. I want to lose myself in her for the rest of the night. Maybe longer. I suck and bite the smooth skin of her supple tits, leaving my marks behind, finding a steady rhythm as I fuck her. They bounce with each thrust of my hips.

"Fucking perfect," I grunt when she clenches around my cock. My balls draw up, ready to release, ready to paint the inside of her tight cunt with my cum. Goddamnit, not yet.

I don't want this to be over. Not yet. Not when there are so many ways I want to fuck her, so many different positions I want to see her curvy body in.

Pulling out of her completely, I lower her feet to the ground, then flip her around so her hands are pressed against the wall. My hands fit in the soft curve of her hips, and I pull her hips back until her ass is flush with my cock.

This ass would bring even the best men to their knees, and right now, if I wasn't so desperate to be back inside of her, I'd drop to mine in front of her and devour her pussy for the second time tonight.

Gripping her ass, I spread her open, line up my cock, and sink back inside of her in one swift thrust, causing us both to groan at the sensation. She's so goddamn tight and squeezing me like a vise.

There's no way I'm going to last pounding into her from behind. My hand slides up her back to the nape of her neck, where I grasp the silky strands in my fist as I fuck her.

My thrusts turn shallow, with each slap of my hips harder than the last, like I'm practically trying to fuck her into the wall. Before I can even reach around to rub her clit, she's clamping down on me and pulling my release from my cock as she comes.

"Fuck yeah," I grunt, bringing my lips to her neck as I empty inside her. Her entire body trembles as she comes, gripping onto my neck until the orgasm quakes through her. She sags against the wall as it subsides, and I drop my forehead to her back, trying to catch my fucking breath.

After a second, I pull out of her slowly, pulling her dress back down to cover her ass.

I'm hoping I can convince her to come home with me so I can spend the rest of the night inside of her when she turns to face me, a knowing grin on her lips.

She says nothing as she smooths her hair down and uses her fingers to wipe at the corners of her lips.

I forget the question entirely when she leans forward, pressing her lips to mine, and pats my chest. "Thanks, Romeo. Have a nice night."

Then, without a second glance, she opens the closet door and disappears out of sight.

What... the... hell... just happened?

THE MOMENT CHANEY sees me walking back to the table, his face transforms into confusion as his lips turn up in a sly grin, "Thought you were headed out? Where you been? And what the *hell* is wrong with your hair?"

Immediately, I reach up and smooth my hair, not realizing that it's fucked, but after what I just experienced... well, the number of times she grabbed on for dear life...

For a moment, I think about not telling him what just happened. She wanted to remain anonymous, but then again... I don't even know the girl's real name. All I know is that I just had the best sex of my life with a complete stranger, and the only thing I know about her is how tight her pussy is and that she's not a hockey fan.

"Yeah, well..." I lean closer, lowering my voice. "I just had the best sex of my goddamn life in a broom closet with a girl I don't even know, and she left me there before I could even put my dick back in my pants."

His eyes widen, comically so, before he bursts out laughing, loud and raucous, causing several eyes to turn his way. I slap him on the back of the head, promptly quieting his dramatic ass.

"*Shut up, you idiot.*"

"Fuck, don't hit me! I'm sorry. I'm *sorry.*" He raises his hands in defense, stepping back slightly before I can hit him again, "That shit is hilarious. Man, have the tables turned, huh? Tell me, Romeo, when's the last time someone hit and quit *you?*"

My eyes narrow as the scowl on my lips deepens. In my post-sex haze, I hadn't even realized what was happening. "You know what? I don't even know why I just told you. Can you please for the love of god keep quiet? Not say shit to anyone else?"

"Your secret's safe with me, *Romeo.*"

The smug-ass grin on his lips tells me that it won't be long until the entire damn team knows.

THREE
HUDSON

Chaos. That's all there is surrounding me. Pure, unfiltered fucking *chaos*. Complete with a bouncy house and a whole-ass petting zoo. No, really, an *actual* zoo. Imagine my surprise when I walked into Reed's mansion this afternoon and saw a fucking goat looking at me all funny.

There's a miniature cow, a herd of baby goats, a couple of sheep, and this little baby pig that keeps squealing like it's stuck the second one of the kids manages to catch it. All of the animals are secured behind a rickety-ass wire fence with a drove of toddlers all fighting to get as close as they possibly can to them.

Without a doubt, this was Holland's idea, and as usual, Reed went along with it because that's just who he is. The guy would give her anything, including his balls in a handbasket, if she asked for them.

"This is fucking wild," Reed mutters, taking in the sight in front of him. It's like *Survival of the Fittest*— toddler edition. I'm pretty sure someone is going to end up with an elbow to the face and a black eye as a trophy.

A chuckle rumbles through my chest as I take it all in, shaking my head. As wild as it is, I wouldn't want to be anywhere else. With my brothers and their families that have become my own along the way. I love these wild-ass kids.

Just as the thought enters my mind, Evan runs past me, with Alex and Olive both chasing after him, giggling.

There's a part of me that can't even believe that it's his *eighth* birthday. It feels like just yesterday, Reed was getting the call, and suddenly, Evan was the center of all of our lives. I've watched him grow from a quiet toddler into a mini version of my best friend, and it makes my chest swell with pride. This is my nephew. Even if we're not joined by blood, we have all loved this kid like he was ours since the very first day.

Time is fucking flying. It feels like every time I blink, there's another kid being born. Someone getting married. Moving away. New teammates. Everything's changing before I even realize that it has.

"Which part? The fact that you have a full-blown zoo in your backyard or the fact that your kid is practically a teenager?" I ask him.

Reed shakes his head, his dark hair falling in his face,

but it doesn't cover the way that his eyes soften. "Nah, don't do that shit to me. He's still got a few years. I can't even think about that yet."

"Yeah, remember what you were like when you hit puberty?" Briggs asks. He's standing beside me with Dexter, his youngest, slumped against his chest and snoring slightly. There's a small spot of drool crusted on the corner of his parted lips.

How the kid can sleep with the commotion going on around us is beyond me, but if there's one thing that I've learned about kids, it's that they are resilient. A lot of times, more than us adults are.

"Fuck yeah I do, which is why I am not looking forward to it. Plus, I just want to keep him little, man. No one tells you how hard it will be to watch them grow up. Part of you wants to hold on just a little bit longer, and the other part can't wait to see the person they become," Reed says, his eyes glittering as Evan runs around his party, a toothless grin on his lips.

Asher nods. "I feel this. Just watching all of your kids and Alex grow up. Bittersweet kinda feeling."

The same familiar ache that's been heavy on my chest for weeks, maybe even months, spreads within my rib cage, and I sigh, bringing the water bottle to my lips and draining it in a single gulp.

"Reed?" Holland squeaks from the cotton candy stand, where she's admittedly looking a bit frazzled at the crowd of kids in front of her. Her long, honey hair is now swept into a messy bun on the top of her head, and she's got a smear of something dark brown and crusty on her face that I'm really hoping is cupcake icing.

"Be right back. Gotta go save my wife from toddler eat toddler," Reed jokes, then jogs over to her, leaving Asher, Briggs, and I alone.

Chaney barrels toward us, a toddler hot on his heels, a look of pure terror in his eyes. "Fuck, save me!" he hisses as the kid giggles and tries to latch onto his leg. He leans closer, lowering his voice. "Literally, help me. I can't do this shit. What do I do with it?"

His eyes widen in fear as his gaze drops down to the giggling little girl currently wrapped around his leg like a spider monkey.

"Nah, everyone does their time. You got this." Briggs grins.

All three of us share a knowing smile because man, did we do the fucking time. I can't tell you how many diapers I've changed, or how many times I pulled unknown *"objects"* from underneath my couch after Evan and Olive stayed over at the apartment with Graham, Asher, and me. Every single one of us has been the fun uncle at one point in time, most of us many times over.

"Please," he pleads, his voice breaking slightly as the little girl squeezes harder and nestles into the fabric of his

pant leg. He shakes his leg as if he's trying to shake off a bug or a small animal.

Taking mercy on the panicked rookie, I squat down, getting eye to eye with the little girl, and whisper conspiratorially, "You know they have ice cream over there?"

When that gets her attention, I lean in even closer and whisper like it's the best-kept secret in the entire town. "*Chocolate* ice cream."

One arm loosens.

"*With sprinkles.*"

Suddenly, she lets go of Chaney's leg and squeals, darting off toward the cake and ice cream table.

"Thank *fuck,*" he mutters as his entire body shudders. "I need a beer. I don't know how you do this. I'll never be a father, ever. Kids are not my thing."

Asher laughs. "Yeah, pretty sure we've all said that, rookie. Better wrap it before you tap it."

My gaze drifts out across the party again, taking in all of the screaming kids, the sound of gleeful laughter, and back again to the fact that I can't seem to shake the heaviness I've been feeling. If anything, it's gotten increasingly worse, and I don't know what the hell is going on.

"You're quiet today," Briggs says, pulling me from my thoughts. When I glance up, they're all looking at me curiously. "Unusually quiet."

Chaney's eyebrows raise, "He's still thinking about his mystery girl that rocked his world in the broom closet at the party. Dude's got it bad for the girl, and he doesn't even know her name."

I scowl at him, narrowing my gaze. Dickhead.

It's been three weeks since that night, and as much as I don't want to admit it, he's right. I can't fucking stop thinking about her, and there's not a damn thing I can do about it.

She wanted one night, and she made that shit abundantly clear when she left me with my dick hanging out of my pants and her panties still damp in my pocket.

All I know is that she was fucking incredible and that I want more than that one night, but I have nothing to go on to find her. Not her name, where she's from. *Nothing.*

"Fuck off," I mutter but don't deny it. There's no point lying about it, not to the guys who know me better than I know myself sometimes.

"What did I miss?" Reed cuts in as he walks back up. He's sweating, his dark hair plastered to his forehead, looking like he just ran a marathon. Guess he sorta did, chasing after those kids.

It appears the kids have moved on from cake and ice cream and are now partaking in pony rides, with Evan currently riding on a bedazzled birthday pony.

"Hudson's got it bad for the girl that ghosted him while his pants were still down," Asher says, smirking.

I swear, these fuckers. I'll never live this shit down.

Reed's eyebrows furrow, and he shakes his head.

"Ouch. I thought you had moved on from your Romeo and Juliet tryst."

"Y'all are fuckers. I am over it. It wasn't a big deal, and you're all making it a big deal."

"Yeah, *ooookay*," Chaney says with a shrug. "Except you've been all moody since that night, so obviously, you're not over it even though you're saying that you are."

"Exactly," Briggs adds. Dexter sighs sleepily in his arms as he drops a light kiss to his sleeping son's head.

"Look, it's just like... I dunno, I felt... *alive*. For the first time in a long time, I felt like more. She was funny as hell, beautiful, just the whole damn package, and I feel like an idiot for not getting her real name or her number. She made me... I don't know. It's stupid." I shake my head. "Just forget it."

"Nah, man, it's not stupid. I get it," Reed says. "She was unexpected, and it took you by surprise."

"It's like I feel like I'm fucking stuck in this never-ending cycle. I play hockey, I go to bars, I spend time with my family, but I just feel like, what's the point? Who am I outside of hockey? What does it matter at the end of the day? What happens when hockey is over for me? What happens when an injury puts me out for an entire season? The league wouldn't take me back after that shit, not with my age. It doesn't matter how good my stats are." I pause, dragging my hand over my face, the emotion of the last few weeks spilling out. "You guys have families. Wives. If it all ended for you, you have the rest of your lives to look forward to with them. Me? I have nothing. I have an empty house. Meaningless hookups with girls I never see again. I just feel like I want more, and I don't even know where to start." I take a breath when I finish.

It all kind of just spilled out of me, these questions that have been flitting through my head over the last few weeks, especially after the night with my mystery Juliet. Try as I fucking might, I haven't been able to stop thinking about her.

She made me question shit.

She made me think about what could have been.

The "*what-if.*"

Not just her... hockey. My life.

That night in a dusty closet changed things for me.

Do I want to continue to live an empty life of *what-ifs?*

"You know what? You remember before I met Mads, how fucking lost I was? All that shit with my brother. I was two seconds from being benched permanently," Briggs says, holding my gaze.

I nod. Of course I remember it.

It was pure agony watching Briggs go through that shit. He walked in on his fiancée in bed with his brother, and now they're married with a child together. When it happened, he fell into a hole so deep even we couldn't pull him out.

"I think the only thing that truly made a difference,

the only thing that saved me, was when I was coaching the kids at Face-Off. I needed to take a step back, and it helped to give back and do something for someone else. I was lost, and getting out of my own head, spending time with them... it was better than any shrink could've ever been for me. You could try to reach out, see if they need anyone."

Me? Coaching kids?

"Yeah, I mean, you're good with our kids. You're their favorite uncle—don't tell Graham, or I'll never hear the end of it. But it might be a good place to start while you're figuring things out. And Hudson... It's not a bad thing to be thinking about the future and what it means for you. Even if it seems hazy right now, I have no doubt that you'll figure it out. Just like we did," Asher says, clapping me on the back. "You'd be great with those kids. You've got more patience than any of us combined."

Reed nods in agreement. "I think you'd be great at it, brother. Asher's right. You've got the patience of a saint. Way more than I do, that's for sure."

"Yeah, me too," Chaney adds.

"That's because you're emotionally still a toddler, Chaney," I say, rolling my eyes. "I don't know. I don't want to bring my shit into coaching, and who knows if I'd even be good at that shit? I don't know if I want to be in charge of a group of kids, and I couldn't be around as much during the season. It all seems like a fuck ton of responsibility."

"It is," Briggs says, pausing to check on Dexter, who has stirred slightly in his arms. "But seeing the smile on their faces when they finally nail a shot or the first goal they score after practicing all week... it does something to you. Trust me, okay? Just check it out, see what you think before you commit. Listen, you're our brother for life, hockey or not, and you know it. We're not going anywhere, and we'll be here to help you figure out your shit."

"Time for presents!" Holland calls across the yard, and the kids go running. I guess that's our cue.

For the rest of the party, I'm lost in thought about what the guys said, and even though I shouldn't, I think of Juliet.

And the *what-ifs*.

I SPEND the rest of the weekend watching baseball on the couch and only leave the house to have Sunday dinner with my family. When I brought up volunteering to coach at dinner, my parents and my sister insisted that I do it.

Although they don't know about my Juliet or everything really going on in my head, they said that it was a great idea and ultimately why I had my agent reach out to Face-Off first thing Monday morning. Even though we've done a few events with the organization as a team before, I hadn't ever worked with them one-on-one. I didn't know what to expect when my agent called back and let me know that he had set up a meeting for the following morning.

Briggs said that those kids saved his life in a way that I couldn't imagine, and thinking back to the shit that he went through, I know how rough he had it. Thank fuck he found Maddison and ended up where he should be, but my best friend fought his way back from hell. And he says he owes it all to these kids and this organization for pulling him out of the darkest place of his life. For helping him heal and be a better man.

That's enough for me, and who knows? Maybe coaching these kids will change me too. I want that feeling. The one where it feels like I have a fucking purpose and a path because right now, I feel like I'm wandering aimlessly in circles with no end in sight.

"Hudson Rome?" I glance up to see a short woman with a black T-shirt that reads Face-Off on it striding toward me, a warm smile plastered on her face. Her blonde hair is pulled back in a clip, and she's got a huge stack of folders and a clipboard in her arms, but it doesn't seem to be slowing her down.

Nodding, I extend my hand toward her. "Hi, yes, I'm Hudson."

We quickly shake hands, and she smiles up at me, "I'm

Laura Atkins, and I'm so glad you're here. When your agent reached out to me, I was ecstatic because we could totally use the help. We're organizing a few big events for the year, and it's a bit overwhelming. In the best way, of course."

The way she says it isn't negative at all, more gracious that she's able to organize it in the first place.

I can't help the grin that tugs at my lips. For the first time in a long time, I find myself nervous but looking forward to what's to come. Excitement strums through my chest.

"I'm happy to be here. Briggs is like my brother, and he speaks so highly of your organization that it was a no-brainer to reach out and see if you guys wanted any help."

"Trust me, the kids are going to lose their minds when they find out they're meeting Hudson Rome. I'm sure you already know that you're a lot of these kids' favorite player."

That makes me feel good. A foreign feeling erupts in the pit of my stomach. Something that makes me proud.

It's nice to hear something like that instead of another backhanded comment about my reputation from whatever gossip site they've read.

The Playboy Playmaker, can't take shit seriously, bad boy of the NHL reputation. The one that feels more damning by the second. A reputation that I used to revel in, and now I can't get away from if it killed me.

"You had more saves than any goalie in the entire league last season. And that shutout against the Rangers? Iconic."

Relief immediately floods me that my reputation as an athlete is what matters here. "Thanks. That was a really good game."

"For sure. Uh, I need to drop these off at my office really quickly, then I'd love to give you a tour of the facility and get you squared away with your team and a loose schedule?"

"Perfect."

She smiles enthusiastically and turns on her heel, motioning for me to follow behind her. As we walk toward the end of the hallway, I notice all of the photos that line the walls. I end up trailing a ways behind while looking, and suddenly she's next to me.

"That's Mason Rice. He's up for the Entry Draft this year, and we're so proud to have watched him become this incredible player. That's why we do this. We meet these amazing kids who don't have the financial means to play hockey, whether it be because they're in the foster care system or because they're living with a relative or even because they qualify for low-income subsidizing. We make it happen, and we give them an outlet. All they want is for someone to believe in them and to give them a chance."

This place is something I can stand behind, without a doubt. Just from hearing her talk about it, admiration shining in her eyes, it seems like a program that I want to be involved in.

"Thank you for allowing me to be a part of it," I tell her sincerely.

And fuck, do I mean it. I've only been here for a few minutes, and I already feel like I have a purpose in being here.

"C'mon, let's get you ready to go, Coach Rome."

After spending twenty minutes touring their facility and meeting a few of the other coaches and staff, we walk back to Laura's office, and I take a seat in the worn chair across from her desk.

Despite the volume of folders that are on it, everything is neat and tidy and seems to be organized.

"So, what do you think?" she says, leaning back in her chair, a teasing smirk on her lips.

I think that maybe Briggs was onto something. That this place is exactly what I was missing, and maybe it's too early to tell, but for the first time in a long time, I'm looking forward instead of backwards.

"I'm ready when you are."

Leaning forward, she pulls a dark blue folder off her desk and opens it, turning it toward me. "Well, I know when Mr. Wilson volunteered, he had the U8 kids, but right now, we're full for the younger age brackets. So, you'd be coaching the U14 kids. I know you'll have less availability once the season starts too, so we'll also partner you with an assistant coach to help out when you're away for the NHL."

Shit. Teenagers? What the hell do I know about teenagers?

My eyes lift to hers. "Should I be scared?"

Laura laughs, shaking her head. "They're great kids. Some of them have a pretty hard exterior that might take a while to break through, but they're still amazing kids with so much talent. You'll be surprised how good some of these guys are."

I nod, chewing my lip in contemplation.

Can I coach a bunch of fourteen-year-old boys? I barely know anything about kids in general, let alone hormone-infested boys who think they're men.

"Give it a chance, Hudson. All these kids want is someone who won't give up on them."

I may not know shit about kids, but what I do know is that since walking into this building, I've felt lighter than I have in months.

"Let's go meet my team, then."

FOUR

HUDSON

"Have a seat, Rome." Coach Evans gestures to the worn leather chair across from his desk. "Or should I just call you *Romeo?*" he says with a glowering look.

My jaw tenses. I fucking hate that name and the stigma that comes with it. It used to not bother me, but lately, I hate it more than ever. Unless it's from *my* Juliet's mouth.

"Rome is fine, sir."

He smiles without a hint of humor and nods, taking a seat behind his desk, his hands folded over his stomach. The top of his desk is littered with folders and papers, along with pens bearing the Avalanches logo.

When he texted me that he wanted to meet with me, I was immediately wary. There are only ever two reasons he wants to see me in his office. One... to bitch me out for something. Or two... he wants to go over gameplay. And since it's the off-season, that only leaves one thing.

"Thanks for coming in today. Sorry to pull you in on your time off, but I need to discuss something with you that unfortunately couldn't wait." He pauses, leaning back further in his chair. "You had a good season, Rome. Hope next year is just as exceptional."

I nod. "Me too. I'm feeling strong. Feeling ready. Looking forward to camp and the season."

It's no secret that even though I perform better than any goalie he's ever had, the man doesn't like me. Never has. He's seen my name in the headlines one too many times, seen what I'm like off the ice. He rode my ass so hard in the beginning of my career because he didn't think my reputation was good for the team or my focus, and it took forever for me to prove myself.

Can't say I blame him. My game speaks for itself now, but the perceptions about my extracurricular activities haven't gone away, and that hangs over my head.

That's the fucking problem. I have this reputation of being a playboy and not taking things seriously, and I want out.

I'm sick of carrying that shit on my back. I want to be known as something different, even if I don't know what the hell that means right now.

So, he can feel however he wants to feel, but he can't

deny that I'm an asset to this team, no matter what they write about me on the internet.

"Glad to hear it. So, as you may have heard by now, since the guys on my team like to gossip like a bunch of women, my daughter moved to Chicago over the summer. She was living with her mother in Seattle, but is relocating to Chicago to attend the University of Northwestern."

My brow furrows in confusion. Not sure why he asked me to come all the way down here to discuss his daughter.

He laughs, shaking his head. "Judging by the look on your face, you're wondering what this has to do with you. Caroline is majoring in sports medicine at Northwestern, and part of her graduation requirement is an internship. Given our partnership with the organization, I set her up with one at Face-Off Foundation. And a few days ago, I got an email from PR letting me know that you've recently started working with them too. Generally, I don't get involved in media stuff unless it's affecting the team, but since you will be working with my daughter, I wanted to have a conversation with you."

Well, at least he's not fucking recommending me for a trade. I can breathe a little easier knowing that.

"Yeah, I've been working with Face-Off for the past couple of weeks. It's been really rewarding. I'm coaching a team of thirteen- and fourteen-year-olds, and they're great kids."

The last three weeks have been like a breath of fresh

air. I'm still figuring my shit out, but when I wake up in the morning, I feel... fulfilled. I look forward to going to the arena to teach them, and it's been a while since I felt this happy. Refreshed.

"PR put you up to this? Are you in trouble that I haven't heard about?" he asks, his dark brows furrowing with distaste, like he wouldn't be the least bit surprised if I found myself in the headlines again. He *would* think that the only reason I'm doing this is because I'm trying to save face.

"No. I just... just really wanted to give back to the community. That's all. Working with the kids on my team has been really fulfilling. I just want them to have the same opportunities that others have."

Coach is silent when I finish speaking, his eyes searching mine like he has something to say but doesn't.

Whether he believes me or not doesn't matter. I'm not doing this as a publicity stunt; I'm doing this because working with these kids is fixing something inside of me that has been off for a long time.

"If you're going to be working with this organization, Rome, I want no bullshit. You hear me? I find you on a gossip site making Face-Off or the Avalanches look bad, I'm going to lose my shit. You wanna do this and be the poster boy for the team? Fine. I'll allow it, but if you fuck up, that's it. The last thing I need on my hands is to clean up a damn PR nightmare. Especially with my daughter working there. Keep it in line. I mean it." He pauses, sighing heavily. "Do right by these kids. You can't half-ass it, and that includes half-ass committing to them. It'll be hard to balance while you're on the road, but you can't shortchange them. They're worth more than that."

I swallow as I nod. "I know that. I have no intention of going anywhere. I'm in it for the long haul, Coach. I'll be on my very best behavior."

"And that includes my daughter. Keep an eye on her and make sure she's okay. She's in a new city, and I worry about her."

Wow, the man does have a heart.

There's a light rap at the door, interrupting his spiel, and his eyes flicker to the small window in the door. He raises his hand to wave them inside, pausing our conversation.

When the door clicks open, then shuts, I'm shocked to see Coach's face transform into a wide smile. I can't remember the last time I saw this man smile like this. Not even when we won the Stanley fucking Cup. It was a half-ass smirk, at best.

I turn in the chair to face the visitor, and the moment my gaze lands on her, my mouth runs dry. I almost swallow my fucking tongue.

Holy shit.

No fucking way.

What?

No. No. No. No. No. No. *No.*

The girl staring back at me with the wide blue eyes, looking every bit as shocked as I am, is *my* Juliet.

The girl whose taste I haven't stopped thinking about since I devoured her pussy in the broom closet of the arena.

"Hudson, this is my daughter, Caroline," he introduces us just as panic claws up my throat, our eyes locking. "Caroline, this is Hudson Rome, my starting goalie. We were just discussing you."

Words escape me. I can't believe who I'm staring at and that I'm seeing her again.

There's no fucking way this is happening right now.

I fucked my coach's daughter... and she's a *college* student...

Caroline Evans...

"Hi," I finally croak, offering her a curt nod. My heart pounds in my chest so hard that I can hear the steady thrum in my ears as I try to stop the entire goddamn room from spinning around me.

She recovers much more quickly than I do and plasters on a fake smile, her pink-painted lips spreading. "Hi... Hudson. Nice to meet you."

Her gaze moves to Coach, her fucking *father*. "Ready for lunch, Dad? I have a meeting at two..."

Fucking Christ. My coach's daughter.

I fucked his daughter. God, I didn't just fuck his daughter —I ate her pussy, sucked her cum off my fingers, and have beat off to the image of her soaked and spent nearly every day since.

My ass clenches at the thought of him finding out. If he hated me before? Pretty sure he'd lose his entire fucking mind if he found out that I defiled his daughter in a fucking broom closet while he drank champagne right down the hallway at the party.

He'd make my life fucking miserable. Go to the GM and demand I be traded because I'm an old fuck who literally slept with his daughter.

Jesus Christ.

My career would be over.

Before I could even blink.

Fuck, I don't think there could be a worse situation to be in right now. Aside from a fucking career-ending injury, and even then...

"Uh... so, I'm gonna head out, Coach. Glad we're on the same page. Thanks for the meeting today," I mutter, rising from the chair. I'm desperate to get out of this fucking room. I can't be in here another second, or I'm going to lose my shit.

He holds up his hand, halting me in my steps. "Wait a second, Rome. Sit."

My ass hits the chair immediately.

Juliet... Caroline, whoever the fuck she is, looks like

she's as uncomfortable as I feel, and her throat bobs as she swallows, her eyes darting back to mine nervously.

"Care Bear, I found out a few days ago that Hudson is currently working with Face-Off, the foundation that I set your internship up with for this year." He drags his gaze from me to Caroline—*my* Juliet—who tucks her hair behind her ear. "I asked him to be here today so you two could meet before you start at Face-Off. He's going to help facilitate things since he's currently already involved there."

She looks like she might actually vomit but somehow manages to half-ass nod at his comment. "Sounds like a *fun* time."

Fuck. Fuck. Fuck.

"Hudson, you'll take care of my girl, right? Make sure if she needs anything, you'll handle it?"

"I—" I bring my hand to my mouth and clear my throat since I can't seem to fucking get the words out. "I can do whatever you need, Coach."

"Great."

He looks entirely too pleased with himself. If he only fucking knew...

If *anyone* knew...

My lips snap shut, and when I glance at her, her eyes have widened slightly in shock.

Yeah, join the fucking club, Bubblegum.

"Caroline, I've got to take a quick call, then we can leave. Okay?"

"Yep," she squeaks, her smile not reaching her eyes. Even I can tell it's fake, but Coach just nods and pats her hand affectionately before turning back to me.

"Thanks for coming in, Rome. I'll see you for camp. If you need something, let me know."

I nod. "Will do."

"Oh, and thank you for looking out for Caroline." He smiles, gazing lovingly at his daughter.

Clearing my throat, I squeak out a farewell pleasantry and slip out the door, desperate to get the hell out of these four walls.

Once I hear the door click closed behind me and I'm alone in the hallway, I suck in a deep breath, trying to keep the panic at bay.

Jesus fucking Christ.

I'm fucked.

Nah, fucked doesn't even come close to what I'm going to be.

How could I be so goddamn stupid?

I've heard him mention his daughter a few times before, casual references at practice or during team meetings, but fuck, I hadn't ever *seen* her. I couldn't have picked her out of a lineup even if I wanted to. I didn't even know her damn name.

Just like she wanted.

Even if that has haunted me since that night. That I was so stupid to not have gotten her name.

How was I supposed to know the sexiest girl on the goddamn planet was his daughter?

And now I have to *work* with her? Goddamnit. How in the hell am I supposed to be around this girl and not want to bend her over and repeat that night?

I sag against the wall, trying to calm the fuck down, when I hear the door open, and Caroline appears, stealing my breath in an entirely different way.

"Romeo? *Really?*" she screeches in a hushed whisper.

My eyes dart around the empty hallway, paranoid that someone will spot us talking, so I grab her hand and tug her into the deserted locker room that's just down the hall from her father's office.

Once we're inside, without prying eyes, I whip to face her.

Her long blonde hair is pulled back from her face in a pink butterfly clip, and unlike the night we met, her face is free from makeup. Today, whether because I know now that she's in fucking *college* or because she's fresh-faced, she looks younger than she did that night.

The pink on her lips is a gloss, making her lips look even more supple, and if I were a better man, I wouldn't want to pull her to me and suck the cherry flavor right the fuck off. She's wearing a plain white T-shirt that shows the smallest amount of cleavage, with a pair of ripped jeans and a worn pair of Chucks.

Nothing like the girl I met that night, and fuck, if I don't like it even more.

This casual version of her.

Goddamnit, Rome.

Get it the hell together.

This is a damn disaster, and lusting after a college girl who's so off-limits it's not even fucking funny is the last thing that I need. Now or ever.

"Did you know? Please tell me you didn't know who the fuck I was that night and that this wasn't some... I don't know... scheme," I say, stepping forward until the toe of her worn Chucks grazes mine, my chest heaving with panic. "You're his fucking *daughter*, Caroline? Or should I call you Juliet?"

Annoyance, followed by anger, flits through her gaze as she crosses her arms over her chest. I ignore the way it pushes her perky, full breasts against the material.

"Oh, that's rich, accusing me of being some... cleat chaser or whatever the hell you call them. Of course I didn't know who you were! I don't know anything about his team. How was I supposed to know you were his *player*? God, I didn't even know your *name*. If I remember correctly, you were the one who volunteered, *Romeo*."

"Because that's my goddamn nickname!" I whisper yell. It wasn't a lie; it was just... not the entire truth.

She pauses, opening her mouth and raising her finger before closing it. "Oh, actually, that makes sense."

Whipping around, I glance behind me at the door, ensuring that it's still shut. Panic rises in my throat as I think of someone coming through the door and finding out what I've done.

I'm not usually this much of an asshole, but the fact that my entire life is flashing before my eyes is making me lose my damn mind. And I just started to feel like I was figuring shit out. Now, I'm knocked on my ass.

"Come on," I hiss, pulling her deeper into the locker room. "Fuck, this is a goddamn mess. Do you realize what would happen if people find out what we did that night? How completely fucked I would be."

"Dude, I had *zero* intention of ever seeing you again or anyone ever finding out. Don't you remember? I'm the one who wanted to remain strangers," she says, her voice laced with irritation. She cuts her gaze to the side, refusing to meet my eyes.

Part of me wants her to face me, to grab her by her chin and force her to look at me after what happened, for her to admit to whatever is still flowing between us right now rather than act like she never gave a shit.

Even though I'm freaking the fuck out and frustrated that I fucked up so royally, I can't help my body's reaction to her.

I'm drawn to her. The soft dip in her sides, her scent

that is driving me goddamn wild, the memory of how she tasted.

The only thing I need to be doing right now is running for the door, putting space between us and whatever the hell happened that night.

I can't even believe she's standing in front of me right now.

"Goddamnit, and you're in college? Are you even legal to *drink?*" I say, dragging a hand down my face before my gaze flits back to her.

She shrugs. "Sure. With a fake ID. I'll be twenty-one... next year."

I groan, rubbing at my temples, which suddenly ache. Fuck, it keeps getting worse and worse. Coach's co-ed daughter, and we got drunk on thousand-dollar champagne she can't even *buy.* "Jesus fucking Christ. You can't even legally get *into* the bar. I'm so fucked. You're his daughter. My *coach's* daughter. And I'm thirty-three. I'm thirteen years older than you."

I realize I'm rambling, but shit. My hands roam over the short, buzzed hair at my scalp. A habit that never left, even after I cut off all of my hair.

"Thirteen is really not that much... Look, why are you making this a bigger deal than it has to be?" she whisper-yells.

Somehow, in the span of our conversation, her back has hit the wall opposite the door, with me towering over her small frame. Her stormy eyes hold mine in a silent face-off. She may be short compared to me, but she's a force.

"We hooked up. Lots of people have meaningless sex, and that's exactly what it was. Meaningless sex, and I barely even came. Not like it was *mind-blowing*. So no worries, Romeo—your secret is safe with me." She says it so sweetly her insult practically drips with the sugar of her words.

So she has a smart fucking mouth, and she's a liar. Two things I've learned in the past few minutes.

"Yeah? Pretty sure you came several times, and one of them was on my fucking face." My voice is low, barely above a whisper, and laced with things it shouldn't. I'm thinking things that I can't be thinking about.

Not my coach's daughter.

Not a girl that's thirteen years younger than me, a girl living a whole different life than I am.

But it doesn't stop my dick from jerking at the thought of the taste of her pussy on my tongue.

"If you want to lie to yourself, fine." I pause, my eyes dragging over her chest, which heaves beneath my stare until I trail my eyes back up to meet hers. "But I know the truth. I know that if I were to reach into the waistband of those panties, I'd find you drenched, just like you were that night. But whatever happened between us *won't* happen again, regardless of whatever sexual chemistry we have. My fucking career is at stake. This isn't just some game. I could lose everything. When we see each other at Face-Off, we keep things strictly professional. Okay?"

For a moment, I see the defiance in her eyes, the need to disobey, and part of me wishes that she would. Just so I could be the one to fuck it right out of her.

But her expression changes as she pushes off the wall until her front is pressed tightly against mine. "Like I said, I was okay with meaningless sex, but you're obviously still hung up on it. I won't be thinking of that night or you *at all*. It'll be like it never happened."

Her soft, supple, forbidden body is molded to my own, my arms caging her in.

"I guess that makes you a liar, then, Juliet."

"I guess that makes you one too, *Romeo*." She smirks. "Thanks for the okay-ish dick."

With that, she ducks under my arm and disappears out of the locker room door, leaving me with a painful hard-on and wishing that she was anyone other than the one girl I can *never* fucking have.

———————

"SO, HOW'D IT GO?" Briggs asks the moment I flop down onto his couch and sigh heavily. "He ream your ass?"

After I got my dick under control, I drove straight to

Briggs' house, and the entire ride here, I thought about nothing but the smart-mouthed blonde. Oh, and the fact that I'm fucked, royally.

I have no idea how the hell I'm going to do this. Be around her and pretend that it never happened.

"About that..."

All of their eyes snap to me, whipping from the video game he, Asher, and Reed are playing.

Chaney's working on some blanket he's knitting because apparently, men who are in touch with their feminine side get more girls. So he's taken up a new hobby. Not going to lie, seeing him with a pair of knitting needles and his eyebrows furrowed in intense concentration is almost enough to make me crack a smile.

I'll have to fuck with him another time.

"I think the universe may be fucking with me because I am completely fucked," I say miserably.

"Told you not to fuck with the universe, dude. How many times did I tell you that?" Chaney mutters, not looking up from the blue yarn in his hands.

"Shut up."

Briggs pauses the game and gives me his full attention. "What happened?"

Reed and Asher follow suit, all eyes on me as I take a deep breath. "I saw *my* Juliet again today..."

Reed's eyebrows raise. "Mystery girl?"

I nod. "Yup. Turns out she's not all that hard to find.

Not that I was looking. She's the coach's fucking daughter, and she walked right into the meeting."

Groans sound around the room, and Reed drops the controller onto the floor in shock. "No. Fuck no. Fuckkkkk no, Hudson," he says as he fumbles for it.

I sigh. "I know. Trust me, I fucking know. I'm completely fucked." I sit up and drag my hand over my hair. "Imagine if Coach finds out."

"I actually do not want to imagine that. You're a pain in the ass, but it's better than you being dead," Briggs says. He sets his controller down on the coffee table and sighs. "Because you know that's what's going to happen when he finds out you fucked his *daughter*, Hudson. His *only* daughter. The one that he gets all weird and starry-eyed about when he talks about like she hung the damn moon. His *baby girl*."

Shit, it sounds so much worse when he says it like that. Imagine if he knew that I fucked her throat and basically called her my slut.

"Christ." I drop my head in my hands and groan, the sound rumbling from my chest. "What do I do?"

"Absolutely nothing. You don't do shit." This comes from Chaney, who sighs like this entire situation is trivial and sets down the knitting needles. "Look, did you talk to her? What happened when you both realized what happened?"

"I mean, I didn't say, 'Wow, you're the girl I tongue

fucked in the broom closet,' in front of Coach Evans, rookie. After I walked out, she followed me into the locker room, and we talked. Well, I guess you can call it talking. I was a fucking asshole and all but lost my shit."

Reed groans as he stands from the couch and starts pacing the room in typical Reed fashion. "Of course you were." He runs his hand through his mop of curls as I speak.

"Listen, I freaked the fuck out, okay? Wouldn't you? It's not like either of us knew who the other was when it happened. At the time, we were complete strangers. She said she never intended to see me again, which is why she never volunteered her name, and she didn't understand why I was freaking out."

"Oooh, bet your ego loved hearing that." Asher smirks from his spot on the couch, where he's still got his sketchbook open on his lap. My best friend is different than he used to be, especially since meeting Auden, but one thing remains: he is a snarky little fucker.

I pick up one of Maddison's frilly throw pillows and chuck it at his head, which he deftly ducks, the pillow hitting the wall behind him.

"Exactly," Chaney interjects. "You're not going to say shit, and clearly, she isn't either because Coach Evans hasn't found you and strung you up by your balls. She's not telling him. So, play it cool. Dude, sex is a form of self-expression. Be. Cool."

I'm getting lectured by a kid that's barely out of his teenage years who's knitting on the couch like my ninety-year-old grandmother. This is the shit that I have to deal with. But he *is* basically Caroline's age, so maybe I *should* listen to him for once.

"He's right though," Reed says, finally pausing the incessant pacing. "Keep your head down, and for the love of god, Hudson, leave her the fuck alone. You fucked up, alright? It is what it is, and yeah, you didn't know, but this is your career. If he finds out, he's going to make your life hell, or worse, he's gonna try for a trade. You know it. We know it."

"I know that. Fuck, I know," I say.

"So no matter what you feel about her, no matter how bad you want to... you have to stay away from her. You can't go there again," Reed finishes.

"Gonna be kinda hard when Coach has her working at Face-Off. Apparently, she's doing her sports med internship there."

Briggs whistles. "Damn. Then, just be professional. Treat her like you would anyone else you work with there."

I nod.

I know they're right, and I'd be out of my fucking mind if I thought about her in any sense that isn't strictly platonic ever again. Hockey is all I have, and even though I'm trying to find who I am outside of that, it's been my life for so long that I can't risk losing everything I've worked for. It's too late in my career to jeopardize the years I have left.

From here on out, Caroline Evans is off-limits.

I just have to get my head... and my dick... on board with that.

FIVE
CAROLINE

"Why are there boys here? I thought this *wasn't* a co-ed house, Caroline?" my father mutters, his gaze narrowing as a guy in a bright white linen polo passes by carrying a cardboard box. "You know I wouldn't have agreed to this... I would've gotten you an off-campus apartment. Boys a—"

"Dad." I cut him off from the spiral that he's very much already going down. I can see the vein in his neck bulging as he turns a shade of red that means his blood pressure is already flying through the roof. "Dad. Take a breath, okay? In... and out."

Since the moment I arrived in Chicago two months ago, my father has been hovering. And by hovering, I mean completely suffocating me.

I know that he means well and that he's overcompensating for all of the time that he's missed. We're both navigating this rocky, foreign territory as best we can, and that's why I get it. I do. I think, in his head, I'm still the little girl he left behind. But that little girl is gone, and I'm a grown woman now.

Reaching out, I place my hand on his arm and swear that I can feel him shaking, "It *isn't* a co-ed sorority house, Dad. I'm pretty sure he's just someone's boyfriend helping move. Calm down, okay? You know the doctor said you need to work on lowering your blood pressure, and you can't have a fit every time something happens or, god forbid, I'm near a man. I'm not a little girl anymore, okay?"

His eyes soften slightly, and a small smile turns his lips up, "Care Bear, you'll *always* be my little girl. Doesn't matter how old you get. I can't help it. I just want you to be safe, and I'm nervous, is all. Chicago is a big city, and I hate that you'll be here all alone."

I notice in the sunlight shining through the high arched windows just how much my dad has aged. His dark hair is now peppered with gray, the corners of his eyes crinkled with lines that weren't there the last time I saw him. It's a reminder of how much has changed since we were together last.

I nod. "I know, but I won't be alone. I have a room-mate, remember? I promise I'll be okay, but I need to know that you're not going to have an aneurysm if I don't answer my phone, Dad. I'm going to be swamped with classes and attempting to meet new people on campus."

The truth is I had no intention of ever leaving Seattle, and certainly not switching colleges halfway through my college career, but my dad called me toward the end of my sophomore year and told me that he had a mild heart attack, and it was a wake-up call for the both of us.

He moved across the country when I was twelve to coach an NHL team after he and my mom got divorced. Our interactions went from nightly phone calls to once a week to birthdays and holidays. We grew apart like the tides, and for a long time, I was heartbroken.

And angry.

Part of me still is.

But I realized that we were both to blame for the wedge that formed between us, and when he called to tell me that he was sick, the rest didn't matter.

All that mattered was the harsh reality that life is short and never promised. At any given moment, he could be gone, and then I'd be left with a lifetime of regret that we didn't at least try to fix our relationship.

It still doesn't change the fact that we're virtually strangers who share the same blood. He remembers me as an awkward preteen, and I remember him as the man who divorced my mother and cared more about hockey than his family.

Even if it wasn't true, I spent the majority of my life believing that. And it broke my heart and left me doing a lot of therapy and healing over the years to get to the point I'm at today.

So now, we're back at the beginning, getting to know each other again and learning each other's boundaries.

"I'm trying, Care. Let's just get these boxes up to your room, okay?" He smiles, and I can tell it's strained, but I nod anyway and offer him a small one in return.

He picks up the box at his feet and heads down the hallway to my assigned room, disappearing into the open door. My phone vibrates in my hand as I follow behind him with a text from my best friend back home.

Lena: Settled in yet? How's your dad?

Me: Slightly suffocating, but it's fine. We're moving in boxes now. I can't believe I *live* in Chicago now. Miss you so much.

Lena: Me either. It feels weird knowing you're not next door anymore, but the plus side is your father coaches an entire team of hot ass hockey players. Have you seen the roster? Daddddddies.

Now is absolutely not the time to confess to my best friend that somehow, I accidentally boned the hottest man I've ever seen in my entire life, and as it turns out... he's my father's hotshot goalie.

Who I absolutely cannot stop thinking about, even though getting involved in something as messy as that is the last thing I need. And turns out he is kind of a jerk, but somehow, I can't seem to stop thinking about the feel of his lips on my skin.

I may have left him in that closet with truly no intention of ever seeing him again, but it looks like the universe has entirely different plans.

So, I haven't filled my best friend in on that tea yet because that is not a conversation you have via text.

Me: Absolutely not. I'm staying far, far away from all hockey players, especially ones that my dad is coaching. Hello, here to fix our fucked up relationship... not make it even worse. That's a one way ticket to "fuck no" for me. *laughing emoji*

Lena: Okay... true, but they're only off limits for you, not me. *winky face*

Lena: Plus, I think most of them are married anyway. Bummer.

Lena: Go move in, and send me pics when your room is done. Oh, and let me know how your new roommate is. Hopefully she stays out of your makeup and isn't a bitch.

I'd be lying if I said I wasn't a little nervous about meeting her. It's always a little nerve-racking when you move in with a total stranger because, let's be real, sometimes people just don't vibe. I truly hope that isn't the case. And if it is, well, I'm determined to make the best of it.

At first, I wasn't exactly sold on moving to Chicago. Of

course I want to spend time with my dad and get to know him again, but I also wasn't really excited to move across the country where I know absolutely no one and am practically starting my life over.

I'm extroverted as fuck, but the thought of moving was daunting, even for me.

I've been in Chicago for only a couple of months, sleeping in my dad's guest room until my room at the house was ready, and I've spent all my free time exploring the city and finding all the best places to eat and shop. I'm lucky that the sorority let me move in a few weeks early to get to know my new sisters and get settled before school starts. Which, thankfully, got me out of my dad's guest room. Now it's time to start my internship and get ready to start my classes. Settle into my new home and life here.

When I round the corner into my room, my dad is smiling, his arms crossed over his chest as he talks to a petite brunette. She's *tiny*, and that's saying a lot since I'm barely five foot one myself.

"Oh my gosh, you must be Caroline." The girl bounds over to me and throws her arms around me, crushing me against her small frame. "I'm Tatum, your roommate!"

"Hi!"

I return her hug, laughing when she squeezes extra hard at the end. There's absolutely no hint of awkwardness or shyness from this girl, and it immediately makes me feel so much better about our new living situation.

"This is my dad, Matthew Evans," I say, gesturing to Dad, who just smiles and shoves his hands in the pockets of his jeans. "Obviously, you've met."

"Yes. Honestly, everyone knows who your dad is. Your dad is practically a legend here in Chicago." She winks at my dad, who seems to turn red under her attention and clears his throat at the praise.

"Well, I think I'll head out and give you girls a chance to get to know each other. Care Bear, don't forget your meeting with the director of Face-Off next week. I'll call you again this weekend to remind you. She'll give you a tour and get you familiar with the practice facilities." He smiles, then disappears through the door.

"Oh, Face-Off? Are you an athlete?" Tatum asks.

"No, it's actually funny—I don't follow much about hockey, even though Dad is the coach. But I am majoring in sports medicine, so I know much more about the injuries and mechanical aspects of hockey vs the sport itself."

Tatum laughs as she hops up on the edge of her bed, letting her Converse-clad feet dangle. "You'll learn, trust me. Every man on this campus lives and breathes hockey and baseball."

I have no doubt about it.

"Ah, well, I am definitely more of a baseball girl. I love it. So that's good to hear. What about you? Tell me about you. And can I just say I'm so excited that we're going to be roommates. I was really hoping to get someone I vibed with," I admit to Tatum.

"Same here!" Her face brightens, and a genuine smile sits on her lips, further assuring me that I seriously lucked out by getting this girl as my roommate. "Well, obviously, I'm Tatum. I'm majoring in journalism, and this is my third year at Pi. My sister was Pi's president a few years ago, so it kind of runs in the family? So, here I am. I love *Gilmore Girls*, early mornings, and running."

"Jess for *life*." I grin, and she squeals.

"Oh, that's my girl! I mean, as if there was another choice though. Tell me about you! I wanna know all the juicy stuff."

I walk over to the stack of boxes in front of my bed and hop on top of it to sit. "I moved here from Seattle this summer to be closer to my dad. I also love *Gilmore Girls* and have *way* too many books. I love romance, and hmm... I'm definitely *not* a morning person? I'm not fully functional until like 9:00 a.m. after a shot of espresso and a Venti cold brew from Starbucks."

Tatum laughs. "Most people aren't. I'm weird. I promise not to wake you up unless absolutely necessary."

"Thank you." I grin. "I'll probably be on the struggle bus for a while with my caseload, so I will need literally every second of sleep I can manage."

"Totally understand. We're going to have the best year ever, I have no doubt. And speaking of..." She hops down from the bed and walks over to her desk, plucking a neon pink flier off her already half-full bulletin board. "This is the perfect way to introduce you to Northwestern!"

I take the flier from her and skim the page. It's a local bar that's doing a back-to-school event in a few weeks, and drinks are two for one if you're wearing cowboy attire.

Now that I can get behind.

I told myself that I would dive into making new friends and falling in love with my new home like I loved Seattle.

Starting with two for one at this pub night with Tatum. I mean, I think I would look so hot in a cowboy hat if I do say so myself.

"You had me at two for one, babe. Now, the question is... what are we gonna wear?"

She squeals, taking the flier back from me, "Oh, I have the perfect outfit. A pair of shorts that will make your ass look *so* good. And you're in luck. I've got the best hat for you from last year's cowgirl-themed rush day. We have plenty of time to have you looking so hot."

Perfect. It's only the first day at a new school, in a new house, with a new roommate, and I already have a feeling this is going to be the best year yet. I'm manifesting that shit.

IT'S FINE. *You probably won't even see him*, I tell myself as I walk through the entrance of Face-Off. I'd be lying if I said I didn't spend the last hour dreading coming here and repeating the same pep talk over and over in the Uber ride here.

It's not that I wasn't excited to be able to work with the youth teams. I'm getting the hours I need for my degree, all while doing something I love. That part I'm ecstatic about. What I'm *not* ecstatic about is seeing Hudson Rome.

I'd prefer to *never* see him again if I can help it.

I was perfectly fine with a meaningless hookup, and after our... creative discussion in the locker room, I'm absolutely dreading coming face-to-face with him again.

But I refuse to let his grumpy, stick-up-his-ass self ruin this experience for me. I'm excited to actually be able to work with kids and even more so to make my dad proud.

Inside the main lobby of the building, there are hundreds of photos framed on the walls of players at various ages, several awards, and even more newspaper clippings. There's a small desk in the front, where a woman sits, working on a laptop. When she glances up and sees me standing there, her face lights up.

"Caroline?"

"Yes, hi!" I rush forward and extend my hand across her desk, which she shakes. The smile on her face immediately quells some of the nerves that are dancing in my stomach, the same feeling that has remained since I walked out of the locker room with my heart in my throat.

"I'm Laura, the program director here at Face-Off. We're so excited to have you here volunteering with us! Your dad mentioned you attend Northwestern?"

I nod. "Yes. I'm a junior getting my undergrad in sports med. Thank you so much for allowing me to intern and learn from your trainers. I'm so excited to be getting hands-on experience."

Laura's smile is genuine as she nods. "That is so exciting. I'm actually a Northwestern alumna myself! Girl, you are going to have a blast. Those years were some of the best of my life. What I wouldn't do to turn back the clock." Her gaze turns faraway as she reminisces on those days before returning to me.

"I am really looking forward to this. I haven't had much of a chance to tour the campus yet, but I plan to this weekend with my new roommate." I smile, tucking my hair behind my ear. I'm thankful that Laura is so sweet and easy to talk to because it's helping with my nerves about seeing Hudson again.

"If you ever need anything, you just shoot me a text and let me know." Her eyes shine with kindness. "But for now, I'll give you a tour of the facility and then let you meet some of the kids." She glances down at her watch, "Practice is about to start for the team Hudson Rome is coaching. I think your dad mentioned you know him?"

I nod. "Uh, we met once in my dad's office briefly, so I wouldn't say I really know him, but yes, I know he's my dad's goalie."

Laura laughs, turning back to the desk and swiping a folder off the tabletop. "Yeah, he's a superstar around here. The kids love him. He's actually coaching the older team—U14. We're going to place you with the U14 team today since your internship will focus on shadowing the teen trainers."

"Sounds good."

It doesn't sound good, not at all, but what could I say? Please don't put me around the hottest man I've ever seen, the one whose dick is obviously magic since I can't seem to stop thinking about it?

He was right when he called me a liar because he did make me come harder than I ever have.

We agreed to a one-night stand, so I'll just have to accept the torture as what it is. And like he said... we're going to act professionally. Which I totally am prepared to do, even if thinking about his magic dick is not in line with said professional behavior.

Easy enough.

It takes about thirty minutes to tour the facility, with Laura pointing out the staff offices, the locker rooms, the weight rooms, and other places I might need, like the sports closet and the restroom.

What they have set up here for these kids is seriously

incredible, and as the tour progresses, I'm even more excited to dive in.

"Now, let's go meet the team," she says, disappearing through the door that leads to the ice. Her blonde ponytail swishes behind her as she steps out into the massive rink, and my mouth drops a little bit.

"Wow."

Her laugh echoes around us as she nods, amusement shining in her gaze. "Tell me about it. Our program has come so far in the past few years, and honestly, the majority of our funding comes from the players. They are very generous, not just with money but with their time, too. The Avalanches guys are responsible for much of this."

She sweeps her arm out and gestures to the state-of-the-art rink full of kids skating. It doesn't take long for my eyes to seek out Hudson.

I tried not to, I really did. I had every intention of pretending he doesn't exist, but the problem with Hudson Rome is that you can't ignore his presence, even if you tried. He has the ability to draw all eyes to him. A magnetic pull that demands attention. Even from the few times we've been together, I can see that. Not to mention how it's captured when he's on the ice. And of course, I googled him the second I got home to attest to that.

As we approach the ice, our arms resting on the

boards, my eyes rake over his body, clad in a pair of gray sweatpants that should be illegal.

God, he's so handsome it is ridiculous.

His dark hair is cut close to his head, and a dusting of stubble ghosts his sharp jaw. Who knew an Adam's apple could be so sexy?

Is that a thing? A sexy neck?

He's in a black hoodie bearing the Avalanches logo and a pair of hockey skates that look like they've been through the wringer, with a shiny silver whistle around his neck.

His powerful legs take him to the far side of the rink, and I try not to think of each of his muscles rippling beneath my fingers as I slid them down his body and into the waistband of his pants in that stupid closet.

"Caroline?"

"Hm?" My gaze whips back to Laura, and my cheeks flame under her stare. "Sorry, what did you say?"

She laughs. "I asked if you wanted to meet the guys?"

"Oh, yes, of course."

A few seconds later, she calls Hudson's name, capturing his attention, and then he skates over, taking his time to cross the ice. I can feel his eyes on me even from across the arena, and I try not to let his attention cause any visible reaction. The last thing I want is this man to see the way that he affects me.

"Laura," he says with a smile that makes my stomach dip. He turns his attention to me and nods. "Caroline."

"The guys are looking amazing out there, really working together as a team. A handful of practices and you're already doing great, Hudson. And you were worried you couldn't handle these guys," Laura says to him with a wink.

"Thanks. They're incredible kids." His throat bobs as he swallows. His eyes drift back to me and then drop to my shirt, the corner of his lips tugging up in a grin, before they lift back to my face. "Nice shirt."

I'm wearing a vintage Mighty Ducks shirt that my dad gave me when I was a kid. It's looking a bit distressed, not because it's in style but because it's been through the wash at least a hundred times. It's my lucky shirt, and I knew walking in here that I'd need all the luck I could get since I was going to be around Hudson for an extended period of time. Not that I was particularly worried about seeing him face-to-face again, not after he was such a dick last time.

A dick that I can't actually stop thinking about, but whatever. He's hot, and I might have hooked up with him again, but his attitude is a big ole nope for me.

"Thanks."

"So, Caroline is going to be with you guys as she shadows Marcus. He's out sick today but should be back next week. If you need anything, get with her. I think she can handle some taping and minor things today." She turns to face me. "Caroline, if you need anything, just give me a holler. I'll be in my office until four."

"Okay, thank you."

She tosses us both a wave and then heads back through the doorway leading to the staff offices.

Silence passes between us before he clears his throat. "Looks like we're stuck together, Bubblegum."

"Mhmm." I avoid his gaze, keeping my eyes on the kids. They're skating and passing the puck to each other in what looks like drills. "Professional, just like you ordered. Remember?"

Something passes through his gaze, but it's gone as quickly as it comes. "Easier said than done, Caroline."

SIX
HUDSON

"Coach Rome, Ms. Caroline needs you. I heard her calling for you," Brent says, skating up to where I'm leaning against the boards, going over my playbook. My guys have come so far in a short amount of time. Honestly, I'm proud as shit. We've spent the last two hours running drills and honing in on what each kid needs a little work on, and now that practice is over, the rink is practically empty now that everyone has cleared out.

My eyebrows raise. "Where is she?"

"The equipment closet, I think? Not sure. See ya, Coach." He skates off with his bag slung over his shoulder, and I set the binder down on the bench. I quickly get my skates off and slide my feet back into my tennis shoes, taking off toward the equipment room.

I've spent the last two hours trying my hardest to focus on practice and not Caroline on the bench. It's impossible to ignore her, to not let my eyes slyly drag down her supple body, lingering on her curves, wishing like fuck we weren't in this shit situation of having to stay between the lines.

I find her in the equipment closet near the back of the rink, teetering on a small rickety stool as she tries to reach a box at the very top, her fingers dangling in midair as the box is just out of her reach.

"You good?" I ask.

My question startles her, and for a second, she sways precariously on the stool but catches herself by grabbing the shelf before she falls. "Fuck! Jesus Christ, Hudson. Don't sneak up on me like that. You scared the hell out of me."

I chuckle. "Sorry. One of the kids said you needed me?"

My eyes drift to the tight black leggings that hug her ass, and my mouth waters, remembering the way she fit into the palms of my hands so perfectly.

I've got to fucking stop. Stop thinking about that night. Thinking about her... and her ass.

"Uh, yeah, I'm trying to reach this box of tape, but it's so damn far back that I can't grab it," she mutters. She says it like I'm the last person she wants to ask for help, but it's just the two of us in the rink today, which left her no choice. "If you don't mind, could you grab it for me?"

"No problem." I step behind her and reach for the box before she can climb down from the stool. I'm six-four. Most people need a ladder for things I can quickly grab, and that's exactly what I do, effortlessly reaching past her to pick up the small box from the shelf in front of her.

I hear her sharp intake of breath as my chest brushes against her back, and my dick jerks in response to the sound. For a second, we're both so still, both of us breathing more heavily than before.

Fuck. So much for keeping distance between us.

It's innocent, but nothing with her feels that way.

I clear my throat, stepping back and handing her the box.

"T-thank you," she says shakily.

"No problem."

I quickly put space between us before I do something stupid like touch her again, consequences be damned.

I don't want to lose my job, and I sure as fuck don't want to be caught lusting after my coach's practically teenage daughter. I have to have more self-control, even if it kills me.

She climbs down from the stool and pushes it back against the wall before turning to face me. Her cheeks are bright pink.

"You did great with the kids, uh... out there today. I noticed how great you are with them," she says quietly, surprise lacing her tone.

I'm honestly surprised she's even complimenting me after what an asshole I was in the locker room the other day.

But fuck, I was *panicking*. I had just found out that my entire career might go up in flames if anyone found out about us.

"Thank you. That's all them though. They're good kids, and a lot of them have more potential than they know." I rub the back of my neck before glancing back down at her. "Look, I wanna apologize... for the other day in the locker room. I was an asshole, and you didn't deserve that."

"No, I didn't," she retorts, crossing her arms over her chest.

"I know, and I want you to know that I really am sorry for acting that way. Fuck, Caroline, I was scared. I can't remember the last time I felt that genuinely scared."

Her eyes soften slightly, and she simply nods. "It's okay. I get it."

"Nah, it's not okay. That's not who I am, and I hate that you got that impression of me. We're going to be working here together for the foreseeable future, and I don't want you to feel uncomfortable or anything."

"I don't. Feel uncomfortable. But thank you for apologizing to me. I'm sorry too. For my reaction. It seems like we were both shocked and behaving badly that day." She shifts from one foot to the other as the words tumble out.

"It's okay. I'm, uh... I'm glad we're clearing the air. I'd rather not make things tense around here." I watch as she nods, and I toss her a smile. "By the way, I wasn't teasing you when I said nice shirt." I walk toward the door and lean against the frame as I grin. "I was always a Mighty Duck fan, back in the day."

She glances down at the logo on her chest and laughs. "This is my good-luck shirt. It's clearly seen better days, but you're a hockey player. You know all about superstition."

"Yep. I'm a pretty superstitious guy myself, hockey or not." My watch vibrates, a text notification from my sister, and I glance back at her. "Shit. I've gotta run. It's my sister's birthday, and I'm late. I'll, uh... see you Thursday?"

"I'll be here."

I nod. "See ya, Bubblegum."

That went better than I planned, but fuck, something tells me that I'll spend the rest of the night trying not to think about her.

The fact that I can't have her?

Only makes me want her that much more.

"YOU'VE NEVER PLAYED hockey before? *Ever?*" one of the kids asks Caroline, shock written all over his face. "B-but *how?*"

She laughs, tossing her blonde hair back as she does. Today, she's wearing a pair of skintight black leggings and a baggy sweatshirt, somehow even more beautiful than she was two days ago when I last saw her.

I've been leaning against the boards, watching the exchange between them for the last ten minutes with a grin that I can't wipe off my face, even if I tried.

"Dunno. Had better things to do, I guess." She smirks.

Caden scoffs. "Like there's anything better than hockey. Can you skate? Please tell me you can at least skate."

"My dad's a hockey coach. Of course I can skate."

"Then how about we teach you how to play, then?" Caden says, skating a quick circle around her. The other guys chime in, taunting her, and her gaze flits to me.

I shrug in indifference.

"Fine. But only if you let me tape you up and give me absolutely no crap next time I need to. I don't want you hurting your knee again, Caden." She says it softly, connecting with him on a level that I haven't quite been able to reach with him yet, by getting on his level and treating him like an equal and not just a kid she has to work with.

"Okay."

"Coach, you in?" Caden asks, his gaze on mine as he leans against his stick.

I hesitate, only because I'm trying my damnedest to keep as much distance as I can between Caroline and myself, except it seems like every which way I turn, she's there tempting me. A man is only so strong.

Before I can even respond, she places her hand on her hip and smarts, "I doubt it. I think Coach Rome is probably too afraid he'll get beat by a girl."

I can't stop the laugh that escapes, my brows rising. "Oh? Game on, then, Bubblegum. No crying when it's over either. There's no crying in hockey."

"Pretty sure that's baseball."

Something passes through our stare, something that I feel in the pit of my stomach, a heavy feeling in my gut that is gone just as quickly as it came.

Before I step out onto the ice, I grab my stick off the boards. Thankfully, Caroline's even smaller than a four-teen-year-old boy, so while the stick isn't the perfect height, it'll work for our playful game.

"Alright, I'm goalie. Caden, you're on left D; Brent, you're on right. Wren, you're left wing. Michael, you're right wing. Jared, forward center." I turn to Caroline as I lean on my stick. "You've got one goal, Caroline. Hit the puck—" I shoot it to her, and at the last second, she stops it with her stick. "—into that goal."

I lift my stick toward the goal behind me and smirk. "Think you can do that?"

Her blue eyes roll in mock annoyance. "How about you just worry about guarding the net, old man?"

Snickers ring out around me, and my smirk only widens into a full-blown grin. I glance over at the guys, who have the same shit-eating grins on their faces, and say, "Let's take it easy on her, shall we, guys?"

"How about you stop talking and block the damn puck," Caroline retorts, slapping the puck at me, which goes right between my legs and into the net with a woosh.

The guys erupt in laughter, slapping their sticks on the ground as Caroline grins, wide and proud of the shot she got right between my legs.

"Easy to hit a puck when I'm not looking, but how about we try it when I am?" I ask her.

She shrugs.

I fish the puck out of the net and slap it back to her as a look of sheer determination ghosts across her face.

Surprisingly, Caroline's quick on her feet and even better with a puck than I expected, making me question whether or not she was honest when she said she'd never played.

She has no problem getting the puck into the net, and each time she does, she smirks and tosses me a wink, leaving me with my jaw slack.

That girl knew exactly what she was doing when she goaded us into a game.

Caden skates up, out of breath after chasing the puck

for the last thirty minutes. "Coach," he pants, bending slightly at the waist, "I think Ms. Caroline *might* have hustled us."

"You *think*?" My eyes narrow at the beautiful girl across from me, her jaw set in self-satisfaction and a sly grin on her lips. "That woman gives NHL rookies a run for their money."

"Mad I made you eat your words, *Coach Rome*?" she says as she taps me with her stick when she skates by, slapping the puck right by me while I'm distracted.

"Shit," I curse as the puck sails straight into the net, her team hollering and whooping as they celebrate their surprising win.

How the hell did this happen?

"Next time, you might want to save the shit talking for *after* you've won. Don't you know that hockey is a mental sport?" Caroline giggles and disappears into the circle of kids chanting her name like she hung the damn moon. And I guess showing up their coach is a reason for her to have hung the moon.

"The guys love you." I nod toward the ice as we sit on the bench, unlacing our skates after the last of the kids have finally cleared out and headed home, leaving us alone in the rink. "You're a natural working with kids."

Her cheeks flush from the compliment while her shoulders lift slightly. "They're easy to work with. I love these guys already."

"Is that what you want to do? Work with a kids team, or do you plan to work with a professional team?"

She pulls her lip between her teeth, hesitation written on her features before meeting my gaze again, lifting her chin slightly as if gathering the courage to share something more personal with me. "Uh, yeah, ideally, I'd love to work with kids. I'd like to work with an organization like this or even for a sports rehabilitation clinic that specializes in younger kids. I'm not really into the hype of professional sports."

I chuckle. "I gathered that when you had absolutely no clue who I was that night."

She shrugs, offering a quiet laugh of her own as she tucks a blonde wisp of hair that pulled free from her pony-tail behind her ear. "I've done my best to steer clear of anything hockey related because of my dad, honestly. It was always a... touchy subject. It's crazy that I chose sports medicine in the first place, but it's something I've always been drawn to. And I don't want to let my dad's career hold me back from something that I'm passionate about and believe in."

I nod. I knew she hadn't ever really been around much, or I would've recognized her that night, but I didn't know she had such a strained relationship with her dad.

"I'm actually really surprised to see how well you work with them."

I arch a brow at her.

"I mean, I just didn't really see you as a kid kinda guy," she says, a quiet laugh slipping by her lips. "But I can see I was wrong for judging you by your reputation. You're patient with them and not too hard on them like a lot of coaches are. It's the reason there are so many injuries in youth sports... because they have unrealistic expectations placed on their shoulders."

"Hockey is supposed to be fun for these kids." I pause, dragging my gaze out onto the ice, which is still scuffed from today's practice. The uneven, marred ice is a constant reminder that you can always start fresh the next day. The next time you step out onto the ice, *you* have the control. I've always been good at control and holding it tightly in my grasp. "I'm here to teach them, but at the end of the day, they're kids. They've got a long time before they enter the draft, and not all of them even have that goal, so to me, teaching them the mental aspect and discipline of the game is just as important as running plays or slapping a puck."

"Well, you're doing a great job. You're practically a god to these kids, *Romeo*." She uses my nickname, causing me to smirk, and her shoulder bumps mine gently. "You may not have struck me as a guy who likes kids, but it's clear that you have something special."

"Helps that all my friends have an entire damn Brady Bunch brood of kids, and I'm stuck hanging out with the daddy daycare."

Caroline's laugh rings out around the empty rink, and I can't fucking help the smile that breaks out on my face.

It's infectious that way. She's infectious in ways that I really didn't understand, even more so now that I've had an actual conversation with her. Her smile, the way her laugh makes me feel a little lighter—it's more than sexual chemistry, which, based on our night together, *obviously* we have no issue with.

"Ah, makes sense now. So, you're the cool uncle?"

"Maybe, for now. Not sure how much longer I'll be cool to them, but I'll take what I can get," I tell her with a laugh. "Either way, they're my nieces and nephews. They may not be by blood, but they are in the only way that matters to me. There is nothing in this world I wouldn't do for them."

Her voice is soft and tender when she speaks, leaning in closer. "That's sweet, Hudson. They're lucky to have you."

Suddenly, her phone pings with a text, and she swipes it off the bench, cursing quietly. "I'm late for dinner with my roommate. See you Thursday?"

"Yep. Apparently, with pizza for the entire damn team since you whipped our asses today." I smirk, showing her that I'm only teasing, and it earns me a sweet smile.

"Don't be a sore loser, Hudson." She stands, grabbing her backpack off the bench. "Maybe next time, I'll let you win. Depends on if you've earned it or not," she says with a wink.

We're dancing on lines that we can't cross.

But damn if I don't love a challenge leaving her smart mouth.

SEVEN
CAROLINE

Slowly but without a doubt, I find myself going from dreading seeing Hudson at our practices to anticipating walking into the rink and seeing him leaning against the boards, with that wooden clipboard in his strong hands.

I shouldn't... but that doesn't seem to stop the thrill swirling in my stomach from starting the second I walk into the rink.

The last two weeks have passed like the first week did. He did his best to remain professional, just as I did, but there is no denying that things are changing between us. Subtle flirting that neither of us can help.

It's almost like we're becoming friends, although neither of us are ready to assume a title that would tie us together in any way.

No, we're both comfortable pretending that night

didn't happen between us, although the tension when we're alone is a constant reminder that it very much did.

We could spend every day dancing around it, but when it's just the two of us, that fact makes itself present, and it is by far the loudest thing in the room. Like the day in the break room when he teased me about my lunch, and the innuendo was so ridiculous we both died of laughter until Laura walked in and asked what she missed.

"Caroline, can you make sure this is straight for me?" Glancing up from my laptop, I see Hudson walking toward me in a fitted black tux that has obviously been custom-made solely for him. The expensive fabric hugs all of the lines of his muscles, showcasing his broad shoulders, and I bite back the urge to tell him just how handsome he looks.

Sorta-friends don't do that, I remind myself.

And that's all we'll be due to his moral compass, even though I still desperately want to climb this man like a tree.

I sigh, abandoning my pencil and notebook where I had been sneaking in extra studying during the quiet times at the rink.

I expected my Friday nights to be much more eventful than they have been, but with the amount of homework I have already, I'm trying to keep from falling behind this early in the year.

"Sure. Big date tonight?" I tease as I stand on the

bench in order to reach the black tie that sits crooked around his neck. This is the first time we've been this close since that day in the closet.

We've been careful to keep a professional distance between us, until now.

My hand is slightly shaky as I adjust the tie around his neck, righting the knot so it sits perfectly center at the column of his neck. His throat bobs as he swallows, and my gaze lifts to the five-o'clock shadow that's dusted along his chiseled jaw.

This is my favorite look on Hudson. His hair short, the lazy, languid vibe of rolling out of bed and forgetting to run the razor over his face. Without realizing, my fingers drift to the silver chain that rests around his neck, fingering it gently as he speaks.

"Not a tux date kind of guy, Bubblegum," he says roughly, his voice husky, the words rumbling from his chest and bleeding out onto me. "I've got a fundraiser tonight for the Pediatric Cancer Society. Gotta wear the damn thing since I'm representing the team. I'd never wear one again if I had it my way."

It would be a sin for a man like Hudson to never wear a tux again. Truly.

All women would weep if they knew they'd never get the chance to see the way the fabric stretches across his broad shoulders and tapers at his powerful waist.

"I see. You know, if the gossip columns get a hold of

this, that playboy reputation you hold might actually be at stake. Imagine if they knew that you volunteered the majority of your free time with a youth team and donated big money to cancer societies," I tell him quietly, my voice laced with seriousness behind my teasing facade.

Every day I spend around Hudson, I realize more and more that he's nothing like what I thought. Nothing like what most people think. He's kind and passionate about those that he loves. He's fiercely devoted to the Face-Off kids.

He might be Chicago's Playboy Playmaker, but underneath, he's just... *more*.

It's a shame that the rest of the world doesn't see those things and that he hides behind the clickbait headlines and the shitty articles attached to his name.

"Nah, reporting on who I'm fucking is far more click-worthy than anything good I do."

I suck in a breath at the mention of him fucking, trying not to let the memory of his powerful body moving against mine assault me.

This was a bad idea, getting this close to him. Not when we have these boundaries that neither of us has tested.

I clear my throat and drop the chain as if it burned me, dragging my gaze back up to his eyes as I notice the corner of his lip tugging up slightly at my reaction.

"Well, I see you, Hudson Rome. All of you, even the pieces that you keep hidden away."

The words escape me before I have time to think about them, the truth exploding out of me.

I do see him, now more clearly than before. After spending the past couple of weeks getting to know the *real* him, I'm starting to see who he really is. The way he cares about the kids he's coaching, how he apologized and owned up to his asshole behavior that first day that we met, how he adores his nieces and nephews and spends all of his extra time with them, and coaching the kids. How important his family and friends are to him.

Part of me wishes that I had stayed ignorant of the fact that despite his playboy reputation, he is actually a good guy.

"Thank you," he says, and I'm not sure if he's referring to what I said or for fixing his tie, but he steps back slightly and shoves his hands into the pockets of his slacks before continuing. "Anyway, why are you still here?"

I step down from the bench and take a seat, pulling my laptop into my lap. "I was going to go to the library, but I figured I would take advantage of the quiet here. Uh, I have a big test coming up, and I really just need to focus. It's actually kind of distracting at the library, and it's impossible to study when my roommate is home."

"I can talk with Laura on my way out, get her to leave you a key at the front desk. If you want."

My eyes widen. "Really?"

Hudson nods. "Of course. I'm sure she'd be fine with it, as long as you make sure everything is locked up and you set the alarm before leaving."

Honestly, studying here seems far more appealing than trying to find a quiet spot at the library or at the house on a Friday night.

"That would be amazing. Thank you."

"Yeah, no problem. I'll see you Monday," he says over his shoulder as he starts walking away. "Be sure to lock up."

"Yes, *daddy*," I smart, watching as he freezes, turning back to face me, his gaze darkening as it zeroes in on me.

Whoops.

That slipped out, but... too late to take it back now. Not that I was going to.

He opens his mouth to speak, and it hangs open for a moment before he shakes his head. "That mouth, Caroline." And he simply walks away, disappearing through the rink door.

True to his word, I'm halfway through my study guide when Laura appears in front of me with a shiny silver key in hand, scaring the ever-living shit out of me.

"Hudson caught me on his way out and said you wanted to stay and study? It's all yours, babe! Just lock up tight when you leave. I'm headed out for the night for a few drinks with my girlfriends."

I reach out and take the key ring from her outstretched hand before smiling. "Thank you so much, Laura—and have fun! I wish I could go out tonight, but there is no way I'm passing this class if I don't study. I swear, each week, I think it's going to get a little easier... it just gets harder."

"It'll pay off. You'll have a ton of career options when you graduate with this under your belt." She gestures around us. "And it'll be a dream. Trust me."

I nod and wave goodbye as she leaves me truly alone for the first time since I started school.

It's so quiet it's almost eerie, but I ignore the feeling and make sure all of the doors are securely locked before returning to my studying. It takes a little while, but I finally get into a groove, relishing in the blissful sound of silence, trying to accomplish as much as I can.

The next time I look up, weary-eyed and losing my steam, it's almost 1:00 a.m.

"Holy shit," I whisper, standing from the bench and lifting my arms above me in a stretch that relieves some of the stiffness from hours of being still.

I didn't realize how late it had gotten, but I'm feeling so much better about this ridiculous test next week. I really want to start the year off right by acing my first test as an official Northwestern student.

Creak.

My eyes widen when I hear something in the front of the building. The lights in the rink are set based on activ-

ity, so most of the building is dark, aside from my spot at a
table in the back near the heater.

What the *hell* was that?

I inch toward the front of the building, fear creeping
into my chest with each step I take.

*I double-checked the doors. There's nothing here,
Caroline.*

You're alone, it's dark, and this building is empty.

You're overthinking.

Quit being a scaredy bitch, as Lena would say.

My pep talk doesn't actually work because halfway
through my tiptoe to the front, there's another loud creak
that this time sounds like a door opening.

I reach for the first thing I can grab in the dimly lit
room, which just so happens to be a hockey stick.

It's a hockey rink. Who breaks into a hockey rink?

Oh god, what if someone knew I was here and they
were waiting for the perfect time to strike and it isn't actually even a robbery? What if they're going to kidnap me?
Would my dad pay the ransom?

Stop.

Get it together.

This is your brain overreacting and reaching, I tell
myself. This is exactly what happens when I listen to too
many true crime podcasts. I get paranoid.

I make my way to the exit door that opens to the front
of the building, and honestly, I'm cursing these stupid

lights and wondering why in the hell they haven't turned on.

It's even darker up here, and I can hardly make out the door handle to grab it with my free hand, my other is occupied with the large hockey stick I'm wielding as a weapon.

Blindly, I feel for the handle, wrapping my hand around the cool metal of it before swinging it open.

When I do, there's a darkened figure standing on the other side, and I don't think.

I react. I spent the last few minutes talking myself out of it being a serial killer who was planning on kidnapping me, and it turns out that I didn't actually talk myself out of anything.

I swing that damn hockey stick as hard as I can until it collides with the looming person in front of me, earning a guttural groan, the man doubling over in pain.

Wow, I didn't realize I actually had that in me.

"What the fuck, Caroline?"

I blink, my brain trying to process the voice and place the familiarity of it, but my heart is pounding so wildly in my chest, fear squeezing so tightly that I can't even breathe over the erratic thrumming in my ears.

"It's Hudson, Caroline! Goddamnit, I think you just punctured my kidney."

Immediately, the stick falls from my hands, clattering onto the ground.

"Oh shit," I say, rushing forward to try and help him,

but it's so dark I can't see anything but his silhouette, and I collide with him instead. "I'm sorry!" I cry, my hands gliding along the expanse of his back as he's doubled over. "You can't just sneak up on me like that! God, I thought you were a murderer or a kidnapper or, I don't know, someone robbing the rink."

I feel his shoulders shake beneath my touch. "And you thought they would be after... *sports equipment*, Caroline?"

"Don't be an asshole. You scared me, okay? It's one in the morning! What are you even doing here anyway? I thought you were at the fundraiser."

Hudson straightens to full height, the stupid lights finally flickering on above us, illuminating his handsome face in fluorescent light. His brow is still furrowed slightly from my hit, and he glances down at the hockey stick near our feet.

"Really?"

"It was the first thing I grabbed," I cry in defense. "You're lucky that I swung blindly, or I might've gotten your face instead, and I don't think your ego could survive a hit like that."

His chuckle vibrates down the hallway, and my stomach flutters.

Why is his laugh that... gravelly and sexy? How can a laugh possibly be *that* sexy?

"Proud of you, Bubblegum, even if my kidney was the

casualty in that hit. Always be prepared." He steps closer before continuing. So close that I can smell the clean, musky scent of his cologne invading all of my senses. "You never know who's lurking in the dark."

With that, he brushes past me into the rink, wearing a wry smirk on his lips as he reaches up and loosens the tie around his neck. His shoulders visibly relax once it hangs open, like he's been itching to be free of the fabric all night.

"And to answer your question, I'm here because Laura said that the alarm system hadn't been armed yet, so I volunteered to come check it out. I wanted to make sure you were okay."

I arch a brow. "You do realize I'm perfectly capable of handling myself, right?"

"*Clearly.*" His gaze darts back to the closed exit door of the rink, where he almost just died by way of a hockey stick. He heads toward the back office, sitting down at the table, where my books and papers are spread everywhere. "It's late as shit. I didn't want you doing something risky like taking the metro or something."

"I lost track of time studying. I didn't even look at my phone until right before you scared the hell out of me."

My stomach growls obnoxiously, echoing around the empty rink, and Hudson's lips turn upward into a smirk like my impending starvation is funny.

"Hungry?" he asks, leaning back in the chair and throwing his free arm around the empty one beside him.

"A little?"

"Liar."

I shrug. "Alright, I'm starving. I planned to be done hours ago, but apparently, biology is captivating because time flew."

Standing, he starts closing my notebooks silently until I speak. "Um, what are you doing?"

"Picking up your stuff. What does it look like I'm doing?"

"I see that you're picking up my stuff, but why are you doing it?" I say, placing my hand over the pink biology notebook that looks small in his massive hands, forcing his gaze to flit to mine.

He leans in closer, eyes holding mine as he pulls the notebook from beneath my hand. "You're hungry. I'm famished. So I'm taking you to eat."

My eyebrows rise. "It's after 1:00 a.m."

"Your point? It's a proven fact that tacos and cheap beer taste better in the middle of the night."

Okay, he's right about that. I can't deny it. My stomach growls again on cue, and I sigh.

It does sound good...

"Like you said to me when we first met, why are you making it a big deal? Come on, it's *just* food, Caroline. I'm not asking you to have a sleepover."

Heat rises to my cheeks as I narrow my gaze. "That would be strictly against your friends-only policy, now wouldn't it."

"Exactly, which is why I'm going to take you to eat, and then I'm going to drop you off at your dorm afterward. Just like a *gentleman* would."

I bite my lip, thinking about how he thrust into me against the wall and buried his mouth in my pussy, whispering dirty words in the dark as he made me come.

"Whatever you're thinking right now, don't, Caroline," he says gutturally. His words are low and rough like he could see the thoughts currently traipsing through my head. "A man is only so fucking strong, gentleman or not."

"O-okay," I say, hastily gathering the rest of my stuff and shoving it into my backpack. We close up the rink in silence and make sure the alarm is set before he leads me to the lone vehicle in the parking lot, opening the door for me to slide inside.

The blacked-out Range Rover screams Hudson. Sleek, masculine, and clean.

"Nice car," I say once he's in the driver's seat and pulling out onto the highway, breaking the silence. "Very you."

"Is it?"

"Yep." I let the *p* pop, reaching into my backpack to take out the stash of strawberry watermelon Hubba Bubba that I always keep on me. Most people have an addiction to sodas or other unhealthy vices, but mine is the bright green and pink bubble gum that you find at the grocery store right by the checkout.

It started as a child, and I've never been able to let it go.

Nor have I tried.

I pop the bite-size piece into my mouth, chewing until it's soft, and blow a bubble that pops loudly.

"Want a piece?" I ask Hudson. His eyebrows raise in question, but he shrugs as he lets go of the steering wheel and holds out his hand for the gum.

I watch as he chews it silently, then turns his head, our gazes locking.

"Strawberry watermelon, right?"

I nod. "My guilty pleasure."

A look passes over his face, and then the corner of his lips turns up slightly. "It used to be my favorite flavor."

That night. The elephant in the room that we avoid, except for tonight, apparently. Tonight, it seems almost impossible to ignore.

"It was the sweetest fucking thing I've ever tasted. Until *you*."

MY OPTIONS ARE LIMITED as to where I can take Caroline since it's after one in the morning, and the last thing either of us need is to have our photos plastered across a tabloid, becoming the latest scandal. I need a place that's better than Five Guys and not as crowded.

It just so happens I know of the best food truck in the entire city.

"Cheesie's?" she asks as we walk up to the bright yellow food truck that's parked on a side street downtown near the riverfront. It's late, so there aren't many people in line, which makes me a little less nervous about someone snapping photos.

"You haven't lived until you've had *The Mac*." I grin when her eyebrows rise in question.

She doesn't strike me as the kind of girl who turns her nose up at a food truck, and that's part of the reason why I brought her here. Cheesie's seems exactly like the kind of place that Caroline would love.

"Fine. I trust you. But don't let me down, Romeo. My stomach is counting on you," she says over her shoulder as she walks over to the picnic table to wait. I quickly rattle off the order and pay, and I stand to the side to wait for our number to be called. It's surprisingly quick, and when I walk over to her with a handful of food, I can practically see her mouth watering. I almost ask her if she wants a beer, but then I remember she can't order one... at least without using her fake ID.

"My god, that smells *incredible*," she practically moans, inhaling the closed box in her hands.

"Just wait till you taste it." I smirk. "Wanna walk by the riverfront while we eat?"

She nods. "Yes, definitely. That's the one place in Chicago I haven't had the chance to really see."

Together, we walk toward the water, and the moment she takes her first bite of The Mac, she *does* moan, causing my dick to stir in my pants. Christ.

"Holy shit. I will never doubt you again, Hudson Rome. This is actually freaking incredible. Oh god, it's so... cheesy. So. Good."

I chuckle, my chest shaking with my laughter, "Told you. I stumbled across it a few years ago after a night out with the guys, and I had my doubts, but it was love at first bite."

"I can see why." She takes another massive bite, and I smile. I love that she's not one of those girls who's afraid to eat around a man. This girl clearly doesn't give a shit, and I couldn't be more attracted to her confidence.

I'll never understand why women feel the need to hide what they eat or how much. We all eat, and trust me, the last thing I'm thinking about is the amount of food Caroline is eating. All I'm thinking about are those sweet moans of pleasure coming from her lips, regardless of how off-limits she is to me.

"So, what's it like being a famous hockey player?" she asks as we walk, her eyes finding mine in the dim light of the streetlamps. "Being in the public eye twenty-four seven?"

"Hockey's always been my life. It's the one thing that always made sense. And the fans, the notoriety, the tabloids... all of that just comes with it. It's something that I've learned to deal with over time, but it's not necessarily something I love. I hate gossip sites, and I hate that I have to duck into a building to escape a camera sometimes." I shrug, taking my last bite before finishing. "But my fans? They're the best fans in the entire world. Their dedication and loyalty never fails to surprise me. It's my favorite thing about playing professionally—besides the sport, obviously."

"I can tell how much you love it. That's inspiring to me. I mean, honestly, I'm kind of winging it eighty percent of the time." She laughs, her blonde hair falling around her face before she tucks it behind her ear.

"You're young—you have a while to figure shit out. It doesn't have to be something that happens overnight. Trust me, lately, I feel kind of..." I trail off, unsure of how to explain the way that I've been feeling without sounding like a gigantic pussy.

"You can talk to me, Rome." Her shoulder bumps against my side, and she smiles. So fucking sweet that it makes my chest ache, further accentuating how fucked I am when it comes to Caroline Evans. "Your secrets are safe with me."

"I feel like I'm kind of just drifting along. I'm thirty-three, and I've played hockey since I was a kid, and I dunno, lately, I just feel like somewhere along the way, I lost sight of me. Who am I without hockey?"

We stop at a bench that faces the river and toss our stuff into a nearby trash can before taking a seat. She sits so close that I can smell the alluring scent of her perfume and feel the heat of her body.

Too fucking close.

"I think you can feel that way no matter what age you are, Hudson," she says softly, turning to face me. "Life is messy that way. Just when you think you've got everything figured out, it tilts on its axis, and you're left to sort out the mess that's left behind."

Wise words from a girl who's still learning all about what life has to offer.

"Sometimes, it takes a shift for us to realize that it wasn't really working before, and it's a wake-up call to change what no longer makes us happy. Life's too short to be anything but happy, no matter what happiness means to you." Her gaze drifts out toward the river. "Kind of how I found myself here... in Chicago and not Seattle."

"Things with your dad?"

It's a subject she's hinted at but never elaborated on, and I haven't felt like it's my place to ask before.

She nods, rolling her lips between her teeth, like she wants to talk about it, but it's heavy. I get it.

"He moved to Chicago when I was twelve after my parents divorced, and our relationship was strained for a really long time. He, uh, had some health scares earlier in the year, and we both decided to let the past remain just that... the past. It's just that we're, like, caught in this weird limbo of remembering who we used to be while trying to learn who each other is *now*. I'm working really hard to let go of my hurt so I can rebuild my relationship with him." Her words are soft. Careful. Emotion hangs on to each syllable.

"Not sure there's a rule book for that one, Bubblegum, but something tells me that the two of you will figure it out. He loves you, and you clearly love him, too, since you moved across the country to be closer to him." I lean back and drape my arm over the back of the bench. My fingers brush along her arm as I do, and her eyes meet mine.

"Thank you... Anyway, enough about me. Tell me about your family? Are your parents still together?" she asks.

"Very. They gross me out on the daily. I'm a grown-ass man, and my parents are basically like two teenagers who can't keep their hands off each other." I shudder at the thought. I love that they're happy—truly, I do. But I do not need to see my parents making out. "I've got a younger sister. Her name's Hailey, and we're really close. We all have dinner together at least once a month, less when I'm on the road, but we make it a point to spend time together.

It can be hard because I'm on the road at least six months out of the year."

She leans back against the bench and rubs her arms as if she's trying to warm them up, so I shrug my jacket off and drape the fabric over her shoulders. The night air is unusually cool, with a steady breeze from being this close to the water.

"Thank you," she says, her smile so bright and blinding. "I bet I would love your family. Especially your sister. If she's anything like you."

"Too much like me. We butted heads a lot growing up, and I had to beat the shit out of way too many guys for looking at her."

Caroline tosses her head back and laughs, her shoulders shaking with my jacket draped around her, swallowing her small frame. I shouldn't love how good she looks in something that's mine. "I can actually see you pummeling all of those poor kids who just wanted to date your sister. That seems like such a Hudson thing. You're intense."

I shrug. "She's my baby sister. It was my job to protect her. And it's the goalie in me, I think. I protect what's mine. I'm a concrete wall—shit's not getting past me." I want to say *except you*, but I can't. Because I can't have her, no matter how badly I want her.

At the mention of Hailey, I realize that while she's my baby sister, she's *still* older than Caroline.

"I think that's incredible, you know. That you're the pillar of strength for your family and friends. I think you're an incredible guy, Hudson, even though I hardly know you."

I lean closer because I just can't fucking stop myself. I can't stop my attraction to her. I can't stop wanting her, even when I shouldn't. Dropping my gaze from hers, I watch as her lips part, and she licks them, her breath quickening when she realizes that I'm staring at her lips like I want to devour her whole, like the big bad wolf.

"Hudson..." she breathes as I lean in, our lips centimeters apart, so close that I could close the distance, finally giving in and taking her mouth like I've been dying to since the night she left me in that fucking closet.

But I can't.

I fucking can't.

I have to be strong. I have to resist her, even if it fucking kills me, because she's my coach's daughter and she's *thirteen* years younger than me... and we're already treading too close to hot water.

Clearing my throat, I stand and hold out my hand. "Time to get you home."

Because it's the *gentlemanly* thing to do.

EIGHT

CAROLINE

"Okay, this was the best idea ever. I am *so* glad we came," I say to Tatum, who took the cowgirl theme to a whole new level with a diamond-encrusted cowboy hat. She raises her tequila shot, and we lick the salt, shoot it back, and suck the lime, both of our lips puckering from the bitter burn.

"Told you!" She grins. "This is my favorite bar on campus, and the fact that they don't look twice at my fake ID is just a plus. I can't believe it took us this long to get here."

Between schoolwork picking up and the internship, I've been swamped. Plus, I had my sorority duties on top of that and haven't had much time for "fun."

So I couldn't turn Tatum down when she said we had to come out tonight. Even if I'll be paying for it tomorrow when I'm dragging ass. And since we're technically not old enough to drink, the fake ID did come in clutch. We're on our second round of shots. Or is it third? I'm not drunk... yet, but I'm definitely feeling the looseness as the alcohol courses through my body.

The bar itself is packed full to the brim, people spilling out of the booths wearing cowboy hats, chaps, and obnoxiously large belt buckles. Obviously, the students of Northwestern take these themes very seriously when it comes to two-for-one drink specials.

Honestly, it's so fun to see everyone dress up like this, and I'm feeling good in the cutoff denim shorts Tatum let me borrow, along with the hot pink cowgirl hat.

"How about we get another drink and go dance? This song is the best!" she says, gesturing to the speakers above our heads.

Oh god.

"Is that... *Jessica Simpson?*" I laugh, shaking my head.

"Yep. These boots were made for *dancing,* baby, let's go!" She grabs my hand and tugs me toward the dance floor, which is quickly filling up with people, the sound of boots hitting the wooden floor.

Tatum and I dance, shaking our asses to this ridiculous throwback "These Boots Are Made for Walkin," but in our case... dancing. I twirl Tatum around, both of us giggling until my stomach hurts from laughing, and when the song fades out, we step off the dance floor, both of us holding on to each other.

"Oh my god, have I mentioned that I love you? No, seriously, I'm so thankful we ended up together as room-mates," she says.

"Not as thankful as I am. My best friend, Lena, from back home was worried I'd end up with someone who likes to go through my stuff when I'm not there or someone who was bitchy, but I got the exact opposite. The universe knew I needed a kick-ass new bestie to survive this year."

Her face lights up as she smiles, and then her gaze flits behind me before widening. "Oh my god."

"What? What is it?" I go to turn around to see where she's staring, but she grabs my arm and shakes her head.

"Hudson freakin' Rome and Noah Chaney just walked through the door." Her voice rises an octave, and she grips my hand as she fangirls like a celebrity just walked in the door.

And I guess to most people in Chicago... he is a celebrity. But to me, he's just... Hudson. Though I can't ignore the swirling feeling in my stomach that fluttered at the mention of his name.

It's been exactly four days since the night we ate fancy grilled cheese by the riverfront and talked about our lives, our fears. When he told me about his parents and how they're the epitome of love and how he grew up in a home filled with love. How his sister is his best friend and how his friends and family make his life go round.

The night when he almost kissed me, even though I

could see the war he was fighting with himself raging behind his gaze as that familiar tension hung in the air between us. I could see how close he was to giving in. And then, he cleared his throat and brought me home, dropping me down the street from the house.

Four days that I haven't stopped thinking about him.

Even when I know I shouldn't.

"Are you going to talk to him?" Tatum asks excitedly, her eyes flicking between the three of us.

Tatum knows that we work together at Face-Off, but she doesn't know what happened between us. It's not that I wanted to keep it from her; there just wasn't really a reason to tell her.

Until now, that is.

"Um, no, probably not. It's not like we really know each other that well."

She sighs. "Care, are you really going to rob me of my dream to be a hockey WAG? Noah Chaney. Let that sink in. Do not do this to me."

I glance over at Hudson, who's now standing at the bar with his friend, not looking in my direction at all.

"How about we go dance again? I *love* this song." I grin, tugging on her hand and pulling her back toward the dance floor. But her feet are nearly glued to the ground, and she stands unwavering.

Shit. She is not going to give up on this. I have to tell her.

"Okay, I have to tell you something. Like right now." Before she can protest, I drag her along to the back of the bar by the bathroom, where it's slightly quieter and tucked off from the packed crowd.

"Before I tell you this, you have to swear on your Cartier bangles that you will never repeat a word of this to anyone. Ever. Under any circumstance."

"Duh. What's happening?"

I let out a shaky sigh before the words fly out of my mouth in a rush. "I slept with him."

She goes completely still, her eyes so wide it's almost comical.

"What do you mean you had sex with him? Wait, which one are we talking about?" she asks like that's the most important part of what I just told her.

"Ugh, okay. So, I went to the cup party. You know, the one when they win the championship?" She rolls her eyes as I continue. "I met him outside, and he was funny, and one thing led to another and we had the best sex ever in a broom closet. I didn't know who he was at the time, and he obviously didn't know who I was. We kind of used fake names?"

"Which one? You still haven't answered that question. God, I'm freaking out, Caroline!"

I rub my temples as my alcohol-fuzzy brain tries to sift through the questions coming my way. "Take a guess, Tatum..."

"Romeo. Got it," she mumbles, shock still written on her face. "Caroline, I can't believe you had sex with Romeo! He's a literal fucking god on the ice. Wait, you had no freakin' clue who he was?" Her eyes turn dreamy as she speaks. "I bet he has the biggest dick ever, and he probably fucks like a god too."

I slap my hand over her mouth as a group of girls walks by us, my eyes widening. "Please do not ever repeat any of that, ever again. Actually, we're just going to pretend I never even told you and that it actually didn't even happen. We're supposed to never talk about it again, ever, so you have to act like you know nothing. Which is why I can't introduce you because I'm trying to avoid him."

"I mean, you've had the man's dick inside you, babe. A little late for that."

Groaning, I drop my head back in exasperation, causing my hat to fall backward slightly, the string around my chin keeping it on.

"Seriously, Tatum. We are just going to pretend we didn't even see them. We agreed to not speak about it again, and we work together now. On top of the fact that he's on my dad's team... it's just messy. We're friends, and I don't want to cause any drama or cross any lines."

She nods as she speaks. "Okay, we're going to go back to the bar, get another round of shots, and act like we didn't even see him." Tatum nods again. "Okay, yes. That's what we will do. God, you're a literal frickin' legend right now, Caroline. You fucked *Romeo* and didn't even give him your name. Do you know how many girls would literally die just to be looked at by that man? Honestly."

"Tatum..." I say in exasperation, and she holds her hands up in surrender.

"Fine. Fine. But if the opportunity ever arises, just know I am so down for that man. Chaney. Not Romeo." She loops her arm in mine, and we head to the bar, where I do my absolute best to look everywhere except where he's standing.

I don't want things to be weird, and even though I think we're kind of friends now, I'd rather just hang with Tatum and do my thing.

The bar is much more packed now, but Tatum flags the bartender down and orders us a round of Jägerbombs.

"So, here's the plan. You need to meet some hot guys, not the two extremely hot but off-limits,"—she lowers her voice—"*hockey players*, and get to know people besides me. So, we're going to take shots, then I'm going to introduce you to a few people."

"Yes, exactly. And I need to dance because that was so much fun."

We wait for our shots, and once the bartender slides them across the sticky bar, we toss them back and head toward a table of people that Tatum says she knows.

"Guys, this is my new roommate and new bestie, Caroline. She transferred here from Washington this year," Tatum says, nudging me as she introduces me to her friends.

Good thing I am one hundred percent an extrovert and love meeting new people because all eyes are on me in this ridiculous outfit. I smile and wave to the table. There are a few guys wearing faux cowboy hats and a girl in the back corner who's smiling kindly at me.

I try to keep up with their names, but the music is loud, and everyone slides out of the booth just as the next song comes on, heading for the dance floor. It's already packed, so I hang back some and watch as everyone partners up and starts swaying to the slow country tune.

"Wanna dance?" someone asks to my left, and I look over to see the tall guy with reddish-brown hair who was tucked into the back of the booth. He extends his hand, and I place mine in his.

"Sure, yeah."

The song only lasts a few minutes, but in that short time, I somehow step on the poor guy's feet no less than ten times. Thankfully, he's a good sport, and once it ends, he leads me off the dance floor to a nearby booth.

"Okay, I had no idea I was that terrible at dancing," I admit, scrunching my nose.

He laughs deep and low, and for the first time, I notice how handsome he is. I mean... not Romeo handsome, but not that we're comparing.

"I'm Jay, by the way, and I'll take you stepping on my feet all day, every day if it means I get to dance with you."

My cheeks heat slightly, and I laugh. "Okay, Jay. Nice to meet you, and I apologize in advance for your toes."

He drapes his arm across the back of the plush velvet booth and leans in closer, dragging his fingers along the bare skin of my arm. "So, you're friends with Tatum?"

I'm not really sure how I feel about him touching me, but it seems innocent enough. "Uh, yeah, we're roommates at Pi."

He nods. "I'm pre-med and on the basketball team. That's how I met Tatum—study group."

Wow. I don't bother trying to hide my surprise.

"That's ambitious," I say. "From what I understand, sports players generally want an easy course load so it doesn't interfere."

I can't imagine a pre-med schedule on top of sports. I can barely keep up with mine while working at the rink, and pre-med is much more strenuous.

"Yeah, well, sports don't exactly run in my family, but medicine does, so it just made sense for me to follow that track."

We spend the next few minutes talking, and I realize several songs have passed in that time. I didn't even notice because honestly, he's easy to talk to. I could totally see myself being friends with him.

I realize I haven't seen Tatum in a while, so I'm

looking around the room for her when I hear Jay whisper next to me, "Holy shit."

When I look up?

Hudson is standing at the table, and the look in his eyes is so intense that I feel it right between my thighs.

NINE
HUDSON

There's only one logical explanation as to why I'm currently at a *college* bar right now. Only one singular reason that I walked into this building that's drowning in cowgirl-dressed coeds with "Save a Horse" playing over the speakers.

Fucking *Chaney*.

My dumb ass answered his call earlier tonight, and somehow, this is where we ended up. The very last place in Chicago I'd ever be if I were alone or with anyone else, for that matter. I was tempted to turn the hell around and walk back to the car, but we were gaining more attention than I wanted by arguing in the parking lot.

"Really, Chaney? Of *all* fucking places," I mutter, my eyes flitting around the crowd of cowboy hats and rhinestone-encrusted everything.

"What? My friend said it's two for one, and look at those Daisy Dukes, dude." He bites his fist as a girl rushes by in cutoff jean shorts and a tied flannel top that barely holds her tits in. This is exactly the kind of place I should've expected the rookie to take me to.

I figured we'd go somewhere chill, have a few beers, and I'd head out. So imagine my surprise when I was greeted by a college-aged version of Dolly Parton the second I walked through the threshold.

"You're a literal millionaire. You're worried about two-for-one beer?" I say, my eyebrows rising in question.

He shrugs nonchalantly. "Rich people don't stay rich by blowing money, Rome. You should know that."

My jaw hurts from clenching it. Don't get me wrong, I like women in short shorts like the next guy, but this place? Not even near somewhere I feel comfortable. I'm at least ten years older than most of the people in this room. Yet another reminder of why I can't have the college girl I can't seem to get off my damn mind.

Chaney stops walking as we get to the bar and turns to me. "Look, you need to relax. And what better way to relax than a night out. Right? Let's have some drinks, meet some bunnies, and remove the hockey stick from your ass for five seconds. Make sure it's not becoming a permanent part of your body."

"I'm about two seconds from sticking that stick up *your* ass, rookie." He's right though. I could maybe unwind some, quit being a moody asshole. I roll my eyes and give him a small smirk. "Fuck it. Let's get some beers. Find a table."

With a clap on my back, his grin widens. "That's what I'm talking about."

After waiting for our beers, we grab the bottles and head through the crowd, mostly keeping our heads down to not attract attention.

That's part of the reason I hate going to places like this. It's next to impossible to blend in. Here, I'm the Playboy Playmaker, all-star goalie. The one everybody wants a piece of.

Chaney finds a table at the back, and he sets the beers down, sliding into the booth.

"Shit, I should've come here sooner. Look at her." He points toward a girl wearing nearly assless blue jean chaps. She's got a pair of bright pink cheeky shorts underneath.

One hundred percent his type. I give him all of five minutes before he's on his way over to her.

I take a pull of the cold, crisp beer, my eyes scanning the crowd, landing on a short blonde with wide hips and a familiar ass that has been on repeat in my mind for the last few weeks.

The girl my dick is obsessed with.

The girl with the soft little breathy moans that I still hear every time I close my eyes and fist my cock in the shower.

Of course she'd be here because that's exactly something that would happen to me.

The universe is dangling the one thing I can't have in front of me, even though there's nothing else I want more.

Her curvy, soft body moves with the music, her hands in the air as she sways in sync with the rhythm. Her eyes are tightly shut, and some asshole stands behind her, his hips too fucking close to hers as they dance.

Fuck me.

"Who are you staring at?" Chaney asks, pulling me from my thoughts, reminding me that he's still here.

"No one."

I didn't want to draw attention to the fact that Caroline is here or that I got caught staring at her in the first place. As far as the guys know, I'm purged of all things my coach's daughter.

I'm supposed to be pretending this didn't happen when, in fact, I'm doing the opposite.

Supposed to be staying away from her, and that's not happening either.

I can't stop thinking about her. It's like she's on constant repeat through my thoughts, even more so knowing that I'll never get the opportunity to touch her again. Not like that night.

"Okay, if you say so. I'm going to get Mrs. Chaps' number." He slides out of the booth, leaving me alone with the half-drunk beer and the thoughts that really shouldn't even be crossing my mind right now.

I watch as Caroline and the douchebag slide into a booth across the room, and he smiles as he scoots in even closer to her.

Every time he reaches out to touch her, my teeth grind.

It's not like I have any say over who touches her, but the thought of another guy putting his hands on her, and touching her the way that I did, makes me fucking crazy.

I'm already fucking crazy for feeling like this.

Before long, my jaw aches from clenching it so hard. My beer has gone warm, and I haven't bothered to pay attention to where Chaney went. My eyes haven't left her.

The last straw is when he leans in, as if he's going to kiss her, his fingers sliding along the expanse of her arm, and I can't take it anymore. I stand from my booth and walk over to them before I even think about what it is I'll fucking say once I get there.

"Holy shit," polo-clad douchebag whispers in reverence when I approach the table, my fists clenched at my side.

Obviously, he's a fan.

Appreciate that, but I do not fucking appreciate the way he's been looking at Caroline like she's his next meal.

When, in fact, she will not ever be. Not if I have anything to say about it.

When she looks up, her blue eyes widen in surprise before she smiles and arches her brow as if to ask, *What?*

The goddamn outfit she's wearing is so distracting I try not to let my gaze drop lower to the obscenely low-cut, tied-off top she's wearing.

Christ, I'm losing my fucking mind. That's what's happening. I've lost it, and standing here just proves it.

"Can I... talk to you for a second?" I say, pointedly ignoring the kid next to her. "Privately?"

"Uh, we're kind of in the middle of something..." the kid mumbles. My gaze flickers to his, and I see him fidgeting nervously.

I don't even bother responding to him. He looks like he's about two seconds away from shitting his pants anyway. I came over here for her, and I'm not leaving without her.

"Caroline," I say.

"Oooookay." She grabs her clutch, then turns to face douchebag. "Excuse me, Jay. Sorry."

The kid nods silently, then watches as she slides from the booth and brushes past me.

I guess now would be the time to decide what the hell I'm planning to say. But the truth is, I don't even know what the fuck I'm doing. All I know is that seeing his hands on her, touching her skin, drove me over the goddamn edge.

One I've been teetering on since she walked into that office weeks ago and I realized who she was.

I couldn't watch it for another second. I *wasn't* going to watch it for another second.

Caroline pushes through the crowd, her small body struggling to get through the sea of people, so I walk ahead of her and make a path to the back of the bar, grabbing her hand to keep us from being separated. I push open the back door, then step out into the alley to give us some quiet and privacy, with her following behind me.

Turning to face her, I get my first real look at her not under the neon strobe lights and darkness in the club.

That fucking top. It's light pink, a color that pairs perfectly with her skin, tied under tits that are seemingly spilling from the fabric. Her exposed stomach is soft and perfect for my hands. The Daisy Dukes with hot pink boots are fucking ridiculous, but fuck, she's pretty, and they showcase her thick, creamy thighs.

"Why do you look so mad right now? You're all red and... weird. What's happening?" she asks, crossing her arms over her chest and pushing her already perky tits up higher.

"I'm not mad."

"Well, it sure seems like it. You were not very nice to J—"

Stepping forward suddenly, I slide my hands along her

jaw, pulling her face to me and slamming my lips into hers without warning. My self-control and small semblance of restraint fly out of the fucking window, along with my ability to give a shit about the consequences the moment I taste her. That fucking watermelon gum that I've been dreaming of.

Am I crossing the line that I so firmly drew in the sand between us?

Fuck yeah I am.

But I can't stop myself. I've been fucking obsessed with her, in my head, in my goddamn dreams, for weeks, and tonight pushed me over the edge. I can't do it anymore.

I don't want to do it anymore. Pretend that I'm not so attracted to her it's driving me insane. Being close to her, smelling that watermelon fucking gum that she's obsessed with, knowing how sweet it tastes. How sweet *she* tastes. *Everywhere.*

I'm done.

The moment that my lips touch hers, she fucking melts.

Right in my hands.

My hands cradle her jaw, and I kiss her with every ounce of frustration I've felt for the past few weeks of denying myself. Knowing that I couldn't have her.

That I still can't have her.

Her hands fly to my chest, where she fists the fabric of my T-shirt in her tiny hands, moaning around my tongue, which has slipped into her mouth, working hers. There's nothing patient or gentle about this kiss. It's needy, frantic, and unhinged, both of us desperate for each other.

Bending, I hoist her up, my mouth never leaving hers as her legs hook around my waist, pressing her right against my cock, which is straining against the zipper of my jeans. She mewls when she feels the contact, the hardness of me pressed against her, only the barrier of denim separating us.

"Wait, what are—" She pulls back, panting, and I use the moment to pepper her jaw with kisses, sliding my tongue lower to her neck, where I suck the delicate skin. "What are we doing, Hudson?"

"Stop talking, Caroline," I rasp, my eyes finding hers. Both of our chests heave as we try to catch our breath after minutes of what feels like only breathing air into the other. "I couldn't watch him touch you for another goddamn second, or I was going to spend the night in a jail cell."

Surprise flashes across her face. "You were... jealous?"

"I don't get jealous, Bubblegum."

"Clearly, you do." She wiggles her hips with each word, and I bite down on my lip so hard that I taste the tangy, metallic flavor of blood. She knows exactly what she's doing.

She knows exactly the effect she has on me, and she's right. I was jealous.

That's why I've got her pinned against a dirty brick

wall in an abandoned fucking alley outside of a goddamn college bar, where anyone could walk out and find us, knowing the consequences of my actions.

I'm fucked. That's it.

This girl has my head *fucked*.

And I don't want it to be any other way.

I just want *her*.

"I want you, and I am so fucking sick of pretending that I don't," I say honestly, my eyes holding hers. "And I think you want me just as bad. I'm giving in. I'm waving the white fucking flag because I can't last another second without touching you. Can I have you, Caroline?"

Biting her lip, she says, "Are you asking for a repeat of the broom closet, Hudson Rome?"

Her words send a laugh rumbling from my chest. "You meant the time I *barely* made you come?"

Her shoulder pops, a flirty smile gracing her lips. "I'm willing to let you redeem yourself. Maybe."

This time, a groan erupts, deep and throaty, and I drop my head against her soft chest. "That mouth."

And then her lips ghost across mine, and I fucking love that she's the one to initiate it. I don't know much about my Juliet, except that she's as off-limits as they come, and the sound that she makes when she comes.

Oh, and that she's a liar, because I made her come several times in the span of just a few minutes, but I'll play her games. For now.

I can tell she's confident and comfortable in her own skin, and I fucking love it.

I deepen the kiss, angling my head to slip inside her mouth, my hands cradling her jaw, and goddamnit, I want her.

I want to take her home and lay her out on my bed, peel each layer off her until she's naked, her honey-blonde hair spread out around her as I devour her, make her come until she's limp and stated, then flip her over and slide into her over and over.

The back door to the club flies open, slamming against the wall near us, causing us both to jump. I lower Caroline slightly and step in front of her, shielding her from whoever stumbled through the door.

When I glance over my shoulder, I see a young couple stumbling toward the street, clutching each other, their backs to us.

Thank fuck.

Jesus, that was close.

The moment now broken, I glance down at her. "That's one way to end up on the front page of a tabloid."

She nods. "Yeah, I, uh... I think I probably need to get home anyway. I have a really long day of studying tomorrow. I'll call an Uber."

"No."

"Uh, what do you mean *no*?"

Stepping back, I pull the cowboy hat further down on

her head and straighten her top, which is slightly askew from my hands. I try to ignore the fact that we just made out and dry humped against the wall like a bunch of fucking teenagers, almost getting caught.

"I mean you're not getting in an Uber. You're dressed like a fucking cowgirl, and you've been drinking. I don't want you in an Uber. I'll take you home."

"While I appreciate your concern, I know how to take care of myself. And I don't have my own car, so Uber is how I get everywhere and will for the foreseeable future."

I shake my head. "Which is fine if you weren't dressed like that and hadn't been drinking all night at a bar. I'd feel better if I was the one taking you home. Plus, I drove here and am going to pass the campus on my way home anyway."

She crosses her arms over her chest and sighs defeatedly, like she realizes already that there's no point in arguing with me because I'm not letting her get into an Uber alone after drinking.

Over my dead body.

I'll pick her ass up and throw her over my shoulder before I let her get into the back of a stranger's car without me.

"You're infuriating, and I hope you know that you can't just bust into my life and take control of things. I don't care how good the dick is."

"Oh? So now you're admitting that you love my cock?"

My eyebrows rise in question, and a smirk slides onto my lips before I can stop it, although I quickly let it drop.

Even though she rolls her eyes in mock annoyance, I can see the grin trying to emerge on her face too.

"I'm admitting nothing. I'm simply giving in to your caveman demands because it'll save me twenty bucks on an Uber, and you being a gazillionaire professional hockey player and all... Remember, I am a struggling *college* student, in case you forgot."

As fucking if I could ever forget that shit.

Gesturing toward the parking garage, she says, "Lead the way, Romeo."

I don't bother to hide my grin this time.

TEN

CAROLINE

When I agreed to come out tonight with Tatum, the very last thing I expected was to run into Hudson, let alone end up crossing whatever line he had drawn between us.

After he slides into the driver's seat and starts the car, he pulls out of the parking spot and out onto the main road. I definitely try not to focus on the way the veins in his forearms seem to pop with his grip on the steering wheel.

God, this man is delicious. There's no other way to put it. He's confident. Bossy. Forbidden.

At over six foot four, he makes me feel *tiny*. And... I'm *not* a tiny girl. Well, I'm all of five feet, but everything else? There's plenty to love. I'm a curvy girl, and I love every single inch of these curves.

Obviously, he does too.

The way he just manhandled me in that alley still has my panties wet and my heart racing.

The memory of the night in the broom closet comes rushing back yet again, and I clench my thighs together against his plush, heated seats, trying to push the thought from my mind.

Out of all the trouble I could've found myself in in Chicago, I stumbled into this man.

"Campus?"

I nod. "Near."

His eyebrows shoot up, but he just nods, then pulls out onto the highway.

The bar we were at is only a few minutes from the house, and we ride in a comfortable, slightly tense silence until I reach out and connect his Bluetooth so I can connect my phone.

If we're going to sit in silence, I might as well grace him with my impeccable taste in music.

I quickly choose a song from my playlist, crank it up, then wait.

A few minutes later, Harry, my one true love, floats through the speakers, and a deep, rumbly growl erupts from my Romeo's chest.

"Why am I not surprised that you're a Harry Styles fan?" he mutters, his distaste obvious.

Ignoring him, I turn it up louder and begin singing along loudly, just to annoy him. Halfway through, his scowl lessens, and I see a grin trying to lift the corners of his lips.

I'm great at a lot of things, including my unwavering love for Mr. Styles, but a singer I am not.

"Take a left here. The big white house to the right."

He looks confused for a second, and then his gaze whips to me. "This is sorority row."

"Acute observation, Romeo. Yes, it is."

"Please, for the love of all things fucking holy, tell me you are not in a sorority, Caroline."

An amused smile flits to my lips, and I lean back, crossing my arms over my chest. "Beta Pi."

The second he pulls to a stop in an empty street spot, his forehead hits the steering wheel, and he groans. "Fuck. Fuck. Fuck. Not only did I fuck the coach's daughter, who's in fucking *college*, I fucked a sorority girl... who can't even legally drink. Do you realize how fucked-up that makes me?"

I shrug. "Those are your morals, not mine. I'm sleeping perfectly fine at night after fucking an old fart."

He picks his head up and narrows his gaze, a scowl taking over. "I don't remember you having this mouth on you the night we met."

"And like I told you in the locker room, I don't remember much about that night. Well, anything *memorable*, that is."

A growl—I swear to god, an actual fucking *growl*—

echoes around the truck as he unbuckles my seat belt and pulls me into his lap before I can even blink. The man tosses me around like a damn rag doll, and I don't know whether to be impressed or worried.

"Hudson!" I squeak when my legs fit to the sides of his hips, and my hands fist into his T-shirt. I glance out of the window, worried that one of my sisters will see me being manhandled by a hockey player. "What if someone sees? I—"

He silences me with his lips, soft yet firm, and I moan into his waiting mouth.

"Windows are tinted," he says when he pulls back, his fingers lacing into my hair. "Just let me kiss you, Caroline. I've spent the last few weeks around you being fucking tortured. Smelling how goddamn sweet you smell, watching you bend over to lace your skates with your ass perched high in the air. I'm a tortured man, Juliet. Put me out of my misery."

I can't help it—I giggle, which only makes his gaze narrow.

"That funny to you?" he rasps, leaning in and brushing his fingers along my jaw as he tugs at the hair at the nape of my neck, pulling me to him slightly.

"It's dangerous," I tell him. My lips hover over his, merely centimeters apart. "Stupid. Reckless." Leaning in, I press them ever so lightly to his. "You could lose your hockey career, Romeo."

He sighs, then reaches to brush back my hair that's cascaded around us off my face. "Then we don't get caught."

His words make me pause. Surely, this is not the man who all but lost his shit in the arena's locker room about how we could never see each other again because he was so worried that his career was at stake.

"Why? You said this was done. Why are you still here, Hudson?" I ask quietly.

"Because I can't fucking stay away."

THANKFULLY, my class load is so full on Mondays that I hardly have a chance to stop, let alone think about Hudson and his ginormous dick, not that he would let me forget, even if I tried.

"I think I might have taken on too many classes," I groan to Tatum as I drop my backpack onto the floor next to my bed, then crawl underneath the covers.

I'm exhausted, and I haven't even begun to look over half the syllabi handed out. I simply shoved them into my backpack and decided that ignorance is bliss.

"Welcome to Northwestern, babe," Tatum laughs. She's sitting across from me on her bed, painting her toenails a pale pink and listening to Harry.

Yet another thing we've bonded over since I moved in.

"What if we go out for dinner after chapter tonight? There's this taco place a few streets over that is literally the best thing I've ever put in my mouth, and I mean that in the least sexual way possible."

My mouth begins to water at the mention of food. I've been so busy today that I truly haven't even stopped to eat. Something tells me that I'm going to be surviving on expresso and energy drinks all semester.

"Please. I haven't eaten today, and my stomach sounds like there's something inside it," I say with my head in my pillow.

Nothing in the world sounds better than a nap right now though. Just five minutes would be all that I need to catch a second wind.

I'm dozing off when my phone pings with a text.

Groaning, I lift my head from the pillow and glance at the notification with sleep-clouded eyes.

Unknown Number.

I swipe open the message.

Unknown Number: Are you playing hard to get, Juliet? You should know that I like the chase most of all.

I jackknife from the bed, my phone fumbling in my hands. It's him.

Part of me thought that he wouldn't text at all. Two days of radio silence after our night at the bar and the conversation in his truck where he said he couldn't stay away from me, kissed me hard, then took me off his lap and demanded I put my number in his phone.

Me: Nope. Just seeing how long it would take you to text. I know you're obsessed with me Hudson, but obsessions are not healthy.

Hudson: Always with that smart mouth. Ask me what I'm going to do about it the next time I get you all alone.

Me: Are you so sure that there will be a next time, Romeo?

Text bubbles pop and then disappear, only to reappear a few seconds later.

Have I left the infamous Romeo speechless?

A giggle escapes my lips. God, how is this my life right now?

Hudson: There will be because you want me just as much as I want you.

The fact that this insanely gorgeous man wants me despite what's at stake for him has my stomach in a flurry.

I don't think I've ever been wanted this way in my life, and it's a feeling I could get used to.

Suddenly, my phone is ripped from my hands, and Tatum is standing over my bed, holding it out of reach when I try to grab it.

"You better spill right now, bitch. You've been giggling at that phone like a little schoolgirl for the past five minutes, and I want *all* the details." When she glances down at the screen and sees Hudson's name, her eyes widen and jaw drops.

"No fucking way."

I use her moment of shock to swipe my phone from her hand and lock it before hopping down from my platform bed.

"Tatum, listen to me." I snap my fingers in front of her dazed face. "You cannot tell a soul, okay? We're just... friends. Promise me."

She stutters for a moment. "God, you're literally *texting* with Hudson Rome. Do you actually realize this right now? Caroline, you have his *phone* number," she whisper squeals, practically rocking on her heels in excitement. "Oh my god, not only is he a famous hockey player, he's like ten years older than you. He's *experienced*. That's so hot."

Trust me, I can't believe this either. Never in a million years did I think that the guy I hooked up with at the practice facility was a freaking famous hockey player. Or that I would ever actually see him again, let alone be flirty texting with him.

"I know, I know. But like I said, nothing is even happening. We're *just* friends. Okay?"

"Ooooo-kay, but you at least have to keep me in the loop. I mean, seriously, Caroline, it's not every day that your new roomie slash bestie is hooking up with a freakin' professional hockey player. I have to live through you because truly, the best thing I'm getting is a frat guy that drinks too much beer and gets handsy in public."

Ouch.

Also *gross*.

"First of all, you are gorgeous and could literally get any guy you wanted. Manifest that shit for this year. You're going to find the hottest, most attentive guy ever, and he will not be in a frat. Let's make that a thing. No frat guys."

She nods. "That I can agree to."

"Now, let's go get some tacos because I'm freaking starving, and I have so much homework I want to vomit."

Begrudgingly, she agrees and heads to the bathroom for a quick shower, leaving me alone.

I grab my phone off the bed and hover over the keyboard.

Me: I can maybe agree to seeing you again. Only for your dick. Just so you know.

Hudson: Ouch. I'm offended, but he's not.

Me: Are you referring to your dick in third person?

Hudson: I'm going to spank your ass next time I see you.

Me: Don't make promises that you can't keep, Romeo.

Hudson: Let me worry about what I'm promising.

**Hudson: Come over. We have things to...
discuss.**

Me: I'm busy. Sorry.

**Hudson: Then come home with me after
practice tomorrow. I'll make you dinner.**

**Me: Fine. But, only because I'm a strug-
gling college student living on ramen. Not
because of your dick, even if he is great.**

**Hudson: Are you referring to my dick in
third person?**

I put my phone down, but for the rest of the night, I
can't wipe the smile off my face.

ELEVEN
HUDSON

"*Again*," I say.

"I'm never gonna get this shit," Wren mutters.

I skate a circle to face him and point my stick at him. "Hey, language. Lose the attitude. Listen, you're never gonna get the shit if you don't keep practicing."

"We've been at it for hours, and I haven't made progress," he says.

"Just because you can't see the progress doesn't mean there isn't any. Now, *again*."

I'm tough on him, but that's because I fucking believe in him, and I just need the kid to believe in himself. I look at him and see more than just a fourteen-year-old kid. I see potential, and the only way to progress his potential is to keep at it. Over and over until he gets it.

I've only known the kid a short amount of time, but

I've got a bit of a soft spot for him. Out of all the kids on my team, he's the one that I've bonded with the most. Maybe because we're both strong-willed and hotheaded, or maybe because I see so much of myself in him. Hence the reason why I've been practicing one-on-one with him for hours at least once a week.

Both Reed and Briggs are spending the week on vacation with their families before we head off to training camp, and Asher is tied up with his girl, so I've been giving all my extra time to Wren and this damn puck.

I slap the puck to him and watch as he drops, and the puck sails straight past his leg into the net.

He groans, tossing his stick down. "Fuck."

"Language."

I skate over to the net, using the bottom of my sweatshirt to wipe the sweat from my brow.

"Alright, your drop was good. Even. Quick. Here's the problem. When you scoop your glove like that, you're leaving too many holes for the puck to fly through. That's what you've got to keep working at. Being a goalie isn't just about blocking a puck. It's about focus. You've got to mentally prepare for every time you step out onto that ice. When you're only reacting to the game in front of you, then it's impossible to be consistent. Your job is to envision every damn scenario that you can think of and how you're going to keep that puck out of the net. It's mental as much as it is physical."

Wren nods, but I can see the disappointment in his eyes. I remember that feeling, and to this day, I fucking hate it.

"You're good, Wren, but if you'd listen to what the hell I'm saying—" I tap my stick against his helmet and give him a wry grin. "—and practice until you feel like you're gonna puke, you'll be *great*. The kind of goalie they talk about years from now."

"Thanks, Coach Hudson."

"It's nothing. We'll get it. Me and you. I gotta get out of here—I have some stuff to do tonight. Your stepdad coming to get you today?"

Pulling the helmet off, he nods. "Yeah, he, uh, should be here soon."

He reminds me of myself growing up. Sometimes, I'd be the last kid at practice because my parents were working late.

I didn't grow up rich. My parents are blue-collar; my father worked in the electrical plant, and my mom's a kindergarten teacher. Sometimes money was tight, and I'd have to reuse skates some years or miss out on a training camp because my parents couldn't afford it. It's why for my entire career, even more so than some, I've never taken for granted what hockey has done for me. I paid off my parents' mortgage and bought my little sister a new car when she graduated from college. It was shit that I could've never imagined growing up, and it means every-thing to me.

It's part of the reason why I'm here, coaching my team. I want to give back however I can. It's also why I donate a huge chunk of my salary to organizations that support underprivileged youth. To schools.

And because I've been on both sides of the coin, I can see the fire in Wren's eyes and see that just because he has what-ever problems at home, it doesn't mean he can't be successful.

I've noticed that he's always the last kid at practice, and when I asked him about it, he just said that his stepdad is on the way. Except he's been over an hour late before, and it worries me that something else is going on at home that Wren isn't telling me. Last year, his mother passed away from cancer.

Shit that I can't imagine a kid at his age having to go through, and now his stepdad has custody of him.

I'm worrying because I've grown closer to him, and it's hard not to be attached.

"Practice Tuesday?" I ask, tossing my stick down onto the bench next to my water bottle, which I scoop up.

"Yeah, I can see if I can get a ride. I could always take the bus."

I pause bringing the water to my mouth. "Hell no. If you need a ride, call me."

"Okay."

"Rookies are headed to training camp Monday, and vets will follow the next Monday, so I won't be here that week to coach, but I left Erin in charge, and he's going to slap you shots."

He eyes me with a smug grin. "You know, if you keep working with me one-on-one, people will think I'm your favorite."

"I don't have favorites. I told you that. I just... I think you need the practice."

"Mhmmm." He heads toward the locker room. "If that's what you need to tell yourself. I mean, I'd be my favorite, too, if I was the coach. I'm the shit."

That little shit. He starts to disappear into the locker room door, and I call, "Language!"

These kids are going to give me gray damn hair.

After grabbing my stuff, I check my phone and see that there's a message from Caroline. She left early to study, and we agreed for me to pick her up tonight. Which is a good thing because lord fucking knows that if she were here, I wouldn't be able to concentrate for shit, and Wren needed that today.

Caroline: How do you feel about biology?

Hudson: If it involves your body, then...

Caroline: Ha ha. Big test Monday. May need a rain check...

Oh, fuck no. She's not getting out of this.

Hudson: If that's your way of trying to cancel on me, try again. I want to see you.

Bring your textbook and I'll help you... study.

Caroline: Something tells me your version of "studying" does not involve a textbook.

Hudson: Maybe not, but it definitely involves a lesson.

Caroline: As long as it counts toward my grade. *winky face*

Fuck.

Once I get home, I spend the rest of the day picking up my house and attempting to figure out how to cook. Turns out most people can't learn how to do that in less than three hours. But I'm an overachiever, and maybe there's a little part of me that wants to impress Caroline with a meal that I cooked.

I had to call my sister, and now she's currently giving me ten versions of the third degree to find out why I'm taking a sudden interest in cooking.

"You can lie all you want and say that you're meal prepping, but I know you have a date. Why else would you want to make spaghetti? That is not something you would eat, Hudson. You spend like twenty hours a week in the gym," Hailey says.

"That's a ridiculous exaggeration, and you know it.

Plus... I like Italian food. I love that place up the road with the meatballs."

She laughs. "Exactly. Takeout. Whatever, we're discussing this more at family dinner Sunday. You will be there, right?"

To sit through an hour of interrogation from her and mom?

Can't wait.

Thankfully, she drops the questions and guides me through making my mom's homemade sauce, which I do actually happen to fucking love, even if I try to eat clean during the season.

There's no way I can keep my body lean if I'm shoveling spaghetti and garlic bread into my mouth on the daily.

I leave the sauce on the stove on low when I leave to pick her up, thankful as fuck I didn't have to fight her on not taking the damn Uber.

When I pull down sorority row, I see the house she lives at lit the fuck up all the way down the street. Apparently, there's a party. Cars line the entire street, causing me to have to park down the road. I send her a quick text, and a few minutes later, she appears, opening the passenger door with a sweet smile.

Fuck, she's so damn pretty.

She's got her hair piled on top of her head in a messy bun, with a pair of black square frames on her face, her bag thrown over her shoulder. She's got on a white tank top that's tucked into the front of a pair of blue jean shorts and a thin pink cardigan over her shoulders.

She looks cute as fuck, and I'm pretty sure I've never been attracted to *cute* in my life, until I met her.

"Hey," she breathes, sliding into the seat and shutting the door behind her.

I take her bag and put it into the back seat, and before she can say another word, I slide my hand along the back of her neck and pull her to me, my lips moving over hers in a sultry kiss. She whimpers against me, and I shudder.

One sound—that's how much it could take to be my undoing.

I pull back, tearing my lips from hers, even though it's the last fucking thing I want to do.

"I've been waiting all fucking day to do that."

Her eyes are heavy-lidded, her gaze raking over me in a way that makes me want to do a hundred on the interstate just to get her home.

"Well, hello to you too, Romeo."

The tiny smirk on her lips makes me grin, and I untangle my fist from her hair, then sit back in my seat. I reach out to drag my thumb along her lips. "Hey."

I realize just how in over my head I am, yet here I am, pulling away from the curb of her fucking sorority house like I've not got a damn thing to lose.

"WOW," Caroline whistles as her wide gaze rakes over the front of my house, "Gotta say, Romeo, I was not expecting you to live in such a... *cute* house. So domesticated."

I hoist her bag higher on my shoulder and scoff. "Yeah, well, that's what happens when you move out of your bachelor pad because all of your friends got married and had kids."

"Makes sense. Playboy Playmaker—perpetual bachelor with a penchant for puck bunnies." Her tone is light and teasing, but it strikes something inside of me I used to never give a shit about until recently. I hate that persona, and all I want is to leave that shit behind.

"C'mon, I'll give you the grand tour."

"Mmm. You know, I've heard that exact line before, and I ended up in a broom closet..."

I chuckle. "Oh? Make it a habit of dragging strangers into closets?"

She shrugs and feigns more interest in the stucco of my house than the conversation we're having. "Sorry, Romeo, I don't kiss and tell."

Without another word, she leaves me standing in the driveway, shaking my fucking head at the mouth on her, and walks to the front door, calling over her shoulder, "Well? Are you coming?"

I join her on the porch and unlock the door, then hold it open for her, gesturing. "After you, Bubblegum."

Amusement shines in her eyes as she slides past me into the foyer and takes in the house. I set her bag down on the last step of the stairs, watching as she looks up at the vaulted ceilings and some of the artwork on the wall.

Definitely not shit that I picked out—I left it up to my sister. All I wanted was privacy and a comfy-ass bed to come home to when I got off the road.

"Oh my god, that smells *amazing*," she says, inhaling deeply before letting out a moan, "Please tell me that's what's for dinner because I am starving. I think I've had approximately two packs of ramen noodles and a Bang Energy drink in the past two days."

"That's not fucking healthy, Caroline. You've gotta eat. The body needs sustenance."

Her gaze snaps to mine, narrowing slightly. "Is this like an old guy thing? Being so bossy and... authoritative? Jesus. I know I need to eat, *daddy*."

I'm fucked for thinking that's so hot, but I don't give a single shit.

I never had an interest in the name until I heard it from her lips. Now, I think I'd like to try it on for size.

My hand itches by the second to spank the fuck out of her. Truly, it's currently twitching by my side. But before I can have her, we need to discuss... ground rules. Or whatever the fuck because all I know is that the second I get her splayed out on my bed, I'm not coming up for goddamn air. There's very much still the fact that no one can know about this and what would happen if they *did* find out.

"I'd lay off the nickname, Bubblegum, unless you want to be screaming it later."

When her eyes widen slightly from calling her bluff, I smirk, then grab her hand and pull her toward the kitchen.

She immediately drops her purse onto the floor next to the barstool and slides onto the wooden stool while I check the sauce and fix us both a plate.

I'm surprised I didn't somehow fuck it up, but it seems to taste okay. Hailey will have a field day with that fact.

"So, you cook?" she asks as I slide the plate across the bar, then grab a wine glass from the rack. Pretty sure this is the first time it's ever been used.

"Not often. I'm on the road six months out of the year, and that doesn't include camps or practice, and then I generally travel during the off-season, so I'm not home much. If I am, I usually order meal prep for the week from a nutrition place the team works with."

She nods. "Makes sense. The muscles and all."

"You been checkin' me out, Bubblegum?" Her eyes roll, and I smirk. "White or red? I got both because I didn't know what you preferred. And being underage and all, I figured you weren't too picky."

"Asshole." She laughs at my teasing, then shrugs. "Uh, honestly? Neither. Beer."

Hm. Well, fuck me, this girl continues to surprise me at every turn. Just like she has since the first day she started at the rink and I began to really get to know her.

Setting the glass down, I walk to the fridge and pull out two beers, then join her at the bar. I pop open her beer, then slide it toward her, my eyes fixed on her as her lips close around the forkful of spaghetti.

She moans, her eyes rolling back as she chews. "My god. This is so good. Or maybe I just haven't had a meal that didn't cost a dollar thirty in like a while, but I'm pretty sure it's fucking delicious."

I toss my head back and laugh. "I think that was the most backhanded compliment I've ever gotten, so, thanks? It's my mom's recipe. Just glad I didn't fuck it up."

"It's amazing. You know, I think this is the first time anyone has ever cooked for me, aside from my mom back home."

My gaze rakes over her profile as she speaks. The soft slope of her nose, her long, dark eyelashes fanning out on her cheeks when she blinks, the faint rosy pink on her cheeks.

"To be honest, this is one of the *very* few times I've cooked for myself. I was fully expecting to burn something or have to call my sister at the last minute."

This time, it's her laugh that floats through the room, soft and breathy. So fucking sweet. "Well, I appreciate the effort. It's definitely noted."

We eat dinner together in comfortable conversation, and then I give her a mini tour of the house, starting with the backyard. My favorite place in the entire house.

"This pool is incredible. I haven't been swimming in so long," she says dreamily, gazing out into the in-ground pool in my backyard. "It's huge."

It's pretty fucking big for a residential pool, but the guy that owned the house before me was huge into swimming, so he invested heavily in the pool. It's got a cascading waterfall, a twenty-foot slide, and a huge hot tub to the side, which helps when I'm sore and tight from practice.

"It's one of the reasons I bought this house. I work out every morning in my basement gym, and when I'm on the road, I like to swim, so when I saw this house, I knew it was the one just because of this setup."

Her gaze drags over the pool and slide, a flirtatious grin hanging on her lips. She reaches up and pulls the tie from her hair, letting it fall down her back, then flicks the button of her jean shorts free and drags the zipper down.

My eyebrows rise in surprise, but I remain quiet and watch as she shimmies out of the shorts and her panties, letting them hit the ground.

"You going to stand there, or are you going to join me?" she whispers, tugging at the hem of her shirt. She pulls it over her head and discards it, then reaches behind her and unclasps her bra. Her tits spill free, and then she stands in front of me completely naked, and my mouth runs dry. It's the first time I've seen her completely naked not in the dark, and I was not fucking prepared.

Fucking Christ.

Her tits are heavy and full. The kind that would fill my large hands perfectly. Rosy pink nipples hardened into taut peaks that beg to be sucked. Her stomach is soft and sexy as it flares into wide hips. Hips that are perfect for my hands to grip while I pound into her. Thick thighs, an ass that makes my cock fucking leak just seeing it.

My eyes drift to the apex between her thighs, and I groan. She's smooth and shaved, bringing back memories of how good she tasted on my tongue. It was dark in that closet, and I couldn't properly admire her body.

But now?

I never want to fucking stop.

She's the kind of perfection that only exists in my goddamn dreams, but what stands out even more is her confidence. She's not shy. She owns every inch of her body, and there's something so sexy about a woman who is unashamedly herself and gives no fucks what another person has to say about it.

"Caroline..." I trail off. I'm trying to be a gentleman, and she's making it harder by the second, testing my restraint. "Put it back on. All of it."

A giggle falls from her lips. "I'm not swimming with

clothes on, Romeo. Nothing you haven't seen before. Or touched..."

That's the fucking point. I can't stop thinking about my hands on those hips, sucking on the sensitive peaks of her nipples.

"Race you to the slide!" She squeals, then turns and dives directly into the deep end of the pool, giving me the perfect view of her delicious heart-shaped ass.

I get naked in five seconds flat and dive in behind her. The water is the perfect temperature, thanks to the heating element. It dawns on me as I resurface, sucking in a deep breath, that I've never actually skinny-dipped in this pool.

"God, the water feels amazing," she breathes, wading up to me as we meet in the middle. "If this were my house, I'd never get out. Ever."

"If this is all it took to impress you, I would've started with that instead of attempting to learn how to cook."

She laughs. "Color me impressed, Romeo."

I close the distance between us, my hands sliding around her waist and hauling her to me. "Yeah? Just think about what I can do with my cock."

TWELVE
CAROLINE

Being around Hudson is easy. It's effortless to lose myself in our conversation. He's funny, charming, and sexy.

We hadn't really discussed... whatever line we crossed, and we needed to at least bring it up, yet for the entire dinner, all I could think about was how hot this man is. I mean, who looks that good eating spaghetti?

Every time he'd pick his beer up and bring it to his lips, the muscles in his arm would ripple.

Actually ripple.

And, well... it turns out my vagina is a fickle bitch, which led us here.

His arms tight around my waist, his lips merely centimeters from mine, my breasts smashed against his wide chest as we stand in the neck-deep water.

Not the position we need to be in if we're going to lay

down rules to whatever this is between us, but god, the mouth on this man.

It's crass and filthy, and it only makes me want him more.

"Yeah? The first time wasn't very memorable, so you'll have to remind me," I taunt. I love how he responds to my teasing, giving me back a dose of my own medicine every time. Water sloshes around us as my arms slide around his broad shoulders, and I lift myself higher, then wrap my legs around his strong waist.

Before I even finish speaking, he flexes his hips, and his cock brushes against my center, inciting a moan before I can stop it. Our bare skin brushing together makes this feel even more forbidden.

"I suggest you stop with the taunting before I fuck the shit out of you right here in this pool, Bubblegum. And that doesn't help with the conversation we need to have, now does it?"

My legs tighten around his hips in an attempt to quell the ache he's awoken between my thighs.

"No, it doesn't," I mumble, then move my hips again, rocking against him once more, unable to stop myself. "We have to talk about it, Hudson... At least lay some ground rules."

He hisses when the blunt head of his hard cock brushes against my aching clit. Gasping at the sensation, I squeeze my eyes shut and toss my head back, my limbs loosening in pleasure.

I could come like this, so, so easily. It's always easy with him.

"Talk now. Lay your rules out so I can bury my face in your pussy and eat you until you come on my face."

Another swivel of his hips has me panting. If we weren't in the pool, already soaked, he'd feel how wet I am for him.

"Caroline. *Now.*"

"Okay, okay," I breathe and let go of his shoulders and drop my legs, then turn to swim to the shallow end.

I can't think straight with his hands on me, and we have to discuss this. Now that we've started again, we can't keep our hands off each other. And therein lies the problem.

Hudson Rome is dangerous, in every way possible.

"I need you to stay over there," I say breathlessly.

I'm still clenching my thighs together as I sit on the concrete step, a shiver racking my body. I can't decipher whether it's the cooler air hitting my exposed shoulders or if it's the lingering effect of his hands on my body.

He's in the shallow end now too, a few feet away, wearing a smirk that I want to kiss right off his ridiculously handsome face. His gaze is hungry, and I feel it directly between my thighs. Water clings to his skin, glistening, beckoning for my tongue to lick every drop all up.

Because he's so tall, the water only reaches his waist, revealing his six-pack... or eight-pack? Can someone have more than an eight-pack because I think he might.

Ten-pack.

I knew he was fit—I mean, he is a professional hockey player, but my god. The sharp V at his hips disappearing beneath the surface of the water has my mouth watering, and it's taking every bit of my self-control not to close the distance between us and finish what we started. There's a line of soft, dark hair that leads lower, and I make a mental note to follow that trail to what I know is beyond the water.

"Caroline," he rasps, his heavy-lidded eyes capturing mine. "Gonna need you to stop looking at me like that."

"Like what?" I squeak.

"Like the only place you need to be is on your knees while I feed you my cock."

God.

Damn.

I am so fucked.

"We—I—" I sputter, momentarily stunned by his filthy words. This must be why girls like older men. Besides the experience. They're not ashamed to say exactly whatever filthy, dirty thoughts they're thinking. Words that could make you practically come in a single minute. But maybe that is just a Hudson thing.

"Why?" The word finally tumbles out in a rush because it's truly the only thing I can think of right now.

"Why what?" he asks. "Gonna have to be more clear, Bubblegum."

Letting out an exasperated sigh, I pop my shoulder. "You wanted to end this. Walk away and never tell a soul. Why are you suddenly now willing to take the risk?"

I let my words hang in the air between us.

Risk everything to touch me.

His gaze holds mine as his jaw works. He doesn't speak for a moment but slowly makes his way over to where I sit on the stairs.

"Why am I willing to take the chance?" he repeats my question back to me. "Why do I close my eyes at night and remember the soft, breathy moan you make when you come? Why was I so goddamn jealous when I saw that douche's hands on you that I almost beat the shit out of a college kid? Why do I not give two fucks that you're more than a decade younger, that you're a little sorority girl still in college? Why am I fucking obsessed with *everything* about you, Caroline?"

Now, he's standing in front of me, his chest rising and falling in sync with my own as he leans down, his thick arms framing me. "Because I'm fucked when it comes to you. Because I can't think of anything else, and for the first time in a long fucking time, I don't want to walk away. I

just want you. It's simple underneath all of the complicated shit."

Holy shit.

Not at all what I was expecting, but it has my stomach
fluttering at the statement.

Even with what's at stake, this sweet, unbelievably
sexy man wants *me*.

"I want you too, Hudson. If this is what we both want,
then we keep it a secret. It's just sex—no relationship. We
keep things fun and get orgasms in the process. I don't
want the messiness that comes with my father finding out,
and you want to keep your position on the team. Easy."

He nods. "I like *easy*."

I nod back, our eyes locked on each other. At least we
both understand the repercussions of our attraction and
can agree that our desire for each other is the easy part.

"We have fun while it lasts, and when it's over, we
walk away and pretend it never even happened. No one's
the wiser, and no hard feelings. So, let's have fun,
Hudson."

"Fun is all you should be having. You're thirteen years
younger than me, Caroline. I'm not going to stop you from
living your life. College is supposed to be about you
making fucked-up decisions, partying, being a little reckless. I'm not standing in the way of that. I wouldn't ask
that of you. But when it comes to sex, you're only having
fun with me."

"Are you claiming me, Hudson Rome?" I say it play-fully, and his gaze turns hungry, darkening.

"If we're doing this, my cock is the only one you'll be sucking. Fucking. Touching." He all but growls the words.

"Fine," I laugh. "I'll be too busy with your magic dick anyways. We keep this casual. No attachments. I'm good at uncomplicated, Hudson, and truthfully, I'm not a rela-tionship kind of girl. I've got daddy issues for days."

"That it, Bubblegum?"

I nod. "Simple."

"Easy. Got it."

I exhale the anxious breath I had been holding. I'm so glad we're on the same page with... whatever we're doing because the sensitive spot between my legs *aches* for this man. A physical ache that I know even if I were to try and satisfy, I would never be able to make it feel even a fraction of the way that he does.

Leaning forward, he brushes his lips against mine before he rasps, "Glad we got that out the way because I want to spend the rest of the night showing you just how good it can be. Starting with that mouth."

His words send a shiver down my spine, causing goosebumps to cascade down the skin of my arms, hard-ening my nipples into painfully tight points. How can just words affect me so easily?

"Who says that I'm done swimming, Romeo? You've got this big slide that's just calling my name." I duck under his arms and wade out of the shallow end, closer to the ladder on the back wall of the pool that leads to the massive stone slide.

He pulls back, his eyes shining with amusement. "Is it?"

I nod. "I remember saying race me to..."

Silence passes between us for a moment before he reacts, diving under the water toward the ladder.

Shit!

I'm closer now... but his strokes are double mine. I dive under the water and kick toward the other side, and when I resurface, I see him leaning against the ladder on his elbows, a smug grin on his face.

"Looks like I won, so... what's my prize?"

I swim up until I'm pressed nearly against his hard body and lean in as if I'm going to kiss him, only to splash him and quickly lift myself off the side of the pool and out of the warm water.

The cool air shocks me as it touches my skin, and my nipples tighten in response.

Shit, it's *freezing*. I almost second-guess my decision to taunt this big, broody man until I look back and see the wry smile on his lips. "Oh, your ass is mine," he says, and I giggle, taking off toward the slide that I've been eying all damn night.

My ass might be his... but he'll have to catch me first.

"YOU'RE RIDICULOUS, you know that? You cheated!" I screech, trying to break free from his strong grip, only for him to tighten his arms around me as he tugs me back toward the edge of the pool with plans to toss me in again.

His lips brush against the shell of my ear, causing me to shiver. "Nah, I'm *creative*. Not the same thing."

I can't remember the last time I had so much... fun. With *anyone*. My stomach hurts from laughing, and even though he cheated, I *totally* let him catch me.

No matter what he thinks.

And it was simply because we stared each other down from opposite ends of the pool, both of us as stark naked as the day we were born, and I tried and failed miserably to stop my eyes from drifting down his toned chest to the ripple of abs that would make even the strongest woman weak.

Hudson Rome makes me weak.

In more ways than I even want to admit to right now.

When his hold on me loosens slightly, I flip around to face him, my arms trapped against my chest and my fingers resting on the broad expanse of his.

The smile fades from his lips and morphs into something completely different. Hunger.

A look that seems to burn through me, causing a fire to

erupt in my stomach that I feel all the way down to my toes.

I feel *him* everywhere.

The spot where his fingers dig into my back as he pulls me tighter against him, like our proximity isn't nearly close enough.

"The chase is the fun part, Juliet. So run all you want. I'll catch you every time, and when I do..." He pauses, leaning closer until his lips ghost across mine, the smallest, barest touch that sends shivers down my spine and anticipation shooting its way through my core.

"I'm not stopping until you're panting, writhing, begging for me to let you come. Until you're desperate in ways you've never known."

"H-Hudson," I pant while asking myself how one person can have so much power over another the way that he does over me in this moment. "Please."

I don't even know what I'm pleading for. Only that I want him, and I don't want to wait another moment to have him.

With one motion, he swoops down, lifts my naked body into his arms effortlessly, and carries me toward his house. Opening the back door, he breezes through like he isn't holding an actual person in his massive hands and kicks it shut with his foot, carrying me directly toward the master bedroom.

He tosses me onto the bed, slamming the door shut

behind him and stalking forward. "Do you know how long I've wanted to see you laid out in my bed like this?" he asks, his gaze raking down my body as he takes me in. "And you're even more perfect than I imagined, in *my* bed, that look in your eyes that tells me how badly you want to get fucked. You're a fucking dream, Bubblegum."

I pull my lip between my teeth, his praise causing anticipation to snake down my spine in thick tendrils. While he takes his time devouring my body with his eyes, I can't help but appreciate the man standing in front of me.

With thick shoulders and an array of hard-earned muscles, Hudson's body was made to be admired, and not just as a professional hockey player but as a raw, masculine specimen of a man. The sharp slope of his jaw that's dusted with hair that he didn't bother to shave. The intense blue of his eyes. The rows and rows of abs that I want to run my tongue along every time I see them, all the way down to the sharp cutouts at his hips that lead down to his cock. And as if he didn't have all of those things already in his favor, his cock is beautiful.

It sounds weird to call a man as masculine and strong as Hudson beautiful, but there is truly no other way to describe it. His thick and long cock bobs against his stomach, covered in thick veins. The kind you want to run your tongue along before taking him as far as you can into your mouth just to see the uninhibited look of ecstasy on his handsome face.

"That look," he mutters, shaking his head. "It makes me crazy, Caroline."

As crazy as he makes me feel, I want to say back, but I simply stare up at him through my lashes, a sultry grin plastered on my lips.

Then, he moves, stalking closer with purpose, and that purpose is to have his hands on every inch of my body. I can see it in his eyes that there will be no repeat of our first night together, no leaving him without a word, no fleeing when it feels too... much.

When his knees hit the bed, he hovers over me, placing his hands on each side of my head. His tongue darts out and flicks the metal bar through my nipple, causing me to gasp at the sensation of his hot, wet mouth. Then, his fingers join his mouth, rolling the sensitive peaks between his fingers, tugging gently at the piercing.

"I love these," he growls, filling his hands with my breasts, squeezing them as he speaks. "I want to fuck them one day. Can I fuck your perky little tits, Caroline? Slick my cock with your pussy, then slide it right here." He trails his middle finger right down the center of my chest, then moves to circle a nipple.

The mouth on this man should be illegal.

"Yes," I breathe when he leans forward and scrapes his teeth over the sensitive tip, causing my back to arch against his mouth and my hands to fly up to fist into his hair.

I've always had sensitive breasts, even more so now

that they're pierced, and it seems like Hudson's picked up on that fact just from the small amount of time he's spent with my body. I think I could maybe even come... *just like this*.

"Not tonight, but I will. Soon," he promises, kissing a path down my stomach, nipping with just the perfect amount of pain, only to soothe it with his tongue. "Right now, I want to eat this pretty pussy because I've been starving for it. You wouldn't want me to starve, now would you, Caroline?"

I'm so turned on, so unbelievably wet and dizzy with lust, that I can hardly form a thought to even respond to his filthy words.

"N-no."

That's all I've got. Two stuttered syllables.

He licks his lips as they curl into a feral grin, dropping to his knees between my legs, then hauls me to the edge of the bed until my feet rest along his broad shoulders.

I'm not sure I'll ever get over the way he's able to handle me like a rag doll, especially when it's so goddamn sexy. Raw, masculine power.

"Open wide, baby. I want to see you," he rasps, using his fingers to spread me open. God, he's so dirty, the way his gaze drags over my pussy. "Look how swollen and wet you are. It's seeping from you. Do you want me to lick it all up?"

I don't even have time to overthink or shy away from

his gaze because he dips his head and swirls his tongue on my throbbing clit.

My legs fly closed at the sensation of his mouth on me, and he pulls back, clicking his tongue as he places a flat palm along my stomach to hold me still. "Be a good girl and be still, or I'll have to stop, and you don't want that, do you?"

Oh god, no. Not at all. I think I might actually die if he stopped right now.

Hudson leans in again, resuming his assault on my pussy by flicking my clit over and over until I'm writhing on the bed, my hands wound so tightly into the sheets that they've pulled free. He flattens his tongue and takes a languid swipe of me, his fingers digging into the flesh of my thighs, all while pressing me down onto the bed, refusing to let me run from the pleasure.

"Hudson," I pant, gripping the fabric harder as pleasure rocks through me, a dull throb inside me intensifying with each swipe of his tongue.

He circles my clit, and I feel his finger prod my entrance before sliding inside me. I clamp down around him, and he hisses, "Goddamnit, the tightest, most perfect pussy I've ever seen."

I don't know whether he's talking to me or to himself, but he stares down at me with reverence as he sucks my clit into his mouth, my vision dancing. My body seizes in the most intense pleasure of my life.

Another finger. More pressure. His teeth graze against my pulsing clit. The wet sound of him devouring me alone is so erotic that it's almost enough to send me over the edge.

"Not yet," he murmurs against my slick pussy and slides out his fingers, leaving me feeling empty. The orgasm that was slowly building inside of me fades out of reach. My body, which was wound so taut, now sags against the bed, and in one quick motion, Hudson flips me over onto my knees, gently pressing my upper half into the mattress. I can feel his teeth graze along the globe of my butt, his fingers deftly sliding along the soft curve of my hip, pulling my ass higher in the air.

His lips graze my lower back, his tongue dipping into the small dimples there before he trails slow, steady kisses up my spine. By the time he reaches my neck and slides his hand along my throat, pulling me back against him, I'm practically panting.

Wetness slides down my legs in a sopping, soaked mess, intensified by his lips ghosting across my skin.

It's erotic and dirty, but I don't care. All I care about is falling over the edge with this man.

Kissing along my neck, he sucks on the sensitive skin behind my ear before taking my earlobe between his teeth and tugging, sending a shiver down my spine. I'm desperate for the release he's denying me.

My finger slips between my legs, sliding through my

wetness to rub my clit, only for him to pull it free and whisper along my back, which is slick with sweat, "You come whenever I say so, Caroline. Not before."

His hand slides from around my throat over my shoulders to the middle of my back, where he pushes me down onto the bed, my face in the sheets, and yanks my hips up higher, burying his face in my pussy. The rough pads of his fingers spread me wide as he circles my clit and shoves two fingers inside of me roughly, possessively taking me like I'm *his*.

I moan, clenching around his fingers as I rock back against him, my legs shaking with pleasure.

My spine arches, and my nails bite into the sheets as I chase my orgasm again, my body quaking for release.

"It's too much..." I gasp.

"Come, baby, soak my sheets, let me taste you," he says roughly, fucking me harder with his fingers and sucking my clit. A tidal wave crests, my entire body seizing as the orgasm hits me so powerfully my legs tremble, my hands begin to ache from gripping the sheets so hard.

"Fuck yes," he says, flattening his tongue, dragging it through my pussy as I come. He circles and flicks my clit until I shy away from his touch, completely spent. With one last lick, he turns me and lays me down on the bed on my back, lying down beside me.

I can see my wetness coating his lips and chin, and

even though I just came harder than I ever have, I feel a sense of heat rush through me at the sight.

"That was..." I trail off, watching as his lips spread in a satisfied smile.

"Incredible? Mind-blowing? I know, baby, you don't have to tell me."

I reach out to push his shoulder, but he captures my hand in his and pulls me on top of him until I'm straddling his waist. His cock juts into my wetness, pulling a hiss from his lips, and I smirk, reaching between us to palm his length. He's impossibly thick, and I just want to feel him inside of me.

Just like this.

Lifting, I notch him at my entrance and slide down a fraction of an inch. We both groan in unison, my hands resting on his chest as I still completely, holding his gaze.

I sink down fully until he's as deep as he can be inside me, and I roll my hips, desperate for the feeling of him rutting against that spot inside of me that has pleasure shooting from every limb.

"Condom, Caroline, fuck." He pauses, his hands flying to my hips to keep me from moving.

Except it feels too good to stop.

I bite my lip as a moan vibrates from my chest. "I'm on the pill." My words are merely a breathless pant, but he hears me, his fingers digging into the soft flesh of my hips. "I just had my annual visit, and I'm clean."

"You want me to fuck you bare?"

Swallowing, I nod. "It feels s-so good." I grind my hips, my clit grazing the soft hair where we meet with each movement.

Nothing has ever felt so good, I'm sure of it.

"Do you have any idea what the fuck that does to me?" he growls, pulling me off his cock slightly only to gaze between us, watching as I slide slowly down on his length. "Seeing your tight little pink pussy stretching around me? Taking all of me?"

He slams me down on his cock, and I cry out from the sensation.

Part in pleasure, part in pain.

Perfection.

"Tell me."

His gaze darkens impossibly as he flexes upward, bottoming out inside of me. He sits up, his tongue flicking my nipples before he pulls it into his mouth, using his teeth to pull on the barbell before he sucks it. Hard.

The sensation, combined with the feeling of him being so deep inside of me, has my orgasm building inside of me once more.

"I'm going to fuck you so hard that when you're in class tomorrow, like the good little college girl that you are, you'll feel me between your thighs. You'll ache from my fat cock stretching your tight little pussy open. You'll be sore for days, Caroline, and I want you to think of me every time you throb." He punches his hips upward as I rise and slam back onto his cock, chasing the bite of pain that comes with how deep he is. "I'm going to fill you up, baby, pump you so full of cum that you'll leak for days."

Oh my god.

I've never heard anything more filthy in my life, and I've never been so turned on.

"Hudson, fuck me, please," I plead.

He doesn't hesitate, pulling me off his cock and laying me flat on the Egyptian cotton sheets. My heels dig into his shoulders while he gazes down at my pussy, using his fingers to spread the wetness that's all over me, circling my clit with it before bringing his fingers to his mouth and sucking them.

"I'll never get enough of this." He groans around his fingers. "How fucking sweet you taste. How responsive you are. How your greedy little cunt is weeping for more."

My back arches when he pinches my sensitive clit between his fingers, sending a bolt of pleasure down my spine. Spreading my thighs wider, he slams back into me, fucking me into the mattress so hard my tits shake, a strangled cry escaping my lips.

"This how you want to be fucked, baby?" he grinds out, using my leg for leverage as he pounds into me punishingly. The sound of our bodies slapping together fills the room, mixed with our labored breathing.

The most erotic soundtrack of my life.

Whimpering, I find my clit with my fingers and make circles, bringing me even closer to the edge.

"Fuck yeah, come with me, baby. Play with your clit and make your pussy ready to take my cum."

When his lips move over mine, his tongue sweeping inside my mouth, swallowing my cries of pleasure, I clamp around him, my spine arching as I come on command. I come so hard that I nearly black out, tiny white spots dancing behind my vision as I dig my nails into his shoulders, holding on for dear life.

He grunts my name once and then again in the sexiest voice I've ever heard, pushing himself deep inside of me with a final sharp thrust of his hips, digging his fingers into my hips as he comes, his warmth spilling inside of me, coating me.

In a way, it feels as if he's marking me as his.

But Hudson and I can never be anything more than what we are at this very moment. I can't really be his.

But after *that* orgasm?

I'm ready for whatever Hudson Rome has to offer.

THIRTEEN
HUDSON

For the first time in as long as I can remember, I dread going to camp, and it has every single thing to do with the hot-as-fuck blonde I had to leave behind.

We've texted back and forth all week, even FaceTimed once when she got home from the library, and fuck... I can't wait to be home.

I scroll back through my messages and click on her name, bringing up our text thread. The ones with her snarky, flirty texts that got me hard with just a sentence. I swipe through the few photos that she sent of her doing the most ordinary shit... A selfie as she was studying, her at the rink wearing a shit-eating smile while she holds my practice stick.

Which, of course, she had to compare to my cock because that's who she is. My dirty girl.

Fuck, this week has been too long, not being able to touch her.

All I can think about is her at home in my bed, the white linen sheet draped across her stomach, her perky tits still brushed red from my beard.

I'll never forget that sight for as long as I fucking live.

"I'm not used to seeing *you* waiting for a text, Hudson. Tell me, how does it feel? I think it was you that said staring at it wasn't going to make her text back?" Chaney smirks, scraping his stick along the ice and slinging a puck toward me.

My jaw tightens as I clench my teeth. "You know, rookie, you sure as fuck are getting *real* brave. Been a while since you got your ass kicked? I think you need to be knocked down a few pegs."

He only laughs, making me that much more annoyed. "If your old ass could catch me, then sure. Gonna be that much harder with an extra sixty pounds of goalie pads." He skates to the other side of the rink, where the new rookies are talking to Coach, before I can reach forward and smack him in the head with my stick.

I swear, these fuckers try me every day of my life, and then I'll be the one who has to do laps or sit on the fucking bench when I beat the hell out of him because our coach already doesn't care for me.

"I can't handle either of you," Reed grumbles when Chaney skates away. "Fuck, I don't want to deal with either of you today." He pauses, glancing down at my phone. "You know how bad this shit is going to blow up in your face, right?"

Glancing back over at Coach, I let out a ragged sigh. This week has been awkward as fuck. Every time I look at him, I think about what would happen if he found out what I was doing with his daughter. A constant reminder of how off-limits she is and how it's likely that it will blow up in my face. "I'm regretting even telling any of you."

"We're your best friends, dickhead. Of course you'd tell us when you were potentially making the biggest fuckup of your career," Asher says quietly.

He's not wrong, but none of them know what it's like to have Caroline.

"Listen, we're just worried, brother. That's all. We're here, always. Just know we have your back," Briggs says.

This week is about showing the coaching staff and Coach how we work together as a team. The new recruits, a guy from North Carolina and a guy from Washington, are being brought on. This is the time they really get to see how the rookies work with us vets. See who does better together on the ice and who doesn't work together fluidly.

Plus, training camp is open to the public, which means an entire week with every eye on you. Which makes me even more on edge since I have a secret that could ruin my entire career.

"Man, I'm ready to be home. I miss Mads and the

kids," Briggs says, plopping down on the bench and reaching for his water bottle, squirting a stream all over himself to cool down. "I hate being away from them."

Reed and Asher both grumble in agreement as they collapse next to him. All three of them have been progressively grumpier as the week wears on, all itching for camp to be over so they can rush home to their families.

I, for one, have never really had that feeling. Someone at home to miss or to want to hurry back to see. Sure, I miss my parents and Hailey, but it's not like they're waiting at my house for me when I walk through the door. And lately, I've found myself wanting it. Wanting to have someone at home waiting for me, and now, specifically, a petite, blonde, curvy bombshell that rocks my fucking world.

"Coach said we're done, so I'm gonna head to the showers. Briggs, are we still having the get-together at your house?" I ask as I turn toward the locker room so I can shower the seventeen pounds of sweat off my body before I head home.

"Yeah, I'll text the group tomorrow. I better not hear from you assholes at all tonight because the second I walk through that door, I am dragging my wife to our bedroom."

"Gross. I'd rather not think of you and your wife partaking in any activities," Asher says. "But same. I'm unavailable until tomorrow. Gotta spend some time with my girl."

And with that, I'm out. I've heard enough about these three fuckers' sex lives. Trust me, I've had enough of listening to them talk about getting their wives pregnant and how at least one of them at any given time wants another kid. Either that, or it's some gross kid shit that makes my stomach turn.

I love my nieces and nephews, but there's only so much I can take.

I take a quick shower and check my bag, ensuring I have everything before tossing a bye to the guys over my shoulder as I walk out of the practice facility. There are a few fans still hanging around the exit, so I sign a few jerseys, take a few selfies, and then I'm home free.

Once I get in my car, I pull my phone from my jogger pocket, checking my notifications before pulling the thread with Caroline up.

Hudson: Can't fucking wait to see you, Bubblegum.

Hudson: I may or may not be thinking about all the panties I'm going to be ripping off once I see you.

Caroline: Maybe I just won't wear any so you can't ruin any more. I'm a broke college girl, Romeo. I can't afford your panty fetish.

I smirk, texting back.

Hudson: Don't make me wait any longer, I

need you in my bed. My pool feels very empty without you...

Caroline: That's because you're stupid rich, and it's stupidly large.

Chuckling, I toss my phone onto the console and turn my car on, then pull out onto the highway.

My house is only a few minutes outside of the city, and the drive is quick when traffic is low, so I'm pulling into my giant driveway less than thirty minutes later.

I might not have anyone waiting at home for me, but I have a king-size bed with fresh sheets that're just calling my fucking name. Once I park, I grab my hockey bag from the back seat and head inside.

Heavy silence greets me as I walk through the door and toss my bag onto the floor in the mudroom. Maybe I should get a dog? Hailey could take care of it for me when I'm on the road, and then I won't have to come home to an empty house anymore.

My phone rings in my pocket, pulling me from thoughts, which is probably a good thing because I probably don't need a damn dog. Doesn't mean I don't want one though, now that I've gotten the thought in my head.

Wren's name flashes on the screen when I finally get it out of my pocket. Swiping, I answer, "What's up, kid?"

"Hey. Uh, are you home from training camp yet?"

I open the fridge, pulling a Powerade from the stocked

shelf. "Just walked through the door. Why, what's up with you?"

"Wanna get a skate in? I... I just wanna get out of my house for a while. It's okay if you're busy. I know you're probably exhausted as fu—"

"I'm in. You need a ride?" I say, cutting him off. Obviously, he's calling because he needs me. It's not like this is a regular occurrence, and I can hear the quiver in his voice.

For a second, he pauses, then says, "I could probably take the bus? It'll take me a bit because I need to check the schedule."

As fucking if I'm letting this kid take a public bus alone.

"Nah, get your stuff ready and give me a few to take care of something, and I'll be on my way. Sound good?"

"For sure. Thanks... Thanks for this, Coach."

My heart does something funny when he says those words of gratitude, and I clear my throat. "Yeah, kid, it's nothing. I'm always here."

———

"YOUR HEAD ISN'T in it today. Doesn't matter how many times I shoot this puck, you're not there, Wren," I say. "What's going on? Let's go sit, get some water, chill for a minute."

He doesn't respond to my question but nods and flings off his gloves, leaving them on the ice in front of the net. When we get to the bench, he pulls his helmet off, then squirts his water into his mouth, his gaze somewhere far off in the distance.

Obviously, something is up. He's not his usual animated self.

"You wanna talk about it?" I ask, taking a seat next to him, leaning my stick against the boards as I wait for him to respond.

I want him to feel like he can talk to me, but I don't want to push too far and make him run. I knew when I heard his voice on the phone that something was off, and the way he's acting and playing today on the ice solidifies that.

"Just an off day," he mumbles, eyes cast downward.

I nod. "We all have them. Been playing hockey since I was younger than you, and I still have off days. Especially when shit is fucking with my head. I always play my worst when my mental game isn't on par with my hands. It's like the two can't keep up when they aren't in sync."

His throat bobs as he swallows, still avoiding my gaze. "I just hate when my bad days affect how I play. I mean... I just have a lot going on, and if there is one steady thing in my life, it's hockey. At the end of the day, it doesn't matter what happens at school or at home. If I have a fight with my stepdad or flunk a test. Hockey is always there. Some-times it feels like hockey is all I really have."

"I get it. That's part of honing your craft, Wren. Learning to leave it at the door the second that you step on the ice. It also helps not to keep all of that shit in your head bottled up. Get it out. Find an outlet to express the way you're feeling," I say, nudging his shoulder with mine, his eyes finally meeting mine.

"My stepdad... he's been drinking more. And some-times he forgets things."

My stomach dips at his confession. Fuck, he's just a kid. He shouldn't have to carry this on his shoulders.

"What kind of things?" I ask.

He swallows, averting his gaze like he's worried about telling the truth, "Just things. Sometimes he forgets to pay the electric bill, and they turn off the electricity for a few days. Sometimes he forgets to buy groceries." He pauses, shuffling on each foot, still not meeting my eyes, and I can feel my rage increasing by the second. "It's just hard some-times, Coach. I miss my mom so much, and it feels like sometimes I don't have anyone."

Sighing, I drag my hand down my face. Goddamnit, part of me wants to beat the shit out of that asshole for being a piece of shit to Wren, and the other part wants to take him away from this situation, but I'm not really sure what my place is here. This is entirely new territory for me. Right now, he looks like he could flee at the drop of the hat, and that's the last thing I want.

"Wren, listen to me. I don't give a fuck what time of night it is, what day it is... I don't give a shit if I'm in the middle of the Stanley Cup game. If you need me, I'm here. Night or day. You hear me? The second you feel like it's not safe for you, if you don't want to call the police, you call *me*, Wren."

He nods. "Thank you... I just needed to get it off my chest. That's why I'm here late sometimes 'cause he forgets to pick me up, and I have to take the bus." Silence envelops us both as we stare out at the rink. I'm struggling with the right decision. There's a fierce part of me that needs to protect this kid. But something tells me the more I push, the more he'll back away. I can see it in his eyes. A human's natural response—fight or flight. "I wish that I could turn the clock back, even for just a few minutes, to when my mom was here, and she could just hug me and tell me everything is okay."

"Wren... I—"

He turns to face me, and I throw my arm around him, tugging him to my chest. I hold on fucking tight, and I don't move when I feel him tense. All he needs is a damn hug, and my heart is breaking listening to him tell me this stuff, knowing I can't take him away. If I tell Laura, what could she do?

Clearing his throat, he steps back, the emotion still hanging on his words. "I don't want you to treat me any differently. I'm still going to bust my ass out there and earn my spot. Look, can you just pretend that I never said anything? Coach, promise me... promise me you won't say anything. I'd rather my stepdad forget a few times than end up in a group home in the foster care system."

"I'm only making that promise if you make one of your own, Wren. You have to fucking promise me that if you ever feel unsafe, you will call me. Immediately. No hesitation."

He nods. "I don't want to end up in foster care. Do you know how many teenagers get thrown into foster care and sit there? No one wants a teenager. No one will want me, and sometimes we have to choose the lesser evil."

Reaching out, I put my arm on his shoulder. "I'm never letting that happen, Wren. I promise you that. Okay? That's my promise. You call me no matter what. With the season starting, I'm going to be traveling a lot, but even if I'm on the road, I don't care. You call me."

"I will. Saved your number under *Old Man*." A small smirk tugs at the corner of his lips when he teases me, earning him a shove to his shoulder. "I probably need to get home," he says quietly, looking down at the beat-up watch on his wrist and eying the time. It's late now, the sun beginning to set outside the rink.

"C'mon, I'll take you. Let's call it a night. We'll get some ice time later this week."

When he skates off to the locker room in front of me, I pull my phone out of my sweats and text Caroline.

After that... All I want to do is see *her*.

FOURTEEN
CAROLINE

Sundays are my favorite day of the week. Mostly because they're a day of rest. It's really the only day of the week where I feel like I *actually* have my shit together, and although it's short-lived, I love feeling like I'm a functioning adult. It's been an extra-long week since we're preparing for our first mixer of the year at the house, so between that and trying to stay on top of homework and studying, I haven't had a chance to come up for air.

Which means less time to think about Hudson.

A week has passed since that night in his pool, and I won't bother lying to myself that I haven't stopped thinking about him. His lopsided grin, the way his hands slid down my body while his tongue made me come harder than anyone ever has, and how my body is all too willing to give itself over to him.

We've spent the week texting back and forth, and I'm not going to lie, every time my phone lights up with a notification, a ridiculous smile hangs on my lips.

He's got that effect about him.

The ability to have me anxiously awaiting his arrival home. Not just for the orgasms but because I actually *like* being around him. He makes me laugh.

"Care, are you listening?" Tatum calls from in front of the mirror, diverting my attention back to her. She's clutching a black minidress to her front as her bright blue eyes drag down the length of the mirror, inspecting her reflection. "I don't want to seem like I'm trying too hard. I mean, it's just a date, right?"

Even from across the room, I can tell how nervous she is, which is quite the contradiction when it comes to my new roommate. Tatum is confident, genuine, and the kind of girl who doesn't hesitate when meeting someone new. She's a lot like me, but underneath her bright smile and extroverted demeanor, she has her doubts. We all do.

"Babe," I say, tossing my iPad down onto my bed and crossing the room to where she stands, then placing my hands on her shoulders. "You are *hot*. He is lucky that you even gave him the time of day, let's be real. This dress is fire and gives bad-bitch vibes. Nothing else. 'Kay?"

She exhales, her eyes darting back to the mirror. A slow smile spreads on her glossy lips. "You're right. What would I do without you? My personal hype girl."

"That's what I'm here for." I smirk. "And wear the red heels. They make your legs look amazing."

Tatum's expression softens, and she takes me into her arms, the dress in question squished between us. "I love you, Care. I know I say that a lot, but I'm serious. So thankful that the universe made us roomies. It's like it knew how much I needed you."

"Me too, babe. Now, go get dressed, and have so much fun." I let go and step back, gesturing toward the door. "I've got dinner with my dad tonight, so I'll be heading out soon too. You can tell me everyth—"

A sharp knock sounds before I can finish my sentence. Tatum walks over to the door and swings it open, revealing Sam, another one of our sorority sisters, carrying a white box with a bright red bow.

"Uh, Caroline, a deliveryman just dropped this off for you. There's no note."

My brow furrows in confusion. "Oh, okay. Thanks, Sam." Smiling sweetly, I take the box from her, and Tatum shuts the door with her foot before she follows me back to my bed. I climb in and sit cross-legged with the box in front of me.

"Who do you think it's from? Please tell me it's Hudson. God, it better be him." Her words are dreamy, and I just laugh. The girl is obsessed with him, in a cute way.

I roll my lips together before a smile breaks out. "Hudson." Carefully, I tug on the red silk ribbon, unraveling it until it falls open on the bed, then lift the lid from the box. Inside, there is red tissue paper matching the bow. I open it, and my jaw drops at what must be a hundred pairs of panties—lace, silk, and satin, mostly in reds, pinks, whites, and blacks.

There's a square note card on the top.

"What is it? Tell me, oh my god..." she screeches, pausing for me to answer her. "The suspense is killing me!"

I pick the note up and begin reading.

I never make promises I can't keep. So, here are your replacements, Bubblegum. There's even a color included that's named after you. I can't fucking wait to see you in them, and I really can't wait to taste you again.

Oh my god.

Of everything I expected or thought this could be... this was not it.

My cheeks flame, and I drag my gaze up to Tatum, turning the box toward her. She ambles over and snatches the postcard from me, quickly scanning the note.

"Oh my *god*, Caroline!" Her eyes dart to the box full of what looks like extremely expensive underwear. "You are literally out here living all of our dreams. What's it like to be God's favorite? Honestly." She sighs, flopping down onto the bed next to the box and tossing a few in the air for dramatic effect.

As they cascade around her, I laugh, shaking my head, "It's just underwear."

"*Just underwear?* Caroline, we have been through this. You are literally boning a hot, professional hockey player who was one of *People*'s sexiest men alive. And as if that wasn't enough, he's funny, and he sends you freaking like five thousand dollars in Agent Provocateur underwear just because he *ripped* a pair. You better give that man the best blow job of his life tonight."

As if it's a chore. I'm convinced he has the best dick on the planet, so...

"Oh!" She sits up and grins. "You should get his jersey and send him a picture wearing a pair. He'd practically come in his pants, I bet."

"I think you might be right. But unfortunately, right now, I have to go meet my dad for dinner and pretend that I didn't just get sexy lingerie delivered by one of his players."

"Go get 'em, girl." She smirks.

After a quick shower and changing out of the clothes I had been studying in, an Uber drops me off in front of my father's modest suburban house, complete with a white picket fence. He offered to pick me up from campus, but I insisted on taking an Uber. Living here for the short time I did this summer before I could move into the house... was weird. Living in the house that my father lived in after leaving my mom and me. The home he created that doesn't include me. The house is a stranger to me, and living here didn't make it feel like my home. I felt like a guest in my own father's home.

I walk up the path that loops through the manicured lawn and raise my hand to knock, only for the door to swing open, and my dad appears.

"Caroline!" he says as he pulls me over the threshold into his arms. I pat his back awkwardly.

"Hi, Dad."

"We really have to discuss you taking an Uber. I hate those damn things. They're not safe, and there's no accountability."

"Dad," I warn, pulling back to narrow my eyes. "I know you worry, but I'm an adult. Remember?"

A frown forms on his lips, the line between his brows deepening, "I know, Care Bear. It's just this world is so dangerous now, and you're my little girl."

Hearing him call me his little girl does something to my already battered heart. How many nights did I wish for this moment? To have my dad back, all to myself, making up for the time that we lost.

It's hard not to feel... abandoned. Where was he all of those years that I needed him? He was with his hockey players, not me. I've spent a lot of years seeing a therapist, learning how to let go of that anger. One of the questions that she asked was if I truly wanted to repair the relationship with my dad, and the answer is yes, I do.

Sometimes it's just hard to look past everything we've been through to get from that point to feel like it's possible to get to a new one.

"Come in, come in. I made your favorite," he says, smiling warmly.

His house is decorated simply, and while I know his salary with the NHL is more than I'll probably make in ten years, you wouldn't be able to tell from his home or what he drives. If anything, my father is frugal. He doesn't drive a flashy car, have a huge mansion, or wear expensive suits.

Imagine the fight we had when he offered to pay for my tuition.

I appreciate the fact that he's trying so hard, I do. Trying to repair our relationship is going to take a lot of work on both of our parts, but I also want to keep the independence that I've worked hard for.

"Here, let me take your bag," he says, and I hand it off to him. He hangs it on the wooden hook near the door next to the coats and umbrellas hanging neatly next to each other.

The walls are painted a pale beige, and there are very few photos or decorations along the wall aside from a few random pieces of landscape art.

"I decided to make homemade pot pie because I

remembered how much you loved it when you were younger. Remember when you turned eight and we asked where you wanted to go for dinner for your birthday? Man, you could've chosen anywhere, but you asked me to make you a pot pie." There's sadness in his tone, the same sadness I feel when talking about the past.

"I remember. Thanks, Dad." I smile, taking a seat at the modest kitchen table. Tucking my hair behind my ear, I watch as he grabs a pair of black oven mitts and opens the oven, pulling out the steaming hot pot pie. "So, how was training camp?"

"Good. We've got a great group of guys, and thankfully, the vets are good guys. They're welcoming to the rookies, and I'm excited to see them work together as a team," he says while he pulls the mitts off and leans against the counter. "I know hockey has never really been your thing, but I was hoping you could make it out to a few games this year?"

Oh god. Seeing Hudson play in the flesh? I don't know if my heart... or my vagina... could take it.

Clearing my throat, I nod. "Uhm, yeah, I'd love to. I just have to check my schedule, you know, with school, internship, and the sorority. If I can sneak away, I will."

His grin is contagious, and I find myself smiling in return. "That works, Care Bear. I'll leave you a few tickets at will call so you can bring Tatum if you want? How's that going?"

"She's great. We get along really well, and being her roommate is honestly one of the highlights of moving here. She's very neat, and she knows that studying is my top priority."

Dad nods and opens a drawer, pulling out a knife to cut the pie. He keeps talking as he cuts. "That's great. I love to hear it. And your classes?"

"They're good. I may... have taken on a few too many classes? I'm a little ambitious, and the course load is killer, but I've got this. It just means less partying and more studying."

"Good. Less partying means less worrying for me. Especially when we go a few days without talking, Care. I can't help but worry. Chicago is a big city, and it's new to you."

"Dad, I've told you a billion times. I'm okay. I'm not a little girl anymore, and I know sometimes you forget that, but you've got to let me stand on my own feet."

He puts the knife down and walks around the kitchen island to me, taking a seat next to me. "I-I just missed so much, Caroline. I wish I could turn back to the clock, start over and be there for every minute that I missed."

"Me too, Dad, but we can't do that, so we have to move forward, and the only way we can do that is to leave the past in the past and to focus on the future."

He nods, sadness dimming on his face. "How about we play Scrabble? After dinner? You used to love that game."

My heart pangs again, emotion rising in my throat, but I plaster on the best smile I can manage and nod. "Sounds good."

After eating dinner, which was amazing and truly is still my favorite meal, we play three rounds of Scrabble until I feel my eyes getting heavy. Checking my watch, I see that it's after ten, and this week has officially caught up to me. Studying, sorority duties, late-night assignments.

"Hey, Dad, if someone wanted to get a hockey player's jersey, where could I get one?" I ask as we're picking up the game.

For a second, he pauses, his brow furrowing. "Like as in my guys?"

I nod, pulling my lip between my teeth.

"I thought you weren't a hockey fan?" he asks, cocking his head.

"I'm not really. It just seems like I'm the only person in the entire city that isn't a fan of the Avalanches. Plus, my dad is their coach. What kind of daughter would I be if I didn't at least own a jersey? You did want me to come to a game—shouldn't I wear one when I do?"

He ponders my words for a second but shrugs with a smile. "I guess you're right. I can get you some merch, sweetheart. Don't spend your money on that."

"Uh, well, I mean, I also wanted to get one for Tatum. She's a huge fan, and, uh, she wanted to get a specific player."

His eyes darken slightly. "And who would that be?"

Shit. Shit. Shit.

I should've known better than to ask him.

"Hudson Rome."

He eyes me carefully before replying. "There's an official merch store near the arena that carries all the vets. But I think it's worth reiterating that both Tatum *and* you need to stay away from my guys, Caroline. The last thing I would ever want is my daughter caught up with any of them. They're too old for either of you and not the settling type. Especially not a guy like Rome. Okay?"

"Yep. Of course, Dad. I was just asking for Tatum. Thank you."

He nods, rising from his chair. "Let me grab my keys, and I can get you back to the house. One sec."

I should feel guilty for hiding this from him and sneaking around with his player.

I should.

Except... I don't. While I want to repair my relationship with my dad, I also don't think he has any right to impose any rules on my life. He's been absent for almost ten years of my life.

It's late when I get back to my room and completely quiet. I had a few unread messages from Hudson and one from Tatum saying she was staying over with her date and, I quote, "getting the D."

Which means I have our room all to myself.

After doing my nighttime skin care routine, I throw on an old T-shirt and panties, then climb into my bed before opening all the texts from Hudson.

Hudson: I'm home and very disappointed that you weren't in my bed waiting for me.

Hudson: Did you like my gift? Currently trying to decide which pair I want to rip off first.

I'm partial to red, I think. But not a picky guy.

Hudson: Are you ignoring me, Bubblegum? My dick misses you. I miss you.

Grinning, I type out a response.

Caroline: Wow, three texts in a row? You're looking a little desperate , big guy. I was having dinner, and I just got home. I'm glad your dick misses me. I was hoping I made a lasting impression.

Hudson: You made an impression alright. It's been a week since I've tasted you. Not sure how much longer I'll survive.

Caroline: I'd hate to be the reason for your untimely death. Too bad I'm all alone in my room and you're all the way over there.

I quickly snap a picture of the faded T-shirt riding high on my thighs, showing just a glimpse of my panties, and send it to him, which immediately prompts a response.

Hudson: Fuck. Goddamnit Caroline.

Caroline: Goodnight Hudson. *winky face followed by kissy face*

Hudson: Goodnight Bubblegum.

FIFTEEN

HUDSON

"Fuck, I missed you," I murmur against her lips, lacing my fingers into her hair. The only thing I do is groan when I taste the watermelon bubblegum flavor on her tongue. That goddamn gum that I've been craving for over a week now. Especially after our text last night, I couldn't wait to get to the rink today, not only to catch up with my team but because I knew she'd be here. "Maybe it's just the Hubba Bubba. I think I might be developing an addiction. This is very serious."

"You've only been gone a week." She giggles as she loops her arm around my neck, standing on her tiptoes. "And I'm pretty sure you're just addicted to giving me orgasms... not the gum, but whatever you say, Romeo."

"A week too fucking long."

My lips move over hers, tasting, teasing, tracing the

seam of her lips with my tongue, desperate to dip inside her mouth.

This is reckless, kissing her here right now, in the closet of the practice facility. I know better—I just couldn't wait another second to touch her. My hands physically *ached* to touch her.

And the last hour has been the worst form of torture... being so close to her yet not able to act on my desire for her.

"We have to go back out there before someone realizes we're *both* gone," she says but makes no move to slide out of my embrace. If anything, her grip on my neck tightens.

"Yeah, we do."

My gaze holds hers, neither of us moving, only breathing each other in.

"Right now. We should do that *right now*."

"Yep."

Then suddenly, her lips are on mine again, a soft moan escaping as she launches herself into my arms, her legs wrapping around my waist. My hands fist in her hair as her tongue strokes inside my mouth, and together, we're lost.

The rest of everything fades out, and it's only this feeling.

We're making out in a closet like we're teenagers—obviously, we have a thing for them—yet, the last thing I want to do is stop. Even though we should. Even though anyone could realize that we're both missing and come looking to find me with my coach's daughter, my team's intern, in the most compromising way possible.

It wouldn't just be my reputation on the line; it would be Caroline's too, which is why I tear my lips from hers and carefully set her back down on her feet as much as I really don't fucking want to.

"Tonight," I promise, dropping my lips to hers once more in a quick kiss. "I'll pick you up."

She nods, giving me the sweetest fucking smile. "You go out first, and then I'll come out in a couple of minutes?"

"Yep. I'll go and distract Laura."

"My Romeo," she quips, a teasing look in her eyes. Those fucking eyes could bring me to my knees if it's what she wanted.

I open the door and quickly slip out, shutting it behind me. When I turn the corner to the hallway, I see Wren leaning against the wall next to the water fountain, his arms crossed and a knowing smirk on his lips.

"What?" I ask.

His eyebrows rise. "You do realize you are not very inconspicuous, right?"

"I have no idea what you're talking about."

Fuck.

Shit.

"Yeah... okay, but, uh,...you've got lip gloss on your face."

Lifting my hand, I swipe at my lips, only for his smirk to widen into a full-blown shit-eating grin.

"*Ha!* I knew it. Is she your *giiiiiirlfriend?*"

"Wren," I warn, my gaze narrowing when I realize there isn't shit on my face, but I accidentally just outed my... relationship with Caroline to him. Not that I would admit it to him.

"Don't worry, your secret is safe with me, Coach. I, uh, came here to ask you something else anyway." He zips his lips and throws away the key as he stifles another grin.

I was not fucking prepared for this, and frankly, it caught me off guard. Now one of my players is involved, and fuck, I want to be with Caroline, but we're already being reckless and careless. I clear my throat and ask, "What's up?"

Wren hesitates, then shakes his head. "Never mind. It was stupid." He pushes off the wall and hikes his bag higher on his shoulder before turning toward the rink.

"Wren. It's not stupid. What's going on?" I say.

He whips back around as his shoulders sag in defeat, "I was going to see if you could help me with this, uh, scholarship paperwork thing I need for school. I need a reference, and I was going to see if you had any time. I know you're probably busy and only in town for a few days. I ju—"

"Nope, not too busy. How's tomorrow?"

The emotion that crosses his face causes my heart to

squeeze. All he wants from me is time, and the moment that I agree, he's shocked, every time.

"Y-yeah, that would be cool," he says.

———

"THAT WAS POSSIBLY the best thing I've had in my life," Caroline groans as she slides into the passenger seat of my car.

I lean over and capture her lips, tasting the salty-sweet caramel still sticky on her lips. I learned tonight it's her favorite ice cream flavor, and seeing the way that her eyes lit up when I made a detour and pulled into the small mom-and-pop old-fashioned ice cream parlor on the outskirts of town was worth it a thousand times over. Made me want to buy fucking gallons just to have delivered to her house knowing it makes her that damn happy.

"Gonna have to disagree on that one because I've had something far *sweeter*."

Her eyebrows rise, and she smirks. "You are a dirty man."

I shrug. "It's true, though. Ready to head home?"

She nods. "I've been dreaming about your huge..." She leans over the center console until her lips brush against mine lightly, using her tongue to trace my bottom lip. "*Hot tub* since I left."

Christ.

I groan when she pulls back and settles into the passenger seat, pulling the seat belt across her chest and securing it. "You are fucking killing me. You can't do that to me after not being able to touch you for an entire fucking week, Caroline."

All she does is giggle, making no attempt to stifle the amused sound from her lips, and the entire ride home, she does her best to tease me until my dick feels like it might punch through my jeans. It didn't help that her hands were everywhere. I could hardly focus on driving.

"Just wait until I get you inside," I tell her, then walk around to the passenger side and open the door. I unbuckle her, easily lifting her from the seat and tossing her over my shoulder, my hands gripping her thighs as I stride toward the front door of my house.

When she yelps and hits my back, I bring my hand to her ass and spank the fuck out of it.

"Oh my god, did you just *spank* me, Hudson Rome?" she squeals.

"Sure as fuck did, Caroline Evans, and if you keep taunting me, I'm going to put you on your knees right here and fuck your throat just so you remember who's in charge."

She goes completely quiet, and I grin, smacking her ass once more just for good measure.

"I can't believe you're *spanking* me." Her voice is laced with disbelief, and I grin even fucking harder.

Once we're inside, I set her on the floor and cradle her face in my hands as she faces me. "Oh baby, I can't wait to show you just how good it can be."

Her eyes widen slightly, her throat bobbing as she swallows. "Is that a perk of dating an older man? The *experience*."

"I guaran-fucking-tee that Jay, the preppy little fuck boy from the other night, has no idea how to worship you, Caroline. He wouldn't even know where to begin when it comes to fucking you the way that you deserve. I can wring the pleasure from your body in ways you couldn't even imagine because it is fucking *mine*. Your cunt is mine."

"Then show me what it's like to be *yours*."

Her words are barely out of her mouth before I'm on her, my lips moving over hers as I take her mouth like it's mine. Like *she's* mine. I back her toward the stairs and pull my lips from hers before stepping back.

"The problem with these young guys... is they lack patience. They aren't willing to put in the work and wait for the reward." My voice is low and hoarse with need, but I continue. "Go sit on the fifth stair."

Surprise flits across her features, but she obliges, stepping back until the backs of her knees hit the stairs, and she sits.

The flowy, floral pink dress she's wearing hangs to her thighs, and she denies me the view of her pretty little covered pussy when she crosses her Converse over the other, closing her legs.

"Spread your legs, Caroline," I rasp.

Immediately, her legs slide open, torturously slowly, giving me what I want. Tonight, her panties are bright red satin, her hard little clit peeking against the fabric.

She bites her lip when my gaze meets hers. "Now what?"

"Pull the dress up."

The pink fabric slides up, pooling around her hips, and she leans back slightly, awaiting my next instructions.

My cock gets harder by the second, not just because she's so goddamn sexy but because she's being obedient, and there's nothing more attractive on this damn planet than this girl sitting on my steps with hunger in her eyes.

Like she's eager to please me.

"Slide your panties to the side and touch your clit."

Her gaze never leaves mine as she hooks her finger into the satin and pulls it aside, exposing the prettiest pink pussy I've ever seen, smooth and already glistening with her wetness. Apparently, me instructing her is making her just as desperate as it is me.

That's my girl.

Using her lilac-painted middle finger, she brings it to her clit and begins rubbing slow, teasing circles. Her movement is unhurried, and her gaze stays on mine as she sucks her lip into her mouth, letting out the sexiest moan I've ever heard.

"Does it feel good, baby?"

She nods wordlessly, her body sagging against the stairs as she plays with her clit, her legs falling open even wider.

"Now, slide a finger inside of you."

Her finger slides lower until she plunges it inside her slowly, gasping at the sensation.

"Look at that greedy little pussy taking your finger like a good girl. Fuck yourself with it. Just like you would if you were at home while I was on the road and you wanted it to be me."

Her hand moves as she begins to withdraw her finger and fuck herself, her breathing labored, her chest heaving in pleasure.

Caroline Evans on my stairs, legs spread wide with her finger buried in her pussy, head thrown back in unrestrained pleasure, is the most beautiful sight I've ever fucking seen.

She's not shy—she's confident and unashamed as she bares herself and seeks out her pleasure for me to watch.

"That's it, baby. Now, add another finger," I tell her as I unbutton my jeans, slide the zipper down, and free my aching cock.

Her eyes drag down to where I'm palming my cock, stroking it while watching her finger her tight little cunt. I would watch her fuck herself all night if I wasn't dying to touch her.

"Do you want me to fuck you, Caroline? Do you want my dick where you ache?" I ask when her soft moan echoes around the foyer, the only other sound aside from her heavy breathing and the sound of how wet she is every time she fucks herself.

Nodding, she lifts her other hand and yanks the fabric of her dress higher, exposing her tits, heavy and full in the same matching red as her panties. She pulls the cup down and tugs on the taut peak, using the metal barbell as an anchor as she plays with her nipples.

"Then make yourself come. If you want me to fuck you, then make yourself come right here."

I expect her to protest, for her to beg me to fuck her, but she squeezes her eyes shut and increases the pace of her fingers.

"Eyes on me."

Her eyes fly open, and then they flick lower to where I'm pumping my cock, spreading the cum that's leaking from the tip, then bringing her eyes back up to my face. I can see it as it happens.

The way pleasure rocks through her body, and she comes, arching against the staircase, letting her head fall back as her pussy quivers and her legs tremble. My eyes roam her body, noting how her nipples are hard and tight.

I can't wait to spend the rest of the night sucking on them, giving each the attention they deserve.

After her orgasm subsides, she pulls her finger out of her pussy and slowly lowers her dress before rising from the stairs and making her way over to me.

"Give me your hand, Caroline," I grunt. She lifts her still-glistening fingers, and I bring them to my mouth, tracing the wetness along my lips before sucking them into my mouth and swirling my tongue around them, sucking them clean. My favorite taste in the world.

Dropping to her knees, she looks up at me through thick, dark lashes as she reaches for my cock. A sharp hiss tumbles from my mouth when she closes her fist almost all of the way around me, thumbing the blunt head as cum leaks from the slit.

"College fuckboys wouldn't know how to teach you to open your throat so it can be fucked," I grit out, bringing my fist to her hair and weaving my fingers through the soft strands. "They wouldn't know when to pull you off when you've had enough, when you're covered in spit from gagging around a cock. How to properly fill your throat full of cum."

Taking my thumb and dragging it along her bottom lip, I ask, "Do you want me to fuck your throat, Caroline?"

I wait for her response, and when she nods, I shake my head. "I want to hear you say it."

"Please fuck my throat."

"Good girl," I praise her, taking my cock in my hand and tracing it along her lips. I slip the head past her waiting lips into her hot, wet heat and groan. She cups my balls in her hand, rolling them between her fingers, and I swear I'm already about to come down her throat.

The sensation of her sucking and playing with my balls is almost too much at once. I wasn't expecting her to be so brazen, so bold.

But if there's anything I'm learning about Caroline... she's not afraid to be uninhibited.

Carefully, I guide her mouth down on my cock until I hit the back of her throat, and she gags lightly. I pull out while she sucks in a breath.

"Do you want to stop?"

"No. I want this. I want you," she pants, reaching for me, guiding me back into her mouth, pressing even further this time. Her hands tug on my balls as she takes me as deep as she can, hollowing her mouth and sucking as she presses her nose against the base of my cock.

"Fuck, Caroline," I pant. "Just like that, baby."

If I died right now, I'd die the happiest man on the entire planet. There's no doubt about it.

The small semblance of control I have slips, and I thrust into her throat, my hips flexing deeper each time. My girl takes it, every inch of me.

When I feel the base of my spine beginning to tingle, my balls drawing up, ready for release, I pull out of her mouth, yank her top down, exposing those tits that I can't get enough of, and pump my cock, spilling all over her chest. Ropes of cum paint her chest, her chin, her lips as I come.

Her tongue darts out at the corner of her lips to taste it, and I groan through my release, my hand slowing as I finish.

Reaching between us, I take her fingers and run them along her chest, through the cum dripping off her, before leaning down. "Now, go upstairs and wait in my bed, and do not wash my cum off of you. I'm not done with you yet."

Heat flares in her gaze, and she nods, sucking her lip into her mouth, tasting my cum as she rises off her knees and saunters up the stairs.

This girl is going to be the death of me.

SIXTEEN
CAROLINE

One thing I was absolutely unprepared for is how I would actually *miss* Hudson when the season started and he was constantly on the road.

Not just the amazing sex, and endless orgasms, but hanging out with him. Laughing with him. Sneaking into closets with him. We just have so much fun together, and we click so easily.

Both of our schedules were hectic between his games, my class schedule, both of us working at the rink, my sorority commitments, and anything else that seemingly came up when he got more than a single day at home. It felt like we were two ships passing each other in the night, our schedules never truly lining up.

"When's your lover boy going to be home again?" Tatum asks as she browses through a sale rack at the boutique we're currently shopping in. An impromptu, last-minute shopping date for an outfit for her date tonight, even though our room currently looks like a category five hurricane hit it after she destroyed her closet. Apparently, things are heating up with her new guy, and tonight's the night she's meeting his friends.

I tagged along for moral support and because there's one thing I really need from today's shopping trip, and that's our next stop.

"He's not my lover boy, and he flies home tomorrow night, I think. A whole forty-eight hours before he's got to leave for another game," I say with a pout.

"Ugh, I'm sorry, Care. At least you'll get forty-eight hours of great dick before he's gone? I know you have to miss him. I'd never be able to date someone who was gone like most of the year." Her eyes are filled with sympathy, a small frown sitting on her clear-glossed lips.

I shrug, pretending to focus on the hideous purple dress on the rack in front of me. "I do miss him, but it's also casual, Tate. We're having *fun*. Once we start involving... feelings and shit, things just get complicated. So, when he's in town and our schedules mesh up, we hang out."

"A built-in dick appointment—I'm here for it. Just... protect your heart, okay?" Tatum says.

"No heart involved. Don't worry."

And that's the truth, mostly. But... being around him is

so easy. When we can shut out the rest of the world and all of the things that are working against us.

Maybe someday *more* wouldn't be so terrifying...

As soon as the thought enters my mind, I push it down.

No. Relationships are not for me, and I *like* things just the way they are. Anything *more* becomes messy and complicated, and I don't do messy.

"Now, what about this?" I hold up the purple dress, and she wrinkles her nose and shakes her head.

"I'm going to pretend you didn't even show me that. I'm not finding anything in here. How about we head home?"

Nodding, I put the dress back on the rack and grab her hand. "Yes, but one more stop before we head back."

An hour later, I've got the bag secured and big plans for it once Tatum leaves for her date.

I check my phone once we're back in our room and smile when I see the unread texts from Hudson.

Hudson: How was your day? Missing me yet?

When his message went unanswered, he sent another, and my smile only widens.

Hudson: Gotta head to the arena to warm up, but when I get off the ice tonight... I want to FaceTime you and see your beautiful face. Miss you Bubblegum.

Caroline: Good luck tonight! I'll be watching, and pretending that I know what's going on when I'll really just be watching the super hot goalie I'm currently banging.

Hudson: Caroline, don't talk about banging before I have to go on the ice. Gonna be kind of hard to play when my cock is hard.

Caroline: I guess you probably shouldn't think about what I just purchased then... Wouldn't want to affect your playing.

Hudson: Stop teasing me woman. Gotta go, I'll call you as soon as I'm back to the room.

Caroline: Knock em dead, *Romeo*.

"Earth to Caroline." Tatum waves her hand in front of my face from beside my bed, and I toss my phone onto the bed, giving her my full attention. She's in a completely different outfit with her makeup done, looking so cute. "I'm headed out, and I'm staying at Zach's this weekend, so I probably won't be back until Sunday. Have fun with your lover boy. Love you. Byeeee." She drops a quick kiss to my cheek before grabbing her overnight bag from the bed and leaving me in a slightly less destroyed room, all alone.

I sprint from the bed, snatch the shopping bag from the top of my desk, and reach inside. My fingers graze the jersey inside, tracing over the letters on the back.

Rome.

30.

I take off my clothes, sliding the jersey over my bare skin, and grab a pair of the sexiest panties from the hundreds that Hudson had sent over. The see-through black lace ones with the bow on the back that remind me of a present waiting to be unwrapped.

When he gets his phone tonight after the game, the first thing he's going to see are these pictures, and I can't wait to see his reaction.

Kneeling down in front of the full-length mirror, I pull the jersey up higher to expose my ass and the thin black string of lace between them, I gather my hair to the side, ensuring his name and number are visible from this angle. I snap a few pictures, then switch positions to take a few more.

A girl needs options, especially when you're sending them to the literal hottest man on the planet, who's a famous hockey player.

God, that feels so weird to say. Hudson's this accomplished goalie, and I'm just a girl... in college... thirteen years younger than him... Us being *together* is weird on the surface.

But it doesn't feel that way when we're together. It just feels right. Natural.

Like he's becoming one of my best friends, and I don't want to question things or complicate them because I love things just the way that they are. Chill.

My finger hovers over the Send button, hesitating for only a moment before I press it and then I pick up the remote and put on his game. I can't help the smile that touches my lips when I see him guarding the net, his hulking body dropping at the blink of an eye to stop the puck.

Onscreen, he moves a lot like he does when he's between my thighs. Powerfully, confidently, assuredly. There's no hesitation in his movements; they're steadfast and graceful.

I'm in awe.

It's the first time I've really seen him play, aside from when he's played at the rink with the kids, and that's completely different. He's Coach Hudson then.

On the screen? Out on that ice?

He's the Playboy Playmaker.

I spend the next two hours attempting to work on my paper, but my eyes keep dragging back to the screen, focusing more on the game and Hudson than the introduction of general chemistry.

By the third period, I've abandoned my books completely and am pacing in front of the TV, chewing my nails nervously. The Avalanches are tied with two minutes left on the clock, and my nerves are completely shot.

Holy shit.

This is intense.

The camera flits back to my dad, who's pacing just like

I am, his charcoal suit slightly rumpled, along with his hair from running his hands through it in exasperation.

This has been a game far more interesting than a shutout, if I do say so myself. The adrenaline has my blood pumping and my heart pounding wildly.

I need them to win. They *need* to win!

With thirty-four seconds left, Reed Davis flies down the ice so fast that I can hardly keep up with the puck. He pulls back, taking his shot into the net.

A second passes. My breath stops. My heart pounds.

Then... the crowd goes wild.

Absolutely feral.

Because the puck sailed right past the goalie's legs and into the net with a whoosh.

The Avalanches win!

"Yesssss!" I scream, jumping up and down. They did it. Holy shit, they did it.

I just watched my first full hockey game since I was a kid, solely for Hudson, but now I can totally see what the hype is about.

Flopping down onto my back on the bed, I sigh. That was incredible.

I pick up my phone and pull up Hudson's messages again, typing a quick one back while my heart is still racketing against my rib cage.

Caroline: You are so getting lucky. You were amazing! Congratulations, Romeo.

He probably won't see my messages for an hour or so since they have to shower and then do media, so I set my phone down and put on *Gilmore Girls* while I wait. Slowly, my heart rate returns to normal, but the smile never goes away.

That's *my* Romeo.

"HELLO," I mumble into the phone groggily, my eyes still shut.

A chuckle vibrates through the speaker. "Hey, Bubblegum."

My eyes snap open and ping around the room, noticing the blank TV screen and darkness blanketing the room.

Shit, I must have fallen asleep while waiting for Hudson to call.

"Were you sleeping?" he asks, and only then do I look down at my phone and realize his handsome face is on the screen, and it's not a phone call at all. He's FaceTiming me.

"Mhm," I mumble, bringing the phone in front of my face and praying I don't have drool somewhere. "I was waiting for you to call, and I think I just crashed from the adrenaline after watching the game."

I'm still half-asleep, my voice low and slightly hoarse.

He grins, "This is my favorite version of you. Soft, sleepy. I can't wait to get home and wake up to that, Bubblegum."

"Mmm. Tomorrow, right?"

He nods, propping his phone up against the mirror of the hotel bathroom. I realize then he's only wearing a small white towel knotted around his waist, and the shower glass is still steamed up behind him. He must have called as soon as he stepped out of the shower. Water rivets trail down his torso, and immediately, I'm more awake.

It's impossible not to look at Hudson and want him so badly I ache.

"Do me a favor?"

"Yeah, of course."

"Wear that jersey for me." He grins, running his hand over his short hair, then reaching around his neck to clasp his chain.

Why are chains so sexy? Something as mundane and ordinary has way more effect than you'd imagine.

Or maybe it's just Hudson.

"Maybe," I tease him, biting my lip.

I can't believe I actually fell asleep still wearing it, but after the adrenaline wore off from the win, I just crashed.

"Oh Bubblegum, after those pictures, the only place you're going to be for the forty-eight hours I'm home is in bed, taking my cock." The commanding tone of his voice causes me to shiver. "What did you think was going to happen when you sent them to me, baby?"

I shrug, the smirk on my lips turning sassy, but say nothing.

I love this between us. The banter, the way he can say nothing at all but make me want... all of it. Without a single word.

He grabs the phone, and the bathroom goes dark as he flicks the light off and walks through the dimly lit hotel room to the bed. He flops down onto the plush white comforter, resting the phone on his chest.

"Do you have any idea how hard I was when I saw you in my jersey in those pictures?"

I shake my head, feigning innocence. "Tell me." My words are a whisper, and when his gaze darkens, his eyes turning heavy, I feel myself growing hotter by the second.

"I was in the locker room with at least forty other men, and I still got hard. I had to tuck it into the waistband of my slacks so no one would see," he says low and hoarse in a way that I feel in my core.

Biting my lip, I nod. "I wanted that. To drive you crazy."

"Mission accomplished, Bubblegum. My dick is still hard," he rasps.

"Maybe... you should make it better."

He grins smugly. "Maybe you should help me make it better."

Suddenly, his camera is flipped around, and I see the hard rivets of his abs, with the trail of hair leading down into the knotted white towel around his waist, where he's very clearly hard, bulging behind the thin fabric.

Oh. My. God.

My body is now on fire, and the jersey I'm wearing is only making it worse. I'm burning up for him, and he's thousands of miles away while I'm alone in my room at the sorority house.

Rethinking my newfound love for hockey.

He palms his length over the towel, squeezing it as he husks, "Turn the light on. I need to see you, baby."

I reach over and flick the lamp on and the light illuminates the room in a warm glow.

His gaze darkens when he sees that I'm still wearing the jersey I teased him with.

"If you only knew how fucking sexy you are wearing my name, Bubblegum. If you only knew how possessive I feel or the shit it makes me want to do. Take it off, let me see you." He grunts, then hisses when I pull it off, revealing my bare chest. "Fuck. You have the most perfect tits I've ever seen. Those little barbells I love to pull with my teeth."

Lying back on the bed, I bring my free hand to my nipple and circle the peak before fingering the tiny metal bar through it.

I know how much he loves them and how much *I* love

for him to touch them. My nipples are sensitive, and when he takes them into his mouth, I'm gone.

Only for him.

"Show me my pussy, Bubblegum. I'm missing sliding my tongue in it, licking up all of your cum."

I shimmy out of my leggings and toss them onto the floor, then lower my phone to where my panties are, propping the phone onto the comforter.

"Mmm, you're making a mess in the panties I bought you." I almost moan when I see the towel around his waist disappear, exposing his cock.

The veins in his arms bulge as he strokes himself in slow, languid movements, making my mouth water.

I want to lick those veins.

"Rub your clit through the panties, Bubblegum. Make it real wet for me." Suddenly, the camera turns around, facing him again, and I see him rising from the headboard and walking over to the small computer desk in the corner of the room. He props the phone up on the desk and sits in the chair across from it, giving me a full view of him.

God, he's so ridiculously hot.

His body is a complete work of art, his chest wide and his arms thick. Everything is cut with muscles that I know he's worked hard for. Flat stomach, chiseled abs, tapered waist, and powerful thighs.

It's how he can toss me around like I weigh absolutely nothing, even though nothing about me is light.

"I want you to watch me fuck my fist and know that I'm thinking about fucking you in my jersey, seeing your tight little cunt stretched around me, taking all of me." He pauses and spits into his hand before bringing it back to his cock.

The motion is so dirty, so absolutely filthy, that I swear I almost come on the spot.

My finger works my clit, dipping below the fabric of my panties as he starts to pump his cock, smoothing his palm over the head, using his thumb to spread the precum seeping from its tip.

"Hudson," I pant. My fingers slip lower and plunge inside my entrance, the sound of my wetness echoing through the room as I begin to fuck myself. I don't squeeze my eyes shut and succumb to the pleasure, no.

I keep them wide and fixed on Hudson as he pumps his cock and watches me slide my fingers in and out of myself. The ragged groan that tumbles from his lips has the orgasm inside of me building and building.

"I'm about to come, Caroline. Need you with me." He drops his head back on his shoulders, his abs tightening as he does, his eyes never leaving the screen. "Come for me, baby. Pull on your piercing."

Following his command, I rub the sensitive peak of my nipple between my fingers, tugging on the piercing as my fingers brush against my G-spot inside, and it sends me right over, pummeling into pleasure so intense that my entire body trembles.

"Oh God. Hud—" I moan, my words cutting off as all of the air leaves my lungs in a woosh, pleasure racking my body in powerful waves.

"Fuck, I wish I were there so I could watch my cum dripping out of you." His head drops back against his shoulders again as he groans hoarsely and erupts, coming all over his stomach in spurts. His cum drips down his abs, coating his fist and fingers.

It's the hottest thing I've ever seen in my life.

When we're both able to catch our breath, Hudson chuckles, grabbing a T-shirt from the ground and cleaning himself up while I pick the phone up and ditch the panties since they're now soaked.

"You are a dirty girl, Bubblegum." He smirks. "I fucking miss you, and I can't wait to be home tomorrow so I can clean you up. With my tongue."

I shiver, even though I just came so hard watching his head thrown back in pleasure as he fucked his fist. I can still feel my clit throbbing.

I'm so in over my head. He's turning me into a sexual fiend.

"Can't wait."

"As soon as I land, I want to see you. *Need* to see you.."

I pull my lip between my teeth before saying softly, "Okay."

"I'm fucking beat. Thank you for the pictures and for being my good-luck charm before the game." He pauses, his smirk turning into a full blinding smile. "And after. I'll text you when I touch down."

"Glad I could be of assistance."

"And Caroline?" he says before we get off.

"Hm?"

"Wear the jersey."

SEVENTEEN
HUDSON

"You teased me to the point of *actual* fucking insanity, Bubblegum. Because that's what this is," I mutter as my feet hit the ground inside Caroline's bedroom. I just fucking snuck through the window of her sorority house because I couldn't walk through the front door. They've got a strict no men after 9:00 p.m. policy, with cameras on the front porch, and a house mother to enforce it.

So, here I am. Sneaking through a sorority row window in the middle of the night like I'm a damn teenager, just to fuck the shit out of my girl after she spent last night teasing the shit out of me while wearing my jersey. Wearing my name on her back. I was home less than five minutes before I dropped my bags, took the fastest shower in the history of the damn world, and then took a fucking Uber straight here so I wouldn't have to figure out where to park.

She giggles, yanking at my shirt and hauling me against her, throwing her arms around my neck, "Mmm, finally."

Yeah, fucking *finally*. She should get her tight little ass spanked for the way she teased me the entire time I was on the road. The sexting, the flirtatious pictures, the desire in her voice when we talked. Hard to focus on hockey with a constantly hard dick.

I waste no time moving my lips over hers, my tongue slipping inside her waiting mouth as I lift her off her feet and walk her towards the bed she points to, laying her flat against the comforter.

"You've been a bad girl, Bubblegum. I think you need a taste of your own medicine," I tell her, my voice an octave deeper and hoarse because of how fucking hard I am for her. How insanely goddamn hard I've been since she sent me more dirty texts as I was getting off the plane tonight and told me to do something about it since her roommate would be gone all night.

I'm fucking doing something about it, alright.

She's driving me crazy, completely out of my damn mind with my need for her. I can't stay away from her.

Deepening the kiss, I grind my hips against the tiny scrap of fabric covering her pussy, groaning against her lips when she snakes her hand into the waistband of my shorts, palming my cock through my briefs.

"Can't wait," she pants, gripping me tightly in her hand, causing my hips to flex as she strokes. "Need you. Right. Now. I want your cock."

Fuck. Fuck. Fuck.

As much as I am ready to slide inside of her, I want to devour her before I do, because there's nothing I love more than the taste of her cunt on my tongue.

I crave her taste.

In one swift motion, I tear the panties from her and drop between her legs, biting and sucking along her inner thighs, my gaze holding hers as I do. I create a wet path with my tongue all the way to her pussy, then spread her open wide and swirl my tongue along her clit, teasing the little bundle of nerves until she's squirming, pressing her pussy to my face.

Only then do I pull back and flip her over, onto her stomach, grasping her hips and hauling her upwards so I can devour her from behind.

I love seeing her like this, ass perched high in the air, pussy glistening and gaping as she waits for me to lick her. My hands grip her ass, spreading her open wide so I can flatten my tongue and drag it from her clit to her asshole, teasing the tight ring with my tongue.

I'm slow with my movements, despite the frenzy

building inside me, because I want to take her to the edge and then pull it away. Make her as crazy as she made me. When I finally allow her to come, I want her to fucking drench me, to soak the sheets with her desire. I want her to explode and be limp with pleasure.

I pull back for a moment, only to grab my T-shirt at the base of my neck and pull it off, then remove my shorts and briefs. I bring my hand to my cock and palm the head, squeezing roughly as pre-cum seeps from the slit.

Fuck, I can't remember the last time I was this hard.

I drop back to my knees, my hands gripping the soft curve of her hips as I yank her backwards and lap at her pussy again, relishing at the sound of her desperate whimper.

"Please, Hudson," she pushes back against my mouth, grinding her pussy against my face.

"Patience, Bubblegum," I rasp, sliding my finger through her wetness before pressing into her wet heat. Her back arches, and she pushes back against my finger as I begin to fuck her while sucking her clit into my mouth. I love watching as her pussy greedily takes my finger. Her moan is loud and throaty, echoing in the empty room around us.

I pull my finger from her and slap her sopping pussy, my fingers grazing her clit as I do, hard enough to sting, but not enough to actually hurt.

Glancing back at me, she cries, "Hudson!"

"Quiet, Bubblegum. You have to be quiet if you want me to eat your pussy."

When her mouth flies shut, I reward her with a long, slow lick, and two fingers inside of her.

I take her to the edge, and pulling her back from coming over and over. Denying her the orgasm she's desperate for. Teasing her to the brink of tears, until finally, she scrambles towards the headboard, and turns to face me. Her hands grasp my shoulders, pulling me down, and my back hits the bed.

I barely have time to register my shock before her leg swings over my hips. She positions my cock at her slippery entrance, nudging it into her tight opening and then impaling herself with my dick so quickly, my vision dances.

We both groan in unison as my hands find her hips to guide her.

"Enough. Teasing," she says as she lifts herself up, hands flying to my chest, and begins to ride me. She swivels her hips, then slams herself down on me again and again, the wet sound of our arousal filling the room.

The headboard begins slapping against the wall in loud thuds, but fuck, we're both too lost to stop.

Bringing my thumb to her clit, I circle it as I watch my cock sliding in and out of her, a sense of possessiveness taking a hold of me as her tight little cunt clamps around me.

I love watching her stretch around my cock.

Nothing in the fucking world is hotter than watching her ride me as she chases her pleasure.

Her nails bite into my chest as she comes, tossing her head back and moaning my name so loudly that I grasp her hips, pulling her down on my cock as far as she can possibly fucking go, and then I let go. I move her hips back and forth as I empty deep inside of her, filling her completely with every drop of my cum.

Goddamnit.

I lift her up just slightly, glancing down between us, watching as both of our cum seeps from her pussy onto my cock, dripping down my balls onto the bed. Making a mess that has me thickening inside of her again already. I pull her off my cock, setting her gently on the bed, and reach between her thighs, using two fingers to push it back inside of her juicy pussy.

There's something about seeing her pink little cunt leaking my cum. I want to keep it inside of her, every goddamn drop. The possessive side of me loves marking her with my cum.

I'm about to shove my fingers into her mouth to make her lick them clean, when a loud knock on the door has Caroline springing up from the bed.

"Oh fuck," she whispers, her eyes wide as she turns to the door, "Uh, yes?"

"Caroline, is everything alright in there? We heard loud banging noises. Can you open the door so we can make sure you're okay?"

I quickly get up from the bed, searching for my briefs, but I can't find them on the floor in my panic.

"Hudson, go... out the window," she whispers. "That's our nosy house mother, and she's not gonna leave without checking that I'm okay. Please, I don't want to get in trouble with the sorority for breaking the rules when I'm still new here. You have to go."

"Bubblegum, I'm butt-ass fucking naked with your cum still coating my cock. Help me find my clothes!" I whisper yell, realizing that this situation just got even more insane.

Caroline is now stifling a laugh, and I narrow my gaze, searching for the black briefs I tossed somewhere in the haste of earlier.

"Here!" She tosses my briefs at me, then swipes my phone off her nightstand and tosses that too, shooing me towards the window.

I get my boxers on in five seconds flat, and climb back out the window I just snuck through, turning back to face her once I'm outside. She hastily kisses my lips. "I'll call you."

Then she quietly shuts the window, leaving me

standing outside with the rest of my clothes still scattered on her floor.

I'm oustide her window in my fucking underwear. In the middle of the night. At a goddamn sorority house with my dick literally still wet with our cum.

Jesus Christ.

I send a text to the only person I know who won't give me shit, and I start walking in the opposite direction of her house to hide between some nearby trees while I wait for my rescue.

Because what else can I do?

Ten minutes later, a dark mini van with a yellow "baby on board" sticker on the back slows beside my hiding place, the passenger window rolled down, and I don't even need to fucking glance over to see who's hanging partially out of the window.

"This must be a real low moment for you, *Romeo.*" Chaney smirks.

I don't even fucking look at him, just start walking to the car, my hand covering my junk.

"Really? You *had* to bring him?" I say.

Briggs shrugs. "He was at the house watching a movie with me since Maddison is having a girls' night. So, I had to bring *all* of the kids...."

The motorized door slides open, revealing Olive and Dexter asleep in their car seats, and I shake my head, sighing heavily.

Poor Olive is clutching her stuffed bunny in her pink pajamas like her life depends on it, snoring slightly. Dexter's clearly milk drunk, pacifier half hanging out his mouth, a dreamy and content look on his little face. Hell, I wish I could be him right now instead of having to have my best friend on a search and rescue mission to pick me up from a sorority house half-naked. I didn't even get to cuddle Caroline after our sexy high.

"You're never going to let me live this down... are you?" I roll my eyes.

"Nope," they say in unison, smug smirks on their faces.

Fucking *great*.

Chaney's grin widens, "Get in, loser, we're going back to the daycare."

Chuckling, I climb inside the van, stepping on a book that starts singing the alphabet loud as fuck, causing both Briggs and Chaney to whip around and "shhh" me obnoxiously loud. Even louder than the fucking book. I flop down onto the seat and rest my head against the headrest squeezing my eyes shut.

It just keeps getting fucking worse.

Briggs shuts the door and pulls down the road, silence hanging heavily in the air, the only sound the little snores of the two kids who are thankfully still passed out.

I know my friends want to fuck with me, I can practically feel it in the air. They're desperately trying to keep it under wraps.

"Just fucking say it." I sigh.

They look at each other, and then fucking die of laughter. Briggs is laughing so hard for a minute I'm scared he might wreck the van.

"Dude, we just picked you up in the middle of the night in your fucking underwear outside of a sorority house in Briggs's daddy mobile," Chaney wheezes. "You snuck out of a sorority girl's window like a creepy old cradle robber. Got a thing for daddy kink, old man?" He's literally struggling to breathe, he's laughing so hard.

"Oh fuck you, Rookie," I say, slapping the back of his head.

His shoulders shake with more laughter, and then Briggs looks back at me for a moment before dragging his attention back to the road. "As funny as this is, brother, I'm kinda worried you're going to get caught. I mean, what if someone actually saw you?"

I shrug. "Trust me, I had a moment of insanity. Won't happen again." Although, that's a promise I'm not sure I can keep since she seems to make me lose all semblance of sanity. "I'm going to be more careful."

He's got a point. I'm sneaking into her room because I couldn't stay away from her. Is this shit really just for fun anymore? Because the way I felt tonight... I *needed* to be with her.

I couldn't go another second without seeing her.

And what's more, I'm disappointed I didn't get to

spend *more* time with her tonight before I was unceremoniously shoved out the window. I wanted to hold her in my arms for a while, to hear about her week, to tell her about mine. To soak up everything about her.

I'm beginning to think that I might be a little *fucked* when it comes to my coach's daughter.

EIGHTEEN
HUDSON

"Do you even realize how fucked you are?" Chaney says nonchalantly while we walk toward my car after deboarding the plane. We're just returning from another stretch of away games.

I got "voluntold" to drop him off because Briggs needed to get straight home. Since I'm the only one not rushing home to a wife and kids, they picked me to chauffeur the rookie around. Lucky me. Don't ask me why a grown-ass man doesn't even have a driver's license. He also has a strong aversion to rideshare because of the privacy risk. That part I don't blame him for I guess, but fuck, hire a *driver*. Or something.

I'm just grumpy because I've been stuck on a plane with other anxious, grumpy hockey players who want to get home to their families.

This time, it's different. I actually have someone to get home to, and I can't fucking wait another second to see Caroline. We barely had two days together since the night that I snuck into her room at the sorority house, and it wasn't fucking long enough before I had to head back on the road for another game.

I haven't stopped thinking about her, and I can't wait to see her in my bed tonight. We agreed to only meet up at my house moving forward, just to be safe. This time, no one can interrupt us and there's no chance we'll be caught. Perks of living alone. But I'm also excited to just be together outside of my bed too, to hear her laughter, to hear about the kids at the rink, to flirt and tease like we always do. I just really like being around her.

"Don't make me leave you here." I stop mid stride and narrow my gaze at Chaney's jab, my lips tightening into a scowl.

Chaney lifts his hands in surrender, but the sincere expression on his face gives him away. "I love you enough to say it, Rome. You've been bouncing around for the last hour and a half, filled with nervous energy, and I know it's got every bit to do with getting home to see..." He looks around, lowering his voice and shielding it behind his hand before he continues. "Caroline."

"Get in the car," I tell him, unlocking the Rover and tossing my hockey bag in the trunk before sliding into the driver's seat.

Once he gets in the passenger seat and shuts the door, he turns to face me.

"Listen, I'm just worried, okay? You're... You're one of my best friends, and I don't want Coach to make your life a living hell. Brother, you are fucked-up about this girl. And not just any girl. Our coach's much younger, very fucking off-limits co-ed daughter. Dude, she was a baby when you were a teenager."

I clench my jaw, averting my gaze. "We're not together, Chaney. We're just having fun. We tried to stay away from each other, and it didn't work, so we're just taking it day by day."

He huffs, flopping backward against the leather of my seat. "Yeah, until you get caught, and guess what... then it doesn't *matter* what kind of shit you two want to label it. Then, it's too late. Coach knows, the media has a field day, and your entire career is on the line. You're playing with fire, and I'm scared you're going to get burned."

Part of me wants to snap on him, my patience already wearily thin, but another part of me sees that the kid is genuinely worried. I can see it on his face and hear it in the tone of his voice. He's actually fucking concerned.

"Rookie, I appreciate you, alright? I do," I say with sincerity.

He nods. "Just looking out for you, Rome. That's all."

"I know. I appreciate that, and as much as I do, I'm sick of looking at your ugly-ass face." I smirk, pulling out onto the highway towards his high-rise downtown penthouse.

He chuckles but doesn't respond, and it leaves me thinking about my brothers and the shit we've been through throughout the years. Somewhere along the way, we just added another to our crew.

The rookie became a part of our group from the moment we met him. Suddenly, he just started showing up to shit. Typical Chaney– he's a persistent fucker. But, he's one of us now.

I think about what he said the entire drive home, even after I dropped him outside of the penthouse.

I don't think he's wrong... and I don't blame him for being concerned.

But when I pull into the driveway, the only thing I can think about is getting inside my house to Caroline. Maybe we are playing with fire, but the more time I spend with her, the more I know I don't want to let her go. When I'm not with her, I spend all my time thinking about her, wishing she was there with me.

I toss my keys onto the table inside the front door and quietly set my hockey bag on the floor in the entryway before taking the stairs two at a time to the second floor, walking straight to the master bedroom.

The door is wide open, the silhouette of the beautiful girl asleep in my bed, causing my stomach to dip.

I lean against the doorframe, my eyes riveted to Caroline, who's bathed in the moonlight from the skylight windows, fast asleep. Her blonde hair is spread out on the pillow, her arms and legs tangled into the sheets.

When I thought about coming home to Caroline in my bed, I thought I wanted to come home to her naked, ready for me to crawl between her legs, but seeing her in an old practice T-shirt of mine that falls midthigh causes something possessive to flare in my chest.

I have no right to feel that way... but it doesn't change the fact that I do. Doesn't change the fact that even the thought of sharing her with anyone else makes my chest tight and my fists clench at my side.

She sighs in her sleep, a soft, breathy sound that makes my lips tug into a grin. I slip off my tennis shoes and cross the room, making my way over to her.

My knees hit the bed, and I crawl over her body, placing a kiss along the back of her thigh that's hitched up over the duvet. She smells so fucking good that I drag my nose along her warm skin, inhaling. Doesn't matter what time it is or where she is, my Bubblegum always smells like her favorite strawberry watermelon flavor.

"Mmmm." She moans softly in response to my touch.

Always so responsive, even when she's asleep.

I lift the worn shirt higher, exposing her bare ass, and plant kisses along the expanse of skin, nipping in places, and that's when I hear her breathing change, picking up.

My girl's awake.

I kiss up her back, softly along her spine, until I make it up the length of her body. When I do, I see the sleepy smile on her face.

"Hi," she whispers, her fingers fisting into my shirt and pulling me toward her until her nose brushes along mine. "You're here."

"I'm here, Bubblegum."

I lie down beside her and grab her waist, pulling her flush against me, feeling her warm, pliant body against mine.

"Missed you," she says, bringing her hand up to my face and touching the shadow along my jaw.

As terrifying as it is to admit it... Chaney's right. I'm entirely fucked when it comes to this girl, and I probably have been since the very first night.

I can't admit that out loud, especially not to her. Not when she's said she's not interested in anything beyond this.

This, which feels more complicated by the second.

This, which is beginning to feel like not enough.

Not nearly enough. I think I want everything with her.

"Missed you too, baby," I say, finally capturing her lips, tasting the sweet, fruity flavor that I'm already fucking addicted to. "I wish I could come home to this every time I get off a plane."

She grins against my mouth, looping her arm around my neck. "Mmmm, getting soft on me? That feels a little *too* relationshipy, Romeo," she laughs. "But I think that we could arrange something here or there. Meeting you here is definitely *much* better than worrying about the close call at the house the other day. Don't ya think? We can bang the bed on the wall and scream as loud as we want. Besides, your bed is so comfy," she winks.

My hand roams down her back to her ass, and I grab a handful, loving the feel of her in my hands. I love her like this— playful and flirty, relaxed in my arms. Sexy as fuck.

I crave her with a hunger I've never known.

"I've got less than forty-eight hours with you, Bubblegum." I dip my mouth to where she's already wet and aching for me. "Gotta make every second count."

And until the sun comes up, I do.

———

WHEN I CRACK my eyes open the next morning, the first thing I feel is the sun beating down on my skin, a blanket of warmth tempting me back into sleep one ray at a time.

I stretch my arms above my head, groaning when the sore muscles ripple from a combination of the game and spending most of the night putting Caroline in positions I didn't even know she could go.

We both finally passed out after three, after exhaustion coated my limbs until I felt like I couldn't hold my eyes open another second, much to Caroline's amusement. She could barely keep her eyes open either, but it didn't stop a lazy, sleepy grin from forming on her lips, her teasing me about being an old man with no stamina. So, then I had to prove her wrong one more time before we crashed.

Sitting up, I drag my hand through my hair, peering around the room and realizing that she's not in the bed with me.

Then, I smell... bacon.

Is my Bubblegum cooking me breakfast?

Smirking, I walk to the dresser and snag a pair of gym shorts and pull them up my hips. I walk downstairs quietly and realize I was right.

Caroline's at the stove, wearing my T-shirt from last night, one that falls down her thighs as her hips sway along to the music she's dancing to, spatula in hand.

For a second, I don't say a fucking thing. I just watch as she dances and scrambles eggs, oblivious to my presence.

Something so simple, yet when she does it...

It's mesmerizing.

I make my way over to her, standing a few inches behind her back, and she still hasn't realized I'm here. "Morning, Bubblegum," I rasp near her ear.

She rears back, letting out a scream as the spatula falls onto the counter. "Holy shit!"

I chuckle as I lace my arms around her waist, fisting the cotton fabric of my shirt to haul her against me.

"Expected a warmer welcome after how many times you came last night."

Whipping around to face me, she narrows her blue eyes. "Well, you scared the shit out of me!"

I shrug. "I like watching you like this." I nod toward the eggs on the stove and slowly trail my fingers up the outside of her thigh, underneath the T-shirt. "Cooking in my kitchen, wearing my shirt..."

Her body sags against mine, her hands linking around my neck, fingering the thin chain. Something I've noticed she does a lot that I'm getting addicted to. "Figured you needed to refuel after the game... and last night," she says saucily.

Trust me, I won't be forgetting the way she rode my cock... with her ass facing me, taking every inch of me, giving me a full view of her cunt taking my cock.

This wild girl that I'm fucking crazy about.

"Thank you for cooking breakfast for me, Bubblegum. I think this is a first." I smirk, dropping a quick kiss to her lips before letting her go and walking over to the fridge for orange juice. I set it on the counter and grab two glasses and pour us each one. "Can't say I've ever had a woman cook me breakfast the next day."

"Shame." She grins over her shoulder, then turns back to the stove and finishes breakfast. All while I sit at the bar, watching her cook, watching her hips sway, and trying not to get a hard-on.

Pretty sure my cock could get hard watching her do anything.

Once she finishes, she puts food on two plates and sets one in front of me, a sweet smile on her face.

"So." She joins me at the bar, fork in hand. "What's the plan today? You fly out again tomorrow right?"

I swallow the bite of eggs, reaching out to place my free hand on her thigh, needing to touch her somewhere. "Yep. But today, I'm taking you on a date." I feel her tense slightly next to me, so I add, "Don't freak out that I'm calling it a date. Just two people who like to have great sex enjoying the day together. Better?"

Her eyebrows raise. "Hmm. And do I get to know where we're going?"

"Nope." I smirk. "Rather keep it a surprise."

"I love surprises!"

"NO WAY," Caroline breathes, her eyes widening as I pull into a parking space behind the stadium. "Please tell me you're about to make my dreams come true of marrying a professional baseball player."

My lips twist into a scowl. "Sure, if he wants to die.

Have you seen me on the ice? Now imagine that but worse for anyone stupid enough to touch you."

She smarts, "For someone who doesn't get jealous, you seem *pretty* jealous, Romeo. You could just pull your dick out and pee on me instead."

I shrug. "Not jealous. Possessive. I don't like people touching what's mine." Leaning across the console, I bring my hand to her jaw, my lips so close to hers that I can practically taste her fruity gum. "And Bubblegum? Make no mistake, you *are* mine. At least for now."

With that, I get out of the car, walking around to her door and opening it, then offering her my hand. But I keep her hand in mine as I guide her toward the stadium. "Now, let's go. We've got a big day planned and no time to waste."

I pause to slap her ass for good measure, causing her to yelp.

"You sure are bossy, Romeo."

Chuckling, I clasp her hand in mine again. "You haven't seen bossy yet, baby."

I don't miss the way she shivers at my words, picking up exactly the meaning behind them.

Once we get to the back door of the practice facility, I pull out my phone and send a quick text before pocketing it back into my gym shorts pocket.

Caroline asked what she should wear for our "surprise," and I told her something comfortable, so she went with a pair of tight black leggings and one of my T-shirts tied up at her hip. Her hair is on the top of her head, and the only makeup she's got on is ChapStick.

Simple. Flawless. And it took her all of ten minutes to get dressed.

That's after a thirty-minute shower where I ate her pu—

"Hudson Rome!"

A voice breaks through my thoughts, and I see Fisher Owens standing in front of me, a cocky grin on his face as he pulls me in for a hug. "How the hell are you, man?"

Third baseman for the Chicago Knights, he's a burly motherfucker, and I'm not a small guy by any means. Six foot four, two hundred and eighty pounds, the dude could probably bench-press me. But truthfully, he's a big teddy bear. A solid brick teddy bear.

We met at an event a few years ago and kept in touch, forming a casual friendship, occasionally grabbing beers when we're both around. So imagine my surprise when I found out that Caroline is actually a baseball fan?

Kismet.

I knew my girl would lose her mind when I planned this date.

"Good, man, I'm good. How are you? Enjoying your downtime?" I ask him.

His wide shoulders shake as he runs his hands over the beard on his chin. "Fuck yeah. I think I'm going to go to

Yellowstone for a while next week. Camp out, wake up to the fresh air. This your girl?" His gaze flits to Caroline.

"Yeah, this is her."

Fisher extends his hand to her, and she slides her small hand in his. "Hi, I'm Fisher Owens. A friend of Hudson's."

"Caroline. Nice to meet you." She smiles brightly. "Do you play for Chicago? The Knights? I think?"

He nods, a deep chuckle rumbling from his chest. "Third baseman. You a fan?"

"I'm a Seattle Sirens fan." She grins cheekily, shifting from one foot to the other. "But now that I'm calling Chicago home, maybe I'll become a Knights fan too."

"If not, then I'll convert you." He grins, turning back toward me and throwing his arm over my shoulder. "Lucked out with this guy. He's never called in a favor from me until now."

Her eyebrows rise in surprise as her cheeks pink, and her gaze slides to mine. "Hmm."

She doesn't say anything else, but I feel her eyes on me when I throw Fisher's arm off. "As much as I want to sit around staring at your handsome face for the rest of the day..."

"Fine, fine," Fisher interrupts before I can finish. "You know where the batting cages are. Practice field is free, so just shoot me a text when you're ready to head out, and I'll lock up behind you."

"Thanks, Fisher. I owe you one," I tell him, taking Caroline's hand and tugging her to me. "Maybe I'll come on *Call Him Mommy.*"

The damn podcast he's been begging me to come on for the last year, which I've declined. Every single time.

"Hey, don't say that shit cuz I'll hold you to it."

I laugh, shaking my head. "How about a *we'll see.* Thanks again."

"Nice to meet you, Caroline. Maybe I'll see you at a game this season." Fisher smiles as he walks backward down the hallway.

"Maybe so."

Once he's gone, I look at Caroline, who's gazing around the practice facility with stars in her eyes. "What do you think?"

"Pretty sure this is going to be the best 'friends who have hot sex and are spending the day together' ever," she breathes excitedly.

Even though my stomach drops at yet another mention of how casual this is, I say, "Not sure if that's really a thing, Bubblegum, but if not, we'll make it one."

I try not to let it bother me as we walk hand in hand through the facility, me pointing out random facts that I've learned over the last few years from Fisher, and Caroline nodding along quietly as she takes it all in. When we get to the batting cage, I let her pick out which cage she wants.

"This one," she says, landing on the very last cage in

the warehouse-sized room. The place is the size of three Costcos, with at least twenty rows of cages spanning the wall.

I turn the machine on and set it on a fairly low speed since I haven't actually hit a fucking ball since I was a kid. Ninety-mile-per-hour fastballs are not my thing, only fast pucks. Trust me when I say they are two different things.

"Ready?" I ask, plucking a helmet off the shelf and handing it to her along with a bat.

She looks fucking adorable in a bright red helmet and a matching bat. "Hell yes. This is incredible!"

When she practices her swing, she gets so excited that the bat slips from her hand, almost taking out my entire damn eye with the bat as it flies my way.

I duck at the last minute, and it hits the fence behind me with a loud clink.

Her eyes widen. "Shit, I'm sorry. Shit." She rushes over, her small hands fisting in my shirt. "I may have gotten a little too excited. Sorry!"

"Bubblegum, it's fine. Remember that time that guy ran into you and almost knocked you the fuck over the first time you met?"

Her smile turns from a frown, only slightly. "Oh yeah, he was a real asshole. Hot, but definitely an asshole."

I wrap my arms around her and pinch her butt, finally getting the smile back out of her. "Let's play. I want to see

how hard you can hit that ball. I've seen you fling the bat...
but I wanna see you hit the ball."

Standing on her tiptoes, she pecks my lips with a
feigned annoyed eye roll and grabs the bat, taking her position. I slip out of the cage and hit the button to start it, and
then I sit back and watch...

She misses every single one.

But not from lack of trying. She swings like she's
standing in the middle of a stadium surrounded by fifty
thousand people and this is her shot at the championship.

After several minutes, she finally almost clips one. But
when it hits the fence behind her, instead of her getting
frustrated and giving up, she lifts her chin, squares her
shoulders, and holds the bat even higher, ready to go again.

It makes my chest swell with pride. She could easily
give up and said fuck it, but nah.

Not my Bubblegum.

Caroline Evans is the girl who looks shit in the eye and
says fuck you. And swings again.

"Raise your elbow a little, baby," I tell her through the
fence. She follows my instructions, standing tall as the ball
flies down the tunnel toward her.

BAM.

She fucking hit it!

"Fuck yes, Bubblegum!" I holler as I throw the door
open and turn off the machine, then rush toward her and

pick her up. I spin her around until she's squealing through her laughter. "I knew you would do it."

Her arms are wrapped around my neck, her lips hovering over mine, a smile on her beautiful face that I'd pay every damn dollar I've ever made to keep there.

"It felt amazing! Holy shit," she breathes, tossing her head back and letting out a scream. "I have like *so* much adrenaline running through my veins right now. I feel like I could bench-press a car."

I laugh, the sound vibrating between us. "Woah there, Stone Cold Steve Austin."

She sighs, a happy, sweet sound against my lips, and I hold on tighter. "Seriously, this was amazing. Getting to see the facility, meet Fisher, bat in a batting cage that freaking MLB players use? The most incredible not-a-date I've ever been on. I feel so... alive?"

My smile widens with her declaration.

That's exactly what I feel like when I'm with Caroline. Alive. For the first time in a long time, I feel like I could take on the fucking world. Like I could face anything just as long as I was with her.

"Just wait till you see where we're headed next."

NINETEEN
CAROLINE

I think first "not dates" are pretty much ruined for any man that will come after Hudson Rome.

Today has been... *magical.*

The kind of "not date" that I couldn't forget even if I tried. It wasn't fancy. I didn't wear the prettiest dress I own paired with my best heels or drink the most expensive champagne in town while eating at a restaurant with a yearlong waitlist.

Yet, it was more incredible than all of those things combined.

It was simple. Low-key.

It was us.

Whatever that means. It was so much fun, and I haven't been able to wipe the smiles from my face all day. I would spend countless days on "not dates" with this man if they were even half this fun.

"You can't be a true Chicagoan without having a Chicago-style hot dog, Bubblegum," Hudson says as we walk hand in hand up to a small cart on the sidewalk. "You look skeptical. Are you doubting my food choices?"

"After Cheesie's? Absolutely not."

He chuckles. "Good. Because this hot dog is like an initiation ritual when you live in Chicago. Gene and Jude's is a rite of passage, really."

My hand clasped tightly in his, he leads us to the stand and orders for us. The man behind the counter hands over two massive hot dogs and an order of homemade chips for us to share.

"Wait, can I get some ketchup?" I ask.

Hudson freezes, his jaw dropping, his gaze sliding to the attendant behind the counter, who looks just as shocked that I just asked for freakin' ketchup.

"Ummm... is that a no?"

"Bubblegum, you do not put ketchup on a Chicago hot dog. You just... you just do not," Hudson sputters, the attendant nodding in agreement.

"Tourists," he mutters.

Tossing my head back, I laugh. "Oooookay, sorry I had no idea that ketchup was such a taboo idea in Chicago. I thought it was like a universal hot dog condiment."

Hudson chuckles, and he takes our hot dogs and leads

me to a secluded table nearby. I get a good look at the hot dog and see that it's on a seeded bun covered in mustard, relish, and... pickles? With peppers, tomatoes and onions.

"Alright, I'm doubting you. This looks gross, Romeo."

"Just try it. Trust me. If you hate it, I'll eat them both." He pushes the plate toward me and leans back, arms crossed over his chest as he watches me pick it up and take a bite.

Okay...

"Holy shit," I mumble with a mouthful of this deliciousness. The blend of flavors is incredible.

Smirking, he cocks his head as if saying *I told you so.*

"Fine." I roll my eyes. "I need two more."

"Anything for you, baby. But finish that first, *then* we'll see about two more."

I scarf down half of it in a matter of seconds and take a giant sip of my Coke before leaning forward on my elbows to look him in the eyes. "So, my dad texted me last night."

Hudson stops with the hot dog halfway to his mouth, his throat bobbing as he swallows slowly. I know that my dad being his coach makes him uncomfortable and nervous, and it's still the elephant in the room between us. We don't really talk about him much, in part because we basically agreed to not let it affect things between us when we decided to start hooking up. I know he's worried about what my dad would think, and even though I'm not letting what my dad thinks hold me back, I don't bring it up because I don't want it to make him feel uncomfortable.

"He wants me to go to tomorrow night's game since I've not been to a game yet. He didn't really give me much notice, and he already booked a room for me at the hotel and wants me to fly up on the plane with you guys. I-I tried to say no, but he insisted, and I kind of want to go? If you want me there?"

He sets his food down and then reaches across the table to take my hand. "Do you know how bad I want to see you in the stands cheering my name? How bad I've wanted that since the first night with you? Come to the game. Have a fucking blast, and know that every time I look up into the stands, I'll be looking for *you*. Be *my* good-luck charm, Bubblegum. So yeah, I *want* you there. We just have to be careful like we have been so far."

Easy.

THE TOWEL in my hand is damp as I wring it around the wet strands of my long hair in Hudson's massive bathroom. The walls are bright white with calming pale blue accents, and honestly, the entire house is gorgeous. But this room? Complete with a deep soaking tub that's the size of my entire room at the sorority house? Yeah, it's next-level.

"You've been eying that tub for ten minutes, Bubblegum. You wanna take a bath?" he asks as he leans against the counter.

I pull my lip between my teeth and drag my eyes to his. "Could I? I mean, look at it, Hudson. It's basically a pool... *inside your house.*"

It has been so long since I've been able to take a proper bubble bath, and in a tub this luxurious? I'm practically drooling. Sharing bathroom space with fifty other girls has been my life for the past couple of months, and I am not the self-sabotaging type of girl.

I need to soak in this tub. Need. Especially since there are muscles in my body that are sore from the batting cages that I didn't even know existed.

Hudson's massive shoulders shake with laughter, "Baby, I'm six foot fucking four. I wanted a tub that could accommodate that, so I had this one installed when I purchased the house."

Shit. That makes sense. He's so tall, and god, his shoulders are so broad and thick. Something tells me that even though the tub is huge, it would still make him look like a giant.

I watch as his large hand closes over the faucet as he turns it on, cranking up the hot water. The tub slowly begins to fill with water, steam billowing in soft tendrils through the air.

"Come here."

His voice is low and deep, causing a feeling of lust to stir deep in my gut. Even with me wearing his T-shirt and boxers, he still eyes me like I'm the sexiest thing he's ever seen. I can feel them as they slide down my body. As if he's physically touching me without ever lifting a finger.

My feet move without even thinking, placing me in front of him. His bare chest is so close that my nipples harden and strain against the fabric of his T-shirt as they brush against the solid expanse of chest, causing me to suck in an excited breath.

We've danced around this part of the *non-date* all night, teasing each other until we were wild with desire.

Taunting.

Leading up to this very moment.

Wordlessly, he slips his fingers underneath the hem of the T-shirt, brushing the pads of them over the soft curve of my hip before slowly lifting it.

Inch by inch. Higher and higher.

I raise my arms so he can pull it off. He casually tosses it onto the floor next to us, all while his gaze holds mine so intensely that I have to squeeze my thighs together to dull the throb. Something that doesn't go unnoticed by him, judging by his eyes flaring with hunger.

I'm standing in front of him wearing only his boxers, which are barely staying up on my hips, and my clit throbbing between my legs.

"Take off your panties, Caroline," he says, his voice deep and growly.

I swallow, lifting a shaking hand to loop in the waistband, slowly dragging them down my hips and shimmying until they fall in a pool at my feet. I can see how badly he wants me, and not just by the way his cock is thick and pressing against the thick fabric of his gym shorts but by the way he is devouring me wholly with his eyes.

I'm convinced that there is nothing better than being eye fucked by Hudson Rome.

Except actually being fucked by him, which should be a given.

"You have no idea the power you have over me, Caroline," he husks, bringing his thumb to ghost along my bottom lip before trailing his fingers along the expanse of my chest, my collarbone, the swell of my breasts. My chest heaves as he moves torturously slowly, completely unhurried as he drags his flat palm down the center of my chest.

A smirk tugs at his handsome—too handsome—lips when I shudder beneath his fingers as he continues his slow trail down my body.

I've never in my life felt so... wound up. Desperate for anyone's touch. So tightly strung. Like the finest thread ready to snap at any given moment.

That's the perfect way to describe what being with Hudson feels like.

Like you're on the edge of a cliff and desperate to

reach euphoria at the bottom of it, no matter if it means plummeting. Regardless of the consequences.

When he leans forward and his warm breath fans across my nipples, goosebumps break out along my flesh, and I lift my hand to reach for him. To finally end this... torturous form of foreplay.

"Not yet," he whispers, dipping his head lower and flicking his tongue against my sensitive nipple before sucking it into his mouth, then letting go with a pop. "This is mine, Caroline. I want to memorize every inch of this body, and I won't be rushed. Not even by you."

God, why is his mouth so... delicious.

"F-fine," I say shakily, somehow finding my voice despite my head being dizzy from the feeling of his mouth on me.

His tongue laves my aching nipples again, and he spends his time nibbling, sucking each one, and then moving to the other to give it the same attention. Then he leaves a trail of wet kisses up my chest, dragging his teeth so tenderly along my collarbone that I whimper.

He's slowly causing me to lose my mind.

With each brush of his scruff along my skin, each stroke of his fingers, he leaves me more sensitive than before.

"Hudson," I plead. Begging him to... *touch* me. To take this ache away that he's created.

Finally, he stands tall, bringing his hands to my jaw

to cradle it before his lips meld with mine, his grip possessive as he kisses me tenderly yet with more passion than I've ever known. He coaxes my lips open and sweeps his tongue inside, stealing the breath right from my lungs.

My heart pounds in my chest frantically, and my pulse flutters wildly when he suddenly tears his lips away to guide me into the massive tub, which is now full of inviting warm water.

"Relax first, Bubblegum. You're going to need it with the night I have planned for you," he smirks with heavy-lidded eyes.

"Oh god," I moan, squeezing my eyes shut as I sink into the water, letting the warmth envelop my entire body until my limbs are loose and languid. When I open my eyes once more, Hudson's standing over the tub, watching me sink further down into the water.

In the blink of an eye, he pulls the gym shorts around his hips down, along with the tight black boxer briefs that were peeking out the waistband. Scooting me forward, he steps into the water behind me and maneuvers me between his legs, pulling my back against his chest and wrapping his arms around me, his hands resting on my stomach. I fit against his chest perfectly, and I'm convinced that this is the most relaxed I've ever been in my entire life.

The warm water, the dim recessed lighting, the soft

floral smell of the bubble bath he used. The embrace of the man behind me.

"Today was perfect," I mumble. "*You* are perfect, Hudson Rome. The best not-date I've ever had."

His chest vibrates with his laugh. "Hopefully you let me take you on another non-date one day, Bubblegum."

"Maybe so, Romeo."

He slides his large hands from my stomach upward to my breasts, where he kneads lightly, his touch calming me in ways that it shouldn't, but I don't question it. I squeeze my eyes shut and exhale the breath I had been holding.

He sits us both up, grabbing the soap and lathering it on the loofah before he begins washing my body, cleaning every inch before moving to my hair, where he massages the shampoo into my scalp gently. His movements are unhurried and thorough, allowing me to relax further into his touch.

The feeling is foreign, someone taking care of me. Handling me like the most delicate thing he's ever held in his hands. Putting me first.

While his touch is intimate... it's not sexual.

It's tender. Gentle.

"Bubblegum," he rasps, followed by his lips planting a soft, sweet kiss behind my ear that has me shivering in his arms. "The water is turning cold. Let's go to bed."

I nod, and I feel him rise from the water behind me

and step out. He grabs a towel from the warmer and holds it open for me as I step out and into the soft, warm fabric.

"Only rich people have towel warmers, Romeo," I tease, a grin hanging on my lips.

He wraps it tighter around me. "I should take it off of you just so I can see those tight little nipples that are pebbled from the cold, begging to be sucked. And then I can spank your ass since you have so much to say with that smart mouth. Turn your ass red, leave my handprints all over your soft, milky skin."

Holy shit.

Even after all of the times this man has fucked me until I could barely walk and has eaten me like a starving man, I will never get over his mouth and how deliciously dirty it is when he says things like this.

I sashay around him and unknot the towel, letting it drop to the floor. "Maybe that's *exactly* what I want."

When I glance back over my shoulder, I see his gaze darkening, growing heavier as he watches my ass sway while I walk away.

I walk out of the bathroom, leaving him standing alone, and head straight for the bag I packed for tonight, pulling out the Avalanche jersey and running my fingers over the embroidered name on the back.

Before I can even put it on, I feel heat meet my back, the warmth of his now dry body radiating onto me. Yet, I still shiver in response.

Because no matter what I do, I respond to Hudson in ways I have no control over. It's visceral.

"Put it on, Bubblegum," he breathes into my ear, his hand meeting my neck, his fingers trailing down my spine, the barest of touches. "I want to see you wearing my name. Let me pretend, even just for now, that you're mine. That you've always been mine. From the moment I left that closet with your panties in my pocket, and your cunt on my tongue."

Mine.

And today I really did feel like he was mine. And that I was his. Something I could never truly be. But when it's just us two, alone in the dark, we could pretend. I can be his here.

Pretending is no drama. Pretending doesn't leave you with a broken heart. Because if there's anything I've learned from loving my dad, the first important man in my life, it's that people can leave you even if they say they love you, and you're left behind to pick up the pieces. So pretending is easier. Pretending is safe.

Pretending would make sure neither of us could get hurt, that we never ruin the fun dynamic we have between us. Even though there's a part of my heart that seems to feel like maybe this is...

I don't know.

Maybe it could be more. Maybe it already is. But I can't let it become that.

Tamping those thoughts away, I turn to face him, handing him the jersey, then raising my arms for him to slip it over me. And he does. Torturously slow, he drags it down my body, then walks me forward until my front hits the wall, and his hands are on me. Everywhere.

Starting at my thighs, his fingers trail upward, gripping handfuls of my ass as he pushes his hardness against me, lifting until he ghosts the pads of his fingers along the sensitive skin of my sides.

And while most of the time, I want him to take the lead, tonight feels... different.

I turn to him, pushing him back slightly, reveling in the surprised look on his face as I drop to my knees before him. My hands tug at the white towel knotted around his waist until it pulls free and pools at his feet, exposing his hard cock.

"Bubblegu—" he starts, but the moment my lips close around the tip of him, his hands thread into my hair, and a sharp hiss tumbles from his lips. "Fuckkkk."

He drags the syllable out the further I take him into my mouth, tightening his grip with each inch. My hands fly to his hips for leverage as I take him down my throat, my fingers digging into his skin. I can feel him trembling beneath my touch, and it does something powerfully possessive to me knowing that I have the power to bring this man to his knees.

Even with his hands in my hair, gripping tightly, I'm

the one that's in control. I bring my hands to his length and wrap around him, pumping his cock as I take him deeper, the head of him bumping against the back of my throat, causing me to gag slightly.

"Goddamn," Hudson pants, his hips flexing into shallow thrusts as he fucks my mouth in earnest. I love this side of him. The rough, slightly unhinged side that doesn't hold back, that doesn't treat me as if I'm breakable.

Usually he pulls me off before he comes, but tonight, when he tugs at my hair, I take him deeper, using both my hands in time with my mouth because I want him to come. I want to taste him.

"Caroline, I'm about to—" He pants. "Fuck, your throat feels so good, Bubblegum. I'm coming."

He flexes his hips upward, shoving his cock all the way down my throat before throwing his head back, grunting his release. I feel his cum paint the back of my throat as I swallow him down.

When he finishes, he pulls from my mouth, leaving behind a sticky trail of his cum and my saliva. Lifting his finger, he spreads it on my lips, his heavy-lidded gaze darkening, "I can't decide what I love more. My jersey on your back or my cum on your pretty lips."

Holy shit.

This man... his mouth. I squeeze my thighs together as anticipation unfurls inside of me. My clit throbs at just the thought of the look of pure pleasure on his face as he just came in my mouth.

"On the bed, Caroline. I'm nowhere near finished with you."

A shiver runs down my spine, and I rise from my knees, headed *straight* for the bed, feeling his eyes on me with every step I take.

I lay myself out on his bed, ready for him to take. Pretending or not, tonight I'm going to soak up every delicious moment with this man.

TWENTY
HUDSON

"Are you freaking out? Because I'm freaking the hell out, Rome," Chaney whisper-yells, his leg bouncing in his seat as we wait for departure on the team plane.

Reed rolls his eyes, leaning across the aisle. "You are so fucking dramatic. The only one who's worried about anything... is *you*, rookie."

Well, not entirely true, but I'm not making a big deal out of the fact that Caroline will be riding with us to Atlanta and attending tonight's game. At least I'm not making a big deal of it *externally*.

Am I slightly freaking out?

Fuck yes.

But the guys don't need to know that.

On the outside, I'm the epitome of cool. Everything's fine.

Pulling out my phone, trying to distract myself, I pull up Wren's text and quickly type out a message to him. He texted earlier that he got honor roll at school, and I'm proud as fuck of him.

Hudson: Proud of you kid. Going to take you to dinner as soon as I'm home. Keep up the good work!

I notice the time as I close the message and realize that Caroline is *still* not on board.

We're taking off in the next fifteen minutes, and if she doesn't get her ass on this plane, it's going to leave without her.

It wouldn't be the first time that our captain, Williams, left someone behind. He's a stickler for punctuality, and if any of us are late, then we have to figure the fuck out how to get there on our own... and then get our asses reamed by Coach for missing the plane.

Fastening my seat belt, I lean back against the seat and close my eyes, drowning my friends' conversation out.

"Hudson, are you listening to me?" When I look up, Chaney's practically an inch from my face, his eyes wide. "Do you have a plan? You need to figure this shit out."

"Chaney, chill the fuck out and sit back. Buckle up. Relax. You're giving me a headache."

Huffing, he flops back against the seat, mumbling to himself.

All the guys just laugh, except for Reed, who's grumbling to himself about having to deal with Chaney for another year.

A few minutes later, just when Chaney's finally calmed down, Coach walks through the door with Caroline behind him, her overnight bag on her shoulder as she tries to catch her breath.

Her eyes meet mine, and I feel Chaney tense beside me.

"For god's sake," he says entirely too fucking loud, but I slap my hand over his mouth to shut him up and offer her a small smile, then purposefully start scrolling on my phone. The way to not draw attention to ourselves is to go on about our business and act like we're just acquaintances. Like I wasn't just fucking her from behind in the shower, pulling on her long blonde hair before coming inside of her as she screamed my name.

That's partially why she's late, if I had to guess, since she was just putting on her makeup when I walked out of the door.

We agreed that an Uber would be the best idea since we couldn't just show up at the airport together.

I see Coach look our way before shaking his head, hands on his hips before turning back to smile warmly at his daughter, guiding her to the seat next to him. With one quick glance at me, she sits beside him and disappears out of view, leaving me to spend the next three hours desperate to get off this plane so I can touch her again.

WE WON, and as amazing as it felt to bring home the win... it feels like nothing when I think about how good it felt to have my girl in the stands during the game, wearing an Avalanches jersey and screaming at the top of her lungs.

My eyes found hers every time I looked up from the ice to the stands, and that sweet-as-fuck, secret smile she gave me made me want to walk right off the ice, take her into my arms, and kiss the fuck out of her in front of thirty thousand people without a care in the goddamn world.

"Fuck yes, that's what the hell I'm talking about, Rome!" Grant, our right wing, claps me on the back in the locker room once we've changed back into our suits.

We're staying overnight in Atlanta, then will head out to Denver tomorrow. And while most of the team will be going out tonight to celebrate, there's only one way I'm going to be celebrating, and it's between my Bubblegum's thighs.

I'm a pussy guy, and I have no fucking problem admitting that.

"Thanks, man," I smirk, tossing the damp towel I used to dry my hair into the bin by the door.

"You coming out with us tonight?" he asks, eyebrows raised.

I shake my head. "Nah. Had a late night last night, and I'm beat. Gonna get some sleep."

"You never come out with us anymore, man. You're always tired, always hanging back when we go to the bar. What's up?"

I steel my jaw, knowing that he's only asking because I really have changed over the last year, and it's not his fault for calling it out. Bars, going home with different women every night... that shit doesn't do it for me anymore, and it hasn't for a while.

Even before Caroline.

But now that I have her?

I can't see anything else but her. After a long day, she's the person I want waiting for me at home. The one I crawl into bed and wrap my arms around, telling about my day. The one I want to celebrate my wins with and even lament the losses with too.

Shrugging, I hoist my bag up on my shoulder. "Not really my scene anymore, I guess. Trying to keep to myself and stay out of the media."

Mostly the truth, minus the part where I'm falling for our coach's daughter. And when he finds out, my entire career is going to go up in literal flames. Not to mention... if the media gets wind of our relationship, they'll spin it as something it's not, like I'm creeping on my coach's college-aged daughter.

Grant nods, his shoulders dipping slightly. "I can

respect that. If you change your mind, you know where to find me. Shoot me a text."

"Sounds good. Have fun."

With that, I walk out of the locker room, fishing my phone from my pocket to pull up my messages, seeing three unread from Caroline.

Caroline: I'm convinced there is nothing sexier than seeing you on the ice. I've been wet all night and it's entirely your fault.

Another one a few minutes later.

Caroline: Congratulations, Romeo. Let's celebrate with me on my knees.

Fuck. Fuck. Fuck. I chuckle, scrolling to the next one, trying not to get a hard-on as I walk to the hotel shuttle.

Caroline: I can't wait to see you.

I quickly text her back.

Hudson: Hey Bubblegum. On the way to the hotel. I can't wait to fuck your throat, and watch you swallow my cum.

She must have had her phone in hand because I see the response bubble moving along the screen, and then her message comes through.

Caroline: What's your room number? I'll be waiting on you.

I start to type it out, and then I remember.

I have a fucking roommate for tonight, and that puts a damper on the plans I had for her.

Hudson: Fuck, I forgot I'm rooming with Reed tonight. My room is out.

Caroline: Come to mine. I have my own.

Hudson: It's risky, Bubblegum… Worried I might get caught sneaking in and have a repeat of that night in your room.

Caroline: I guess that means I'll just take off your jersey and go to bed all alone and horny then…

Seconds later, she sends over a photo with her lips in a pouty frown and her hand resting on her stomach under the jersey, her fingers ghosting along the waistband of her pink panties, dipping in slightly.

Hudson: Fuck. You little minx. No risk, no reward. Be there in twenty.

Caroline: 405.

After I drop my bag off in my room, I all but sprint to her floor.

I'm on edge the entire ride down the elevator and from the moment I step foot onto her floor. There's a reason she's not on the same floor as us. Because Coach wants to keep her locked away in an ivory tower.

If he only fucking knew.

Glancing behind me more than once, making sure no one has seen me, I sneak to her door and knock quietly. Seconds later, it swings open, and my mouth runs dry because she's still only wearing my jersey and a smile.

"Hey, Romeo."

I smirk. "Hey, Bubblegum."

Thick, heavy tension fills the air between us as a beat passes, our eyes on each other.

Suddenly, her hands fist into my shirt, pulling me toward her into the room, the heavy door swinging shut behind us.

"Fuck, how can I miss you this much when I just saw you this morning?" I ask her as I bring my hands to her jaw, cradling her as my mouth moves over hers. I sweep my tongue inside her mouth, drinking her in, tasting the sweet, fruity flavor left on her tongue that lets me know she's just finished a piece of Hubba Bubba.

My Bubblegum.

Fuck.

Reaching down, I lift her off her feet, and her legs wrap around my waist, locking around me.

I'm already hard, straining against the fabric of my slacks and desperate to get inside of her. It was the most bittersweet torture knowing she was in the stands watching me play. And now, my plans for the rest of the night include making her come as many ways as possible before I have to slip out and back to my room.

"I think I kind of like this being on the road with you thing." She smiles against my lips.

I pull back and grin. "That so?"

She nods, her eyes shining with adoration. "You were

incredible out there, Hudson. Every time I see you on the ice, I'm in awe."

"It's only because I saw you in the stands, cheering me on. I think I've made you a real hockey fan."

Her fingers brush along the short hair at my nape, causing me to shiver slightly. I can feel her warm, wet center against me through the fabric of my pants as she rubs her panty-clad pussy over my hard cock, and it's taking every bit of restraint I have not to rip my pants off and immediately thrust inside her.

"Mmm... or maybe I'm just a real *Hudson Rome* fan. Charming, ridiculously large co—"

I silence her with a laugh and a kiss, my tongue swirling along hers, swallowing the soft moan that she mews. Within seconds, I peel the jersey off her body and pull back to admire her, my eyes roaming over her soft curves.

She's fucking perfect.

Every curve, every inch.

I want to memorize it.

Her hand palms my cock through my pants as I shrug off my suit jacket and unbuckle my pants, shucking everything I have on as quickly as possible.

Gently pushing her back on the bed, I climb over her body, my size even more noticeable as I tower over her. I dip my head to her chest and drag my nose along her tits, pausing over her tight, erect nipples. The shiny metal of her barbells gleam in the light, her hands flying to my shoulders.

"Want you, Bubblegum," I mutter as I suck her nipple into my mouth, tugging on it gently.

My eyes meet hers, and she nods. "Need you, Romeo."

I give her tits my full attention, sucking, biting, nibbling at the creamy skin before kissing down her stomach. The taste of her skin only makes me more frantic.

My fingers tangle in the waistband of her panties. Before I can help myself, I drop my head and run my nose along the wet spot in the center of the red satin, inhaling her luscious scent. My craving for her overtakes me, and with one hard tug, I rip the panties right off, unapologetically tossing them aside without a second glance.

All I can focus on now is her sweet, little pink pussy, just inches from my mouth. She's already glistening and wet for me. I want to devour her.

I use my fingers to spread her pussy lips open so I can look at all of her. So I can see her desire leaking out of her, beckoning me to have a taste.

"Hudson," she begs, her hands flying to my head and pushing me toward her waiting pussy.

"Please what, Bubblegum?" I ask, a wry grin on my lips as I gaze up her body and look into her heavy lidded, lust filled eyes. "What do you need?"

I blow on her pussy lightly, the cool air causing goose bumps to erupt on her inner thighs.

She squirms and flexes her hips up toward my mouth, groaning in frustration when I pull back.

"Say it, Caroline. If you need it, tell me what you want."

She sits up on her elbows to gaze down to where I'm lying between her creamy thighs and traces her foot along the expanse of my shoulders playfully. "I want you to eat my pussy, Hudson Rome. Eat it until I come on your face."

When I don't move, she gives me a saucy pout. "Please."

My grin widens into a full-blown smile that you couldn't wipe off my face even if you fucking tried. I ghost the pad of my finger along her clit.

"*Please*," she begs again.

Happily, I oblige, only because my girl asks so nicely. And because I'm desperate to get my mouth on her pussy. Flattening my tongue, I drag it through her wetness, groaning the moment I taste her.

I'm torturing her with how slowly I'm dragging my tongue along her, circling her clit, and I know she's getting frustrated that I'm not moving quicker.

I can tell in the way her nails begin to dig into my shoulders, biting into the skin, and how she arches closer to my mouth, moaning my name.

When my teeth graze her clit, nipping at her, she cries out. "Oh god."

I love that she's so fucking responsive.

Dragging my tongue lower, I circle her entrance and push it inside, lapping at the creamy wetness before I start fucking her with my tongue, spearing her tight hole until she's writhing.

"Yes, right there, Please..." She pants, thrashing on the bed. "I'm..."

My mouth latches onto her clit, sucking hard, and my fingers thrust into her, hooking upward to set off the orgasm building inside of her.

"That's it, Bubblegum. *Good girl.* Come for me."

Knock, knock.

I halt at the sound and pull back from her pussy to look at her. She groans quietly, dropping back onto the bed with a frustrated sigh.

"Keep going. They'll go away," she whispers in desperation.

Can't have my girl unsatisfied, and I want to taste her cum on my tongue, so I lean down, spreading her with my fingers, and begin lapping at her p—

Another knock.

She groans. "Ugh, *eventually*, they'll go away."

I laugh, dragging my teeth along her clit gently, her back arching as she pushes her pussy against my mouth.

KNOCK KNOCK KNOCK.

"Caroline, it's Dad."

We both freeze, and I scramble up so quickly that I get tangled up and trip in the sheets around us, barely catching myself on the wall next to me, causing a loud thud to echo around the room.

"Fuck," I hiss quietly.

Caroline is biting back laughter, her hand covering her mouth as she gets up from the bed, searching for her jersey.

"Uh, one second, Dad."

I find her jersey by my feet and toss it to her, pocketing the panties since they're fucking shredded.

Fuck, this is bad.

What if he finds out I'm in here?

My chest begins to tighten in my panic, my dick deflating by the second. Nothing kills your hard-on like the possibility of your coach finding you in his daughter's hotel room while you're in the middle of eating her pussy.

Goddamnit.

Caroline turns to face me after sliding on a pair of cotton shorts from her bag. "Hudson, breathe. It's okay. I'll get rid of him." She whispers it quietly, but it's too fucking late. I'm panicked as fuck, and I can't just pretend that I'm not.

The consequences of being here are too fucking great.

I scamper to the bathroom, swiping my slacks off the floor in the process, and shut the door behind me. A few seconds later, I hear her swing the door open and greet Coach.

"Hey, Dad."

"Hey, Care Bear. What took you so long to answer the door? Everything okay?"

I crack the door open slightly and watch the interaction through the small sliver.

She clears her throat. "Nothing. I was just in the shower and had to throw some clothes on."

He's not believing that shit.

We're fucked.

"Oh, okay. Well, I thought I heard a commotion in here. Anyway, I wanted to see if you had dinner, and if not... we could grab a bite? You don't have to spend the whole night in your hotel room alone, you know?"

She nods. "I just have a headache. If it's okay, I'll take a rain check? I kind of want to just crash. I'll probably just order room service and catch up on sleep."

"Of course, sweetheart. Get some rest—I know you've been working really hard. I'll see you in the morning. Call me if you need anything."

I hear him kiss her head. "Thanks, Dad. Oh, and good game tonight. The team looked great."

"Thanks, Care Bear. Night."

"Night." She visibly sighs once she gets the door shut, and I let out the same breath I've been holding since he first knocked on the door. Stepping out of the bathroom, I head back into the room and sit on the edge of the rumpled bed.

I just freaked the fuck out. But as I was panicking in

the fucking hotel bathroom, hiding from Coach, I realized that I was actually more afraid of whatever is happening with Caroline ending than Coach actually finding out we're together.

It wasn't even that there was a huge chance he'd ask for me to be traded; it would be what would happen to Caroline and me if that happened.

I wouldn't be able to have her waiting for me in my bed.

I couldn't take her around the city I love and show her my favorite food spots.

I'd miss her laughter, how light she makes me feel.

How whenever we're together, I feel like we've known each other forever.

I would lose her, and there wouldn't be a damn thing I could do to stop it.

That's what has my chest feeling tight right now, what has my stomach in knots.

"He's gone," she says softly, sitting down next to me.

All I can do is nod as I stare blankly in front of me. Fuck, my hands are still shaking, and there are so many thoughts flitting through my head so quickly that it feels like it's actually spinning.

"Hudson?"

When I lift my head, my gaze meets hers.

"What's wrong?" she asks, reaching out to take my hand.

"I just... that was so fucking close, Bubblegum." I swallow, my throat feeling tight. "I guess I haven't really wanted to say this to you because I don't want you to feel like you're caught in the middle or to make shit worse with your dad..."

"Tell me. Whatever it is." She squeezes my hand in hers reassuringly.

"Your dad fucking hates me, Caroline. Like, really doesn't like me," I tell her honestly, and when she opens her mouth to say something like "oh I'm sure he doesn't," I shake my head, stopping her. She needs to know that this is more than just her dating one of his players.

"No, he *hates* me. There's been tension between us since he became our coach. Listen, when your dad came on, I was younger, a cocky rookie who liked the fame and liked to party. My reputation, especially as reported by the media, has always been a fucking mess. When he first started coaching the team, I was in the headlines a lot, partially because I was being careless, not giving a shit what they had to say about me. Even if all of it wasn't fully true, it still didn't look good. So we kind of had a rocky start to our relationship that never left."

Pausing, I blow out a breath and run my hand over the short hair on my scalp.

"Surely, my father doesn't hate you because of that. Plenty of players end up in the headlines for silly reasons," she says, disbelief lacing her tone.

"He came down hard on a few of us. He really fucking hated that we were making the Avalanches look bad with our behavior, that we were distracting from what we were all here to do: play hockey. Being in the headlines, the whole 'Playboy Playmaker' shit, reflected badly on his team, and he was a new coach walking into that shit. I was more of a hothead then. We argued a lot early on, once in front of the team, which I shouldn't have done... because it undermined his authority.

"Honestly, it's a miracle that he didn't recommend me for a trade back then. But I'm an asset to the team—then and now. I'm the best damn goalie he's had in ten years. Things have been a little less tense between us since then, but he's never forgotten those days, and I don't think he's ever fully trusted me. But as long as I keep my shit straight and keep playing like I have been, he doesn't say anything to me."

Caroline shakes her head, digesting what I'm saying, her eyes widened with her hand clasped tightly in mine.

I hold her gaze as I continue. "So, imagine if he found out what was going on between us? He would lose his fucking mind. You thought I was overreacting that day in the locker room, and partially I was, but only because I know how much he hates me. Out of any guy on the team, I'm the one he'd never want to touch his daughter."

Standing from the bed, Caroline puts her hands on her hips and shakes her head. "I mean, did he even try to get to

know you before making these assumptions? Hudson."
She pauses, dropping to her knees before me, taking my
face in her hands. "You're amazing, and he's being an absolute idiot if he doesn't see that."

I chuckle, pressing my lips to hers. This fucking girl.
Her response makes me feel like a god, but it also reminds
me how young she is. Because sometimes the way people
see us isn't fair.

But it's life.

If she only knew that I want to throw every fucking bit
of it away to be with her, to make her fucking mine. That I
want her more than anything else.

She'd tell me I'm crazy, as crazy as I fucking feel.

But it doesn't matter because it's the truth.

I'm falling for her. I'm crazy about my Bubblegum,
and tonight feels like the catalyst for... something.

And that something?

Fucking terrifies me.

TWENTY-ONE
CAROLINE

A week passes after the night in the hotel room in Atlanta with Hudson, and I've been so swamped with schoolwork and my internship at the rink that I feel like I haven't taken a full breath since then. And it sucks that I haven't been able to see him at all since he had back-to-back games and has been on the road.

We've texted daily and have been having a nightly FaceTime, but I miss him and am beyond excited that he lands late tonight. He already asked me to be at his house when he got there, so I'm packing a bag to spend the night with him.

"I feel like we haven't seen each other in like a year," Tatum says from her bed as she watches me toss clothes into my overnight bag. "Every time I get home, you're leaving to stay with your lover boy. I miss you."

I laugh, shaking my head. "Babe, we literally live together. Plus, I'll be home tomorrow night anyway. He only has one night home. Let's hang out?"

"Yes. Oh! We should go to Zeta Alpha for their party."

I have yet to venture to any fraternity parties, sticking mostly to the house whenever I'm not with Tatum or Hudson, but it sounds fun.

"Sure, let's do it. I'll be home a little early tomorrow, and you can put me in whatever outfit you want since you love it so much." I'm teasing her, but her eyes shine with anticipation when she hears me say she can be in charge of my outfit. There's nothing Tatum loves more than dressing me up with absolute free rein.

"Say less, boo." She smirks and glances down at her phone while I finish packing my toiletries, then checking the rideshare app to see when the car will be here to bring me to Hudson's.

I finish throwing everything in my bag, give Tatum a quick peck on the cheek, then head out the door to the Uber.

Hudson's supposed to get in earlier tonight than the last time I waited for him, so I'm having a few groceries delivered so I can cook him an actual dinner.

Not that I really know much about cooking dinner. But I'm going to make it work because after a grueling game and a plane ride home with my father, I know

Hudson will probably be completely exhausted and starving.

Plus, I feel like doing something nice for him since he'll need his energy for all the orgasms I'll be getting later.

It's the least I can do.

When the Uber turns into Hudson's neighborhood, passing by all the large suburban houses on his street, it's a stark reminder of how different our lives are. He owns his own house, has an established career complete with a 401K, and tons of professional accomplishments... and half the time, I don't even know what I'm having for dinner that night. I guess it's just easy to forget that we're in completely different places in our personal lives when we're having fun together.

Pulling up at the curb, I grab my bag and thank the driver before walking up the driveway. I quickly put in the code at the front door and walk inside, turning off the alarm and letting my bag slip from my shoulder to the floor in the entryway.

I'm still not used to how massive his house is—way bigger than any I've ever been inside. It's eerily quiet, so I walk over to his surround sound and Bluetooth my phone to it, putting on some Harry to fill the empty space.

While his house is gorgeous and ridiculously large, the decor is also kind of... generic. There are no personal touches. Nothing on the walls, no framed photos of his family, nothing on the fridge except one lone takeout menu from a local restaurant.

I make a mental note to help this man add some color or something more "him" when my phone pings with a notification.

Groceries. Perfect timing.

I quickly get them from the porch and carry them to the huge island in the kitchen, immediately getting to work on dinner. I only have a few hours to throw something together, something that's hopefully edible.

Once I start working, I get lost in the motions.

"Bubblegum?" I hear, followed by the front door slamming. Shit, I completely lost track of time.

"In here," I call out, trying to blow the hair that's slipped out of my clip from my face. I can't use my hands because they're currently covered in sticky cookie dough.

I'm not entirely convinced that dinner will be edible, so when I raided his pantry at the last minute and found the ingredients for cookies, I started throwing them together.

At least dessert will be edible.

Hopefully.

When Hudson walks through the door of the kitchen, his hair combed back, dressed in a dark suit with a light gray button-down, my mouth runs dry.

I can't believe I get to ride this man's dick weekly.

"Hi," I say, suddenly breathless at the sight of him.

He smirks. "Hey yourself, Bubblegum. Whatcha doin'?"

I shrug. "Just making cookies..."

He walks directly to me and grabs my face, planting a not-so-chaste kiss on my lips that somehow steals even more breath from my lungs. I keep my hands to myself so I don't dirty up his expensive-looking suit, and he clearly notices my unusual restraint. He grabs one of my hands, bringing a batter-covered finger to his mouth and sucking, swirling his tongue around the pad.

"Mmmm. Good, but nowhere near as good as *you*, Bubblegum," he says, hauling me against him and lifting me off my feet in one swift motion. "Need a taste."

Squealing, I toss my head back and laugh, "Put me down, you big oaf. I'm covered in flour and dough."

"Even better." His voice is deep and growly, my favorite version of my Romeo. "Don't worry, Bubblegum." Dipping down, he trails his tongue along my collarbone. "I'll get you all clean. I promise not to miss a spot... and then I'll dirty you up all over again."

And he makes true on his promise, just like I knew that he would.

"TELL me something no one else knows about you. Not even your best friend. A secret," Hudson says as we lie in his bed, me partially draped over his body, his fingers tracing along my skin as he speaks.

I feel like I've hit the jackpot with this man. He makes me come harder than I've ever come in my life, and he's sweet, attentive.

Easy.

"Secrets cost, Romeo." I grin up at him cheekily, my eyes shining bright with amusement.

He shrugs. "Fine, give me a secret, and I'll give you one. Tit for Tat."

For a moment, I'm quiet as I think about a secret that I've never told anyone, but I keep getting distracted by how good he feels beneath me. This feels... intimate. But it also just feels right, and I don't want to stop to question it.

"I cheated on my fifth grade spelling bee."

"That's your big secret?" He chuckles, shaking his head.

I sit up, raising my eyebrows. "Listen, I *still* feel guilty about it. I thought about writing a letter to my old school and admitting it. Maybe a confession would make me feel a little better."

"Baby, if cheating on a spelling bee is your biggest crime, then you have nothing to worry about."

He's teasing me, and I just grin, not bothered in the least.

I can take whatever he dishes out, and with grace.

I love bantering with him. It makes me all hot and bothered.

"Your turn. I have a feeling this is going to be juicy. Make it good," I say excitedly as I sit up and peer into his dark eyes, resting my chin on his chest as I wait for a response.

"Fine. But take it to your grave, Evans, you hear me?"

I nod. "Scout's honor."

"I have a Beanie Baby collection. In my parents' attic. I've been collecting since I was a kid, and I don't actively seek them out anymore, but if I stumble across one... I'll buy it. Sometimes on eBay for thousands of dollars..."

My eyes widen, and I try to keep it under control. I really do, but I fail. Miserably. My laughter explodes out of me full force as I completely lose my shit.

You're telling me this hulk of a man with more muscles than I've ever seen on *any* man collects freakin' Beanie Babies? The little vintage stuffed animals that used to come in Happy Meals back in the '90s? Way before my time.

"B-beani-e-e Babies-s, Hudson?" I cackle, bringing my hand to my mouth to stifle the laughter.

"Don't you judge me. You wanted a secret no one knew, and now you've got one. Not even the guys know, and they *never will*. Right, Caroline?"

I nod, trying to hold it together before I fall apart again, and he just shakes his head, pulling me towards him and swallowing every giggle that leaves my mouth until suddenly, my laughter becomes a moan.

"I have something to ask you," Hudson says softly as he trails his fingers up and down my arms as we lie cuddled up in his bed once again. The soothing motion almost has me falling asleep, exhausted from having the best sex of my life. Apparently, I should tease him about his Beanie Baby collection more often if it results in *that*.

"So then ask me, Romeo," I reply sleepily.

He chuckles, the sound vibrating against my back where it meets his chest. "So, I was thinking. I have dinner tomorrow at my parents', and I want you to come. My sister, Hailey, and her boyfriend will also be there."

I freeze, my entire body going rigid in his embrace. I'm awake now.

Meeting his family? Going to a family dinner? That is the literal definition of being in an official relationship and is definitely the last thing that I was expecting him to ask.

"Uh, what do you mean?" I say, scooting away slightly to slip out of his arms. I think this is a conversation that should happen face-to-face and not under the influence of the laxness of our post-sex haze. I sit up, turning to face him. "Meeting your parents, Hudson? Aren't you the one who said no one could know about us... sleeping together? Isn't that what we agreed? I mean... I know that some of our friends know. But they're your *parents*, Hudson. They'll know I'm your fuck buddy..."

His brow furrows. "It's just my parents, Bubblegum, not TMZ... It's not like they'd tell anyone that we are together if I asked them to keep it quiet. And I mean, would it be that bad if we did tell more people?"

"As in...?" I ask. "What are you saying?"

"What if we came clean, Caroline? What if we told your dad and said fuck what everyone thinks? What if we were together... publicly. Together for *real*. A couple. Not fuck buddies. Not casually hooking up. Whatever you want to call it. Just... *more*."

I scoff, shaking my head. "Oh, tell everyone that we've been sneaking around behind their backs for months? Because this *isn't* a relationship, remember? We agreed that we would keep things fun. Easy. Uncomplicated."

With that, I jump up from the bed and start looking for my clothes. I have no idea what is happening right now, but I feel like I need clothes for it. I'm pacing the room, trying to find the things he took off me that are strewn around his bedroom.

I just... I don't understand where this is coming from. I thought we were both on the same page. I thought we wanted the same thing. I thought he liked how things were going.

When did that change? Have I not been reading the room right this entire time?

Because what he's asking? It's not what people who

are "hooking up" do. It's what people who are dating do... after months of dating.

"Hudson, I'm in college. What would your parents say about you sleeping with a girl nearly half your age? Your coach's daughter. I feel like you're saying things you're not thinerking through."

"You're making it sound so... taboo. We're fucking adults, Caroline, in a consenting relationship. Who gives a shit if your father is my coach or if you're in college. Seriously, who gives a fuck. I don't. Not anymore."

I laugh without a hint of humor, shaking my head. "You're thirteen years older than me, Hudson. You're a whole-ass adult with a mortgage and adult responsibilities. I'm a college junior whose only responsibilities are keeping my grades up enough to get a degree and accumulating student debt. You and I both know... this would never work as anything more than casual fun. And not just because of my dad... we're in two very different places in our lives. You're delusional if you think anything different."

I can feel his anger from here. It hangs in the air, draping around us, suffocating us both. His fists are clenched by his side, his jaw set in anger.

"That's bullshit." He seethes. "Complete fucking bullshit, and if that's the excuse you want to use, fine. But it doesn't change shit. It doesn't change the way that I feel. How I think you feel too."

I'm beginning to feel like an animal trapped in a cage, and with each word he throws at me, the enclosure is getting smaller, hindering my ability to think rationally. To process what he's really saying.

"You have lost your mind," I say, pausing my frantic pacing. "Completely lost it, Hudson. Why are you making this more than it is?"

He finally stands from the bed, reaching out for me. "Caroline, just stop for a second, okay? Just listen to what I have to say."

I pull my shirt on, sans bra, my gaze drifting to his.

"You're it, Caroline, do you hear me? I'm fucking *crazy* about you," he says, walking over and cradling my jaw in his hands as he speaks. "I fucking want you, and I don't give a shit what I have to sacrifice to have you. You are worth it, Bubblegum. You're worth whatever the fuck happens when I tell the world you're mine."

Swallowing, I try to push down the emotion that's welling in my throat.

"Who cares if I'm older than you, that we're in different junctures of our lives. People do it all the time— you just figure it out," he adds when I don't reply.

"I thought this was just... just chill... just hooking up, Hudson. And now you want to tell my father? Tell the world? Make it more complicated!" I cry, stepping back, trying to ignore the hurt in his eyes. That's what I didn't want to happen. Drama. For either of us to be hurt.

We agreed on fun. Fun I was good with. Great with, even. But when it gets messy and tangled and feelings are involved, that's where I draw a line. Where I thought we had drawn a line.

"Well, shit changed, Caroline, and I know you feel that. I can't be the only one that feels this way," he says, running his hand over his hair as his eyes search mine.

Shaking my head, I back up a step. "You can't just change things up on me out of the blue, Hudson."

"I can't help that I'm falling in love with you," he yells, his voice raising in frustration. "I cannot fucking help that somewhere along the way, I started to fall in love with you, Caroline. So here we are. I'm asking you for more."

"You don't love me," I whisper, reaching onto the floor for my shorts, then dragging them up my hips, avoiding his gaze. "We agreed from the very beginning that all that would ever be between us is sex, and now you're talking about relationships and love, meeting your freaking family, and I just—I can't do this, Hudson. I can't." I start throwing the rest of my things into my bag roughly, desperate to get out of this room, away from this conversation that's making me question everything.

He's making me question everything.

"What are you so afraid of?" he asks. "I'm risking everything to be with you, Caroline, every single fucking thing, and you're not risking a goddamn thing. So, tell me, what are you so afraid of? So afraid that you're pushing me away. That you're so desperate for someone to *not* love you." His voice is low, hoarse, and full of emotion. I know I'm hurting him, and I hate it. The broken look on his face, the anger in his eyes. But I'm just *so* overwhelmed and have to get out of here.

"I'm afraid of it all," I force myself to say confidently, even if I feel anything but right now. "Falling in love isn't for me, Hudson. You're asking for something that I can't give you. Something that you have known from the start wasn't in the cards for us."

He's asking for something that I can't give him.

My heart.

It was the biggest risk of all.

"Tonight is exactly what you need, Care. Let your hair down, and by let your hair down, I mean let your tits out, drink a shit ton of tequila, and make sure that man is the last thing on your mind," Tatum says as she wraps a piece of my hair around the curling wand. "It's girls' night, and that means it's me and you, babe. No one else. We're drinking till we puke."

Laughing, I try not to move so she doesn't burn me... again. "Um, that does not sound fun. Like, at all, Tate."

I can see her smirk in the full-length mirror I'm sitting in front of. "I mean, it'll be fun while we're doing it, just not the puking part."

Honestly, tequila does sound like it could be the answer to my problems. At least, right now. For tonight.

My heart twinges. I can't believe I'm even referring to things with Hudson being a problem.

And okay, fine, maybe tequila *isn't* the answer because I don't know what the answer is to my confusion, but it will make me feel better for the time being. Help me just be a carefree college student tonight as I try to forget the fight that may be our ending.

I hate how I left things with him, and I hate that we haven't spoken at all since, but even if we did, I'm not sure what I would say. I just need some time to think about all he said, all he sprung on me, when I thought we were both on the same page. But maybe not...

"I don't know, maybe I should just stay here? I don't want to ruin your fun. I feel so... blah."

Tatum stops her curling, shaking her head vehemently. "No way. You are going, Caroline. You cannot sit around here all night alone being upset. You need to get out with your friends and have some fun. You can think about the rest later."

When she says it that way, it does sound perfect. A night out with my bestie and lots of tequila. At least, I keep trying to convince myself of that.

"Look, you look seriously so hot tonight, and there is no way I'm allowing you to let this outfit go to waste. Every guy who sees you tonight is going to lose his mind," Tatum says, eying the outfit she put me in.

A black leather skirt and a satin cowl-neck cami that

shows just the perfect amount of cleavage, paired with the cutest hot pink blazer to *ever* exist. I'm wearing my favorite pair of black heels, and I really do love the outfit she picked. It accentuates my curves and makes me feel hot as hell.

If only my heart felt up to the party tonight. Isn't that the problem, though? The fact that my heart is feeling the brunt of what's happening? That I'm *this* upset over "just a hookup"?

Clearly, I have some type of feelings for Hudson that are much deeper than what I thought, or I wouldn't feel this way.

Right?

My head's all screwed up, and the more I try to sort through everything, the more confused and conflicted I feel. Our dynamic always felt easy, so why does this feel so hard now?

"Maybe I fucked up, Tate," I say quietly, my gaze meeting hers in the mirror. "I mean, it feels like I fucked up? Is he right, that I'm scared and pushing him away? If it means that he's no longer a part of my life, then that isn't what I want. I do know that..."

Tatum sighs, setting the curling wand down on the table next to her before wrapping her arms around me from behind and resting her chin on my shoulder. "I think you just have to decide what you want, Care. It seems like he's laid it all out on the line for you, and you did kind of run, babe. Not that you were wrong. I'm definitely on your side no matter what, but it sounds like you need to take some time to think through things before making any rash decisions."

"I just felt blindsided, and I still kind of do. I'm trying to sort through all of the stuff he threw at me at once. We never talked about this being anything more than casual, and he didn't even give me a chance to wrap my brain around it. And the worst part is that I miss him already, Tate. I miss him so fucking much, and I feel like that means *something*, right?"

She laughs, standing. "I think sometimes it just takes a little while for our head to catch up with our heart. Either way, it sounds like you have feelings for Hudson. Not just that he's your dick appointment and gives you great orgasms. *Real* feelings. And those are messy and complicated at times."

I sigh, the weight of the last day feeling heavier by the second. "It's just... I've never actually had that. Never had a real relationship before, and this all feels brand-new to me. Plus, it's not like I've actually had a great example of what a stable, loving relationship should actually look like, so I don't even know what that is."

"I know, babe, and I feel like that's why more than anything, you need to think about what it is that you want. Clearly, you care about Hudson and don't want to hurt him, so it's only fair to him to take your time to sort through your shit. Which... you can do *tomorrow*. After a night out having fun with me and our friends. You need to clear your head and start fresh."

"Wow." I shake my head, standing from the beanbag. "This was a good talk, Tate."

Her shoulder dips slightly. "I read a lot of self-help books when I'm bored."

My head falls back as a laugh escapes me. The first time I've laughed in what feels like ages, even though it's been less than twenty-four hours since I left Hudson's. But it feels like the longest day of my entire life.

And I think Tatum is right. About all of it. I need a night out with my friends—maybe that will pull me out of this funk and put me in a better headspace to have an actual conversation with Hudson. Because the one thing I do know right now is that I'm not ready to let him go.

"You know, I think you're right, Tate." I smirk, tossing my hair over my shoulder and taking another glance in the mirror. "I think a night out will do me good."

"That's my girl!" she says as she makes a beeline for her closet.

Once Tate finishes her makeup, a dramatic red lip that pops with her dark hair, we grab our purses and start the trek to the party along with a few other girls from the house.

Zeta Alpha is only a few houses down from Beta Pi, so it's just a quick five-minute walk to the large, looming white colonial-style house. There's a large banner stretched across the front two pillars that says "Zeta Life." People are already scattered across the front yard and the driveway, loud music booming down the street.

"Ready?" Tatum asks, looping her arm in mine.

I can't say that I'm really excited to go tonight, but I didn't want to let her down by flaking at the last minute, and she's right... If I stayed in the house, then I would just watch reruns of *Gilmore Girls* and cry into my ice cream, and it's a proven fact that shit never helped anyone.

I just *miss* Hudson. But I know I need to figure out what all of these feelings mean for us.

Even though I'm completely thrown off by everything that is happening, I just... I wish we could go back to how things were. To when we were having fun, and everything just felt right. Like it was supposed to. I'm not sure that's even possible. But I know I need to get my head straight before we talk again. I owe that to him to figure out what I want.

"Care?" Tatum snaps in front of my face, pulling me from my fog. "You okay?"

"Uh, yeah, I'm good." I plaster on the best fake smile I can muster. "Just get me shots, and I'll be *great*."

AN HOUR AND A HALF LATER, I am *drunk*, and Tatum is nowhere in sight.

And I am like *wayyyyy* more drunk than I intended to be.

And everything feels... wobbly.

And I have to pee, like right. Now.

"Tate?" I look around for my roommate, but in doing so, the entire room spins so badly that I reach out to steady myself on the wall just as another person bumps into me, almost sending me sprawling to the floor.

"Sorry," the stranger mutters in passing, and I scoff.

Yeah, thanks for the apology, dick.

God, my head is spinning. I think I drowned my sorrows a little *too* much tonight. I bring my hand to my head to try and stop the room from spinning around me. I feel like I'm floating on top of my body, and I can't seem to get my bearings.

Where the hell is Tate?

Finally, I make it down the less crowded hallway and fling open a door. Not the bathroom. Damnit.

Squeezing my eyes shut, I try to keep my balance, but with my head being so dizzy and these heels making my steps more uneven...

I walk to the bed in the middle of the room and sit on the edge before I fall down and embarrass myself.

Reminder to self...

Never drink again. Ever.

Blackness dots my vision, the room spinning completely out of control, and the last thing I can remember is wishing that Hudson was here to hold me.

Hudson

MY PHONE RINGS for the third time on my nightstand. I fucking swear if this is Chaney calling me again in the middle of the night because he's drunk and lost downtown, I'm going to lose my damn mind. All I want to do is sleep off the feeling of watching Caroline walk away. From me. From *us*.

Because it fucking sucks.

I glance at the glowing red numbers on the alarm clock, seeing that it's after midnight, and shake my head as I reach one arm out for my phone.

"I swear," I grumble, swiping across the screen, "Chaney, this better be life or fucking death."

"Uh, hi... this *isn't* Chaney." A woman's voice comes through the speaker, and I squint with one eye open at the screen, trying to make out the number, but fuck, I'm still half-asleep. "This is Caroline's roommate, Tatum, and, uh... I think she needs you to come get her."

I jackknife from the bed, my eyes flying open. "What's wrong? Is she okay?"

I'm already climbing from the bed and pulling on my clothes at breakneck speed while I wait for her to respond.

"She had a little too much to drink tonight, and she's kind of out of it. I'm worried and don't think I can get her home by myself. I didn't want to call her dad, and my boyfriend is out of town, so I didn't know who else to call."

Fuck. Fuck. Fuck.

Obviously, it's bad if I'm the one she's calling after how Caroline and I left things.

Doesn't matter because I'll be there if my girl needs me, no matter fucking what. Whether she wants to be with me or not, I'll always help her.

"Text me the address. I'm walking out the door," I say, grabbing my wallet from the nightstand, then taking the stairs two at a time.

"Thank you for coming, Hudson," she says. "I know things are... weird with you two right now, but she needs you. It'll mean a lot to her that you came."

"I'll always come for her. *Always.*"

We end the call, and a few seconds later, a text pops up with the address, and I'm already in the car. I click the address and put it in my GPS and see that it's only a few houses down from Caroline's sorority house.

She's still on sorority row, and that just makes my stomach twist in knots. So fucking close to home, and yet she feels so goddamn far away. Out of my reach.

I make the twenty-minute drive in ten, my hands

aching from clenching around the steering wheel so tightly by the time I pull down the street. The entire road is lined with cars and drunk people walking around, and because of that, it takes me fucking ten minutes to find a spot to park.

"Where is this house?" I show a passerby douche in a blue polo and boat shoes, who drunkenly points to the house that's side by side with another house that's also filled with people. It seems like the entire street is partying, and all I want is to find my girl.

All that fucking matters is getting to her and making sure she's okay.

I sprint toward the house, pushing my way through crowds of kids playing beer pong and doing keg stands in the front yard until I finally make it through the front door. Loud, pulsing music is playing inside. Pulling my phone out, I call the phone number that her roommate called from, and she answers on the second ring.

"Hello?"

"Where are you? I'm here," I grunt, trying to scan the crowd for Caroline to no avail.

"I'm heading back towards the room I left her resting in. I needed to grab her some water and a cool rag—I think she was about to be sick. Second door to the right on the second floor."

I hang up and take the stairs two at a time, weaving my way through the crowd until I make it to the second floor, which is thankfully less packed and less loud, finding the door Tatum mentioned. I swing it open without knocking and walk inside.

The first thing I see is Caroline lying on the bed with her eyes closed, a soft groan leaving her lips as if she's in pain. The next thing I see is a guy hovering over her prone body, his hand just above her thigh.

"What the fuck?" I roar, my vision turning red, a poisonous and uncontrollable rage coursing through my veins. I can't control it.

And I don't fucking want to.

The piece of shit scrambles up and turns alabaster white. Good, he should fucking be scared. Instantly, I cross the room in two giant steps, grasping him by the collar and lifting him clean off his feet. I want to kill this fucker.

I hear a gasp and turn to see a short, dark-haired girl just inside the threshold, holding an unopened water bottle and a cloth in her free hand, the other covering her mouth in horror. The look on her face tells me everything I need to fucking know.

I turn back to the douchebag struggling in my grasp. "What the fuck do you think you're doing?" I'm so close to his face I can practically feel the motherfucker shaking in my grip.

He stutters, "She-e... I..."

"I suggest you fucking speak. Use your big-boy words," I warn.

"He was *not* in here when I left!" the girl cries, stalking forward, "I have no idea who this asshole is, but I left Care alone in here for just a second to go grab her a water. Omigod, did he touch her? I'm so sorry. God, I shouldn't have left her side."

So, she's the roommate.

His throat bobs as he swallows. "I was j-just checking on her." His voice is a nasally, full-on fucking whine, and it makes me even more enraged. "She was pa-assed out—I just wanted to make su-r-e she was okay."

My fingers tighten in his collar, cutting off his air supply further, earning a whimper.

I glance toward the bed, directing Tatum with a tilt of my head. "Check on her. How much did she have to drink?"

Her roommate shakes her head. "I don't understand how she's so drunk... we only had a couple shots. I just don't understand." She presses the damp cloth to Caroline's head. She's still fast asleep but groans and turns to the side, curling into a ball.

"Wait... what if someone put something in her drink?" the girl whispers, her gaze darting to the motherfucker I'm two seconds away from killing, and her eyes widen.

Oh fuck no.

Fuck no.

"N-n-o..." he stutters, fear flitting across his face, and when my fist tightens, he looks like he might actually piss his pants. "Holy fuck, no! I was-s just checking on her!"

I'm fucking done with this asshole, with this entire thing, and am raising my fist to beat his goddamn face in when I hear my name being called, soft and shaky, a hoarse whisper that has me snapping out of it. My anger dissipates into thin air.

"Romeo."

I drop the asshole on his ass, and he scrambles away on all fours. My girl needs me. I make my way over to Caroline, who moans when I run my hand over every inch of her face, checking to make sure she's alright.

"Bubblegum. Are you okay?"

She shakes her head, mumbling something incoherent, and I turn to her roommate. "We need to get her home. Did you drive here?"

"No, we walked. It's only a few houses down."

I nod, reaching under Caroline and scooping her up into my arms. She burrows into my neck, her hands fisting into my shirt, and I place a gentle kiss to her brow. "Let's go."

Tatum turns, flinging the door back open, and I follow behind her, carrying Caroline out of the room. There's a crowd hovering near the door, curious glances thrown our way as we make our way downstairs.

"Holy shit, that's Hudson Rome!" someone says. "The

Avalanche goalie! He's a *legend!* Hey, Playboy Playmaker!"

Chaos fucking ensues.

The crowd thickens around us, but I don't stop. Not when paper is thrust into my face, not when flashes go off.

Fuck no.

There's a time and place for shit like that, and this is not it. Not with my unwell girl in my arms.

Finally, we step outside and down the stairs of the frat house, making our way down the curving path of the sidewalk. I could get my car and bring them home, but by the time I make it there and through the horde of people in the road, it wouldn't make any sense. I can get her there faster by walking. Part of me wants to just take her home with me, but after how we left things, I'm not sure she'd want that.

"Are you going to carry her?" Tatum asks, eyes wide. "*All the way there?*"

My gaze narrows. "I'm a fucking hockey player, Tatum. I could carry three of her."

I head in the direction of the sorority house, leaving Tatum with her jaw hanging open until she ambles toward me, picking up the pace so she can keep up with my strides.

My one and only fucking goal is getting my girl home and into her bed safely. Tonight was a shit show, and I saw my life flash before my eyes with that guy in my hands. I could see myself in a four-by-four jail cell for the foresee-able future with how pissed I was, how close I was to destroying that kid. I don't think I've ever felt so much rage in the thirty-three years I've been on this fucking planet.

We walk down the street, Tatum practically jogging to keep up with me, until we get to the sorority house. Unlike the frat house, it's dark and quiet, and I feel inherently better knowing she'll be home in her bed, where she's safe. I'll still worry but a little fucking less knowing that she won't be around some douchebag frat fuck.

Tatum pulls out her keys and unlocks the front door, then turns to me and holds a finger in front of her mouth, ensuring that I'm quiet as we step over the threshold and she leads me to their room. Once we're inside, she hits the light, and I carry Caroline to her bed, setting her down gently on the light pink comforter, pushing her hair from her face.

She sighs sleepily, her makeup smeared, never stirring, even when I bring my hand to her face, cradling her jaw tenderly.

God, I fucking *love* her. I'm gone for her.

Every wild, carefree inch of her, and fuck, yeah... nights like tonight make our age difference more apparent. I remember being her age and what I was like, freshly drafted into the NHL, the world at my fingertips. The only thing I chased was girls and a hockey puck. She's not wrong—our lives are different. But I know that this girl is meant to be *mine*. How do we make that happen? I don't fucking know. My world is better with her in it, and I want to figure this out.

I want her however I can have her.

I'm staring down at her sleeping form, absent-mindedly swiping my thumb along her jaw, when Tatum clears her throat. When I turn, her gaze is on me, her arms crossed over her chest as she leans against the wall opposite Caroline's bed.

"Thanks for helping, but you can't stay, Hudson..." she says softly, "I... I know that you two are going through stuff, and I don't know if she would want you to."

I nod. "I know. Thank you for looking out for her and loving her enough to make decisions like that when she can't. I just want to make sure she's okay before I go." Pausing, I glance back at Caroline, then turn to Tatum again. "Can I get, uh... a makeup wipe? She hates sleeping with it on..."

Tatum nods, her face softening at my words. "Yeah, of course. Here." She walks over to a table with tubes and bottles scattered across it and grabs a wipe from a little pouch in the drawer, handing it to me.

I may not be able to stay with her tonight because I respect and understand that we're not together right now... and I'm supposed to be giving her space. But I want to make sure she can at least rest well. I use the wipe to delicately remove the makeup from her face, then unstrap the heels from her feet and grab two Advil from her desk, setting them next to her with a bottle of water. I make sure the trash can is within reach, then lean down and press my lips against her forehead, lingering for a moment as I breathe her in.

I fucking miss her so much there's a spot inside my chest that aches after only one fucking day apart. I hate that I can't stay and take care of her. That I can't take her in my arms and hold her all night. Keep an eye on her as she sleeps it off. Show her how fucking crazy I am about her. But I understand why I can't. Not tonight.

If there's one thing I will never do... it's go against her wishes. I will always respect her enough to put her first.

Tucking her into the covers, I whisper into her ear, even though she's completely out and probably won't remember this in the morning, "I love you, Bubblegum. It's ripping my heart out of my fucking chest to walk away from you right now, but I love you enough to do it. Because you deserve that man. The one who respects your wishes unequivocally. The man that respects your needs more than his desires."

I sigh, standing straight and turning toward Tatum. "Please call me if she needs anything, okay?"

"I will. Thank you. For everything. You're a good guy, Hudson."

I nod but don't respond, instead walk to the door and turn the knob, opening it.

"Hey, Hudson?" Tatum calls as I step over the threshold.

When I turn back to face her, she's got a soft smile on her face, and she's getting into bed with Caroline. "She loves you, you know? It may not be in the loud, over-the-top way you want right now, but she does. Give her time to find it."

"I'll wait. I'll love her in every way she deserves, even if that means from afar."

TWENTY-THREE
HUDSON

I slept all of three hours before my phone started going off so much that it vibrated right off the nightstand and fell to the hardwood with a crash that had me jolting upright in the bed, my heart pounding in my chest.

"Holy shit," I mutter, reaching down and grabbing it from the floor, my eyes widening when I see the hundreds of notifications on the screen before it rings again in my hand.

Reed.

"What the *fuck* is going on?" I ask, running a hand over my hair, trying to shake off the fog of sleep.

"Turn the fucking news on. TMZ. Right now." He says it so loudly that I pull the phone back from my ear, squinting at the sudden burst of noise.

I feel for the remote on the nightstand and click the

TV on, turning to *E! News*. Two newscasters are in conversation, talking animatedly, but I can't hear what they're saying until I turn the volume up, and the screen flits to...

My phone drops from my hand into my lap.

No. No. *No.* Fuck. No.

Scrambling for the phone, I pick it up and bring it back to my ear. "Tell me this is not fucking happening."

He scoffs. "It's fucking happening, brother, and it's on every major outlet there is. Every social media platform. Every streaming service."

I press the speaker button and go straight to the browser, ignoring the notifications pouring in, and pull up the first article that comes up when my name is typed in. Of course it's fucking TMZ.

PLAYBOY PLAYMAKER PREYING ON CO-EDS?

Hudson Rome seen carrying a busty blonde co-ed bridal style out of a fraternity house last night at Northwestern University and now we want to know... Who is she? And is she just another score for Chicago's star goalie?

There's a photo of me with Caroline in my arms, her face nuzzled into my neck, and the look on my face is grim. I knew photos would probably be taken, but what the fuck else was I supposed to do?

Thank fuck you can't make out Caroline's face, so at least I know she's protected from this shit.

I don't generally give a fuck what the media has to say, but this shit looks really bad, and I don't want her in the middle of a media scandal.

"This is so fucking bad," I mutter. "So goddamn bad, Reed. Like the worst possible goddamn scenario."

God, I hope she's okay and still sleeping last night off. I hope she hasn't seen this shit.

His sigh is long and ragged. "I know. Chaney's having a fucking heart attack, and I was about to drive to your goddamn house since you haven't answered anyone's calls or texts."

Dropping my head back on my shoulders, I blow out a breath and try to think. I have to get on top of this. I've got to go to Coach, first and foremost. I'm going to come clean, tell him I'm in love with Caroline. Tell him why we kept our relationship a secret, smooth over whatever I can so it doesn't hurt their relationship. Assure him that I'd never do anything that would hurt her and that I would do anything on this fucking planet to protect her. And that's what we should focus on.

Protecting her.

Whatever comes back on me comes back, and I don't give a damn as long as she's okay.

"I was asleep. I got home late as fuck and just passed out the second I got inside. Caroline..." I say, rubbing the back of my neck, "She got drunk last night, and her room-mate called me and asked me to come get her. She was worried. I got there, and some fucker was hovering over her like a creep. I almost killed him, but I had to get her out of there and get her back to the house. She was passed out the entire time."

"I figured something happened. Fuck, we know what's going on, Hudson, but the rest of the world doesn't, and shit like this makes it look bad. Real fucking bad."

"I know. Fuck, trust me, I know. At least they can't make out who she is," I say. The one saving grace of this absolute goddamn mess. The only way I'm even remotely going to be able to fix this is by going straight to Coach and getting PR on this. Try to find a way to clear this up and not hurt the team without anything falling back on her. "I've got to go to Coach, Reed. I've got to come clean and set things straight. Caroline will probably hate my fucking guts after, but it's the only way to fix this and protect her too."

"As much as I don't want that to be true, I agree. But Hudson, he's going to lose his mind. You realize that, right? You'll probably be suspended in the middle of the season."

Getting up from the bed, I pad to my closet to throw clothes on as we talk. "Look, I hate that the team gets flak because of this shit, but all I care about is protecting Caroline. If my reputation takes the hit, fuck it, I don't care. I'll sit out, I'll take the trade... I'll do whatever it takes to keep her out of this and make sure it never touches her."

He sighs again, remaining quiet for a second. I can hear Holland in the background, talking quietly. "Holland is threatening to cut my dick off if I don't say this, but she said you better fix this and get your girl, or she's going to kick your ass."

Typical Holland. I shake my head. "I'm getting dressed now. My phone is blowing the hell up. I'm going straight to Coach's office and pray he doesn't kill me in the process."

"We've got your back, brother. Keep me posted."

After a quick goodbye, I set my phone down on the bathroom counter, my hands gripping the granite as I try to take a deep breath.

This is the worst possible scenario when it comes to Coach finding out. Publicly and blown up in our faces.

My phone rings again, vibrating against the counter, and his name flashes across the screen. Time to face him. I sigh as I swipe across the screen, squeezing my eyes shut.

"Hey, Coach..."

"You have thirty goddamn minutes to get into this office, or you are done, Rome." He says it so calmly, so fucking deadly, that I'm actually a little fucking scared.

"Yes, sir." He disconnects the call without saying anything further.

That means I've got twenty minutes to get to his office.

He didn't even give me a choice to check on Caroline

first, and that makes my stomach twist with anxiousness. I want to make sure she's okay.

Sixteen minutes later, I walk through the hallway of the practice facility with every eye in the building on me. Some look sympathetic, others simply curious, wondering if I'm actually guilty of what the media is accusing me of, and some avoid eye contact altogether.

Coach's office is toward the end of the hall, so it takes me a minute to get there, and when I do, I knock only once before it swings open, revealing the man who holds my future in his hands in more ways than one.

His face is beet red, his jaw firmly set, his eyes revealing every bit of his anger.

"In. Now."

I immediately step through the door, and before my ass even hits the seat, he's on me.

"You wanna tell me what the fuck this is?" He throws down a printout of the TMZ article with that horrid fucking headline, spittle flying, his face turning even more red. "I thought we were done with this bullshit. You told me you were serious and you had your shit right. Clearly, you're still that irresponsible kid that I first met. Did you even think about your team? You wanna tell me what in the absolute goddamn hell you were thinking, Rome? Huh?"

I swallow, my knuckles turning white with how hard I'm gripping the armrests of the chair, trying to keep in mind that he has no idea what actually happened, and all he is seeing are these false narratives. Even though it stings that he immediately assumed the worst in me.

But I have a feeling his blood pressure is about to skyrocket when he actually hears the truth.

"I want to start by saying that... that—" I gesture to the paper on his desk. "—is a completely false narrative, and I would never put myself in a compromising position like they're insinuating. I have too much respect for women to do that. That's not who I am, and *nothing* about that is true."

He scoffs, pacing behind his desk as he tugs at the gray strands of his hair. "Well, I suggest you get to explaining, Rome. Because the circumstances and pictures are pretty damn incriminating. What were you even doing there? Do you know what a goddamn circus this is? Do you even know how many phone calls, emails, text messages I have gotten this morning about this? It's a literal goddamn nightmare."

"I understand that we have had a rocky history, Coach. It's no secret, and I think this conversation should be one of honesty, not beating around the bush. You've disliked me from the very first day you became the coach of this team, and I don't blame you."

His gaze narrows as he leans over the desk.

I clear my throat, continuing. "I don't blame you for feeling that way because if I was in your position, walking on to a new team with a player who was constantly in the headlines for shit, then I would have felt the same way. But I also am nothing like the man you met all those years ago. I'm nothing like the man that you knew a year ago, and while I don't need recognition for my growth, what I do need is respect." I pause as I gauge his reaction, but his face remains blank, and fuck if that isn't what makes me slightly more on edge. "I have worked hard as fuck to prove myself to you, not only as a player but as a man, and you've never changed your opinion of me no matter how hard I've tried. I know this situation sets us back, but I hope that you'll give me a real chance to explain everything. It is not what it seems."

"I'm still sitting here, Rome," he grumbles.

"I hate being called the Playboy Playmaker, more than you know, and I've been trying to free myself of that shit for so long. It was cool when I was a rookie, but I'm not that guy anymore, and I haven't been for a long time. The girl in that photo is someone I love. Very fucking much. Someone who I was trying to protect from a scary situation she found herself in."

His expression changes to one of surprise, his brow furrowing. "You're dating this girl?"

I hesitate before responding, shifting in my chair as I try to find out the exact way that I need to phrase this. "Not *exactly*. Coach, the girl in that photo is Caroline. I am in love with your daughter."

He laughs humorously. "Is this a joke? Are you fuckers playing a prank on me and this is your version of funny? This is serious, Rome. Quit fucking around."

I shake my head, my jaw tightening along with my hands as they grip the chair. "Caroline and I met at the Stanley Cup party, and neither of us had any clue as to who the other was. We never expected to see each other again after that night, so the day that we met again in your office, we were both completely... knocked off-kilter. I want you to know that I did not know she was your daughter, and when I found out, I did not pursue her... well... at first."

"Rome, I'm going to fucking kill you." He seethes. "You've been sleeping with my fucking daughter? She's in goddamn *college!* She's my *daughter!*" He comes around the desk, and for a second, I think he might actually hit me, which I would take, but he just shakes his head, his fists clenching at his side. "Tell me why the fuck does she look like she's unconscious?"

"I'm not sorry for falling in love with her. I never will be. I won't apologize for the way that I feel about her because it is so pure, the best thing I've ever known. I'm sorry that we had a relationship behind your back, behind everyone's back. I am. But I would do it again and again for her. I'm sorry you had to find out this way—it's not how I wanted to tell you. But when I realized I was in love with her, I knew I had to tell you... I was going to tell you."

"What the fuck happened to my daughter? Tell me why she looks like that in this picture," Coach interrupts, frantically running his hands through his hair.

"First, you need to know that she's okay. She's safely sleeping in her bed at the sorority house. I made sure of it." I pause, dragging my hand down my face. "Last night, she was out with her roommate at a party, drinking. Her roommate called me to come pick her up from the party because Caroline seemed really drunk and out of it."

"*What?* Why would she call you and not me? I'm her father!" he cries angrily. I can hear the emotion in his voice, and I understand where it's coming from, but I also want to protect my girl, even now. Especially now.

Nodding, I continue. "I don't know, but her roommate thought it was better to call me. She was worried about getting Caroline home safely. Asked me to come get her. And I did. I walked in, and there was a guy standing over her while she was passed out on a bed, and I almost lost my mind. I think that's what drew attention, me yelling at the guy, and when I picked her up and carried her back to her sorority house... people recognized me and took photos. It looked bad, but I was *protecting* her, Coach."

"Is she okay?" Coach looks beside himself with worry. "Fuck, tell me she's okay."

"I got her home safe and put her to bed. Her roommate stayed by her side. I haven't gotten to check on her yet today, but she was home and safe, and is probably still sleeping it off."

He swallows heavily, staring off into space.

"Listen, sir, I had every intention of coming to you today when I saw the headlines, but you called me here first. So there you have it... That's what really happened, and I know that you're probably going to suspend me and, fuck, go to GM and ask for me to be traded, but I want to be clear that I would do it again if it meant keeping her safe, if it meant getting to be with her. I will always put her first. Over hockey, over any fucking thing. I love her, and I would do anything for her."

When I'm done speaking, he's stopped the pacing and is looking at me with something unfamiliar shining in his eyes.

"She's my little girl, Hudson," he says quietly, his voice breaking slightly. "She needed help, and I wasn't there. How many times have I not been there for her? I've messed up for so goddamn long. I want so badly to do it over, but I can't. I've only got the time left I have with her. I'm trying to be there for her now."

"I know, sir. Caroline is amazing. She's everything good in this world, and I'm lucky to even be a part of her life. I want to be there for her too. Your relationship is between the two of you, but you can still be there for her now, Coach."

Rising from the chair, I take one last look at him. Our

conversation is over. I'm not going to beg him to forgive me or to beg for my spot on the team.

I did what I did because it was the right thing to do. I protected the girl that I love, and at the end of the day, that's the kind of man I want to be. And when it comes down to it, the only thing I need is Caroline.

"I know that my spot on the team might be in jeopardy, and I'm genuinely sorry that the gossip sites are spreading lies and making your job even harder than it already is. I never would want anything I do to hurt my team... my brothers. But I will never apologize for loving Caroline. I want to give her the world, and if she'll let me? I'm going to."

Caroline

"RISE AND SHINE, SLEEPING BEAUTY."

I groan into the pillow, pulling the comforter tighter around me as I burrow deeper into the mattress. I need at least another twelve hours of sleep. No, make that sixteen.

"Care, you've *gotta* get up. C'mon."

Seconds later, the blanket is pulled off, the cool air hitting my bare legs and arms, making goose bumps spread on my chilled skin. I crack one eye open and see Tatum standing over me, holding a bottle of water and two little blue pills in the palm of her hand, her eyebrows raised as if to say, *Try me.*

Begrudgingly, I sit up and rub the sleep from my eyes. "What time is it?"

"Three," she says, extending her hand toward me for me to grab the pills, then the water.

I take both and crack the bottle open, tossing the pills down my throat and chasing them with a swig of water.

"Like a.m.?"

She shakes her head, "No, as in like p.m. As in you slept for twelve hours. As in you need to get up like *right now.*"

I reach under my pillow in search of my phone, and then I realize just how hungover I am. My head is pounding incessantly, and my mouth is so dry that it feels like I swallowed an entire piece of cotton.

Jesus.

"How much did I drink last night?" The night itself is completely gone from my memory. I vaguely remember arriving at the frat house and taking a shot of tequila with Tate, and the rest... poof.

Gone.

A black hole in my brain.

Which means I blacked out, and that is slightly concerning since I have only done that maybe once in my entire life.

Tate laughs drily. "Oh, Caroline, darling." Her ass hits

my bed as she shakes her head. "It was bad. Like, really, really bad."

Groaning, I flop backward. "Please tell me I didn't do something stupid like call Hudson and cry. Please, god."

"Worse."

My eyes widen. "No. No. Tell me now. Seriously."

Tatum recounts last night in vivid detail, not leaving out a single horrid aspect, and by the time she's done, I feel like I might *actually* puke. She's right. It is so bad. I feel so stupid.

"God, you should have seen how he was with you, Care. I have never seen a man be so... gentle? He took your freakin' makeup off. He remembered how much you hate to sleep in it, so he asked for a makeup wipe and took it off. Then, he put the Advil and water by your bed. He even took off your shoes and tucked you in. Tell me what man does that so tenderly that you could actually weep."

My stomach plummets. *Hudson.*

I can't believe I got so drunk. I'm beyond embarrassed that he had to freakin' come get me from the frat house and carry me out. Mortified. I don't think I'll ever actually be able to face him again, which is sad because I miss him. So much.

"He's head over heels for you, girl," Tate adds. "You better go get your man and stop denying that you have feelings for him because by the time your father gets done with him, he might not even be in Chicago anymore."

"Wait, what?" I croak. My words are as scratchy as my throat currently feels. "What do you mean?"

She sighs, sitting up. "So, uh... about that." Pulling out her phone, she scrolls and then turns it to face me. A TMZ article is front and center on the screen.

I snatch the phone out of her hand and cover my mouth with my other hand.

Oh my god.

There's a photo of Hudson carrying me out of the frat house. He looks so mad, like... he could actually murder someone. The title of the article is insinuating...

"Oh, Tate," I whisper, tears immediately welling in my eyes. "My father is going to have him traded. He'll be suspended. His career will be over, his professional reputation ruined. What about the kids he coaches... Oh god, I have to fix this. He was so worried when we started hooking up that somehow my father would find out. That the media would make it something scandalous. I thought he was just overreacting." Thrusting the phone in her face, I cry, "Clearly *not*! God, how could I be so stupid? I just cost the guy that I'm in... that I'm seeing his career, all because I had to get plastered at a damn frat house because I wasn't ready to talk to him about my feelings." My face is completely wet from the tears streaming down my face.

"Babe, I'm the one who called him, not you. You were very much incapable of doing that. So, technically, this is my fault. And I'm so sorry I left you alone even just for a minute to get your water," Tatum says sheepishly, remorse heavy in her teary eyes.

"No, stop, Tate. You did exactly what I would've wanted you to do. Thank you. For taking care of my drunk, sloppy ass and for calling him. I... It scares me to think of what could have happened with that guy had you guys not walked in..." My entire body shudders as that thought flits through my mind, and then it turns back to Hudson. Who took care of me. Who showed up even though I hurt him.

"I care about him... I think I might even love him, and knowing that... knowing that I'm the reason the media is portraying him this way and that he's probably going to no longer be an Avalanche? No. I have to fix this. Now."

I stand from the bed so quickly my head spins, and I head straight to the bathroom. I let the scalding water wash away last night, quickly brush my teeth, then throw clothes on before I walk back out to the room.

"I'm going to see my dad," I tell her, grabbing my phone and shoving it into my back pocket.

"Right now?"

Nodding, I walk toward the door, desperate to make it to my dad and make this right. To fix whatever I've fucked up. "Yes, right now. I'll be back."

"Give 'em hell, baby..." Tate smirks, pecking my cheek.

I'm going to need it.

BY THE TIME I make it to his office, the building is quiet. Most people aren't working on Sunday, but I know today's the day my dad likes to review plans, and he prefers to do it in his office so he won't be distracted.

My stomach is in complete knots, my palms are clammy, and my heart... it feels like it's shredded. I feel so guilty, so embarrassed and ashamed of last night. I can't even stomach looking at another article that has Hudson's name on it. Apparently, I'm into self-sabotaging because I looked his name up in the Uber and couldn't stop the tears from falling for the rest of the ride.

My Romeo.

The man who I foolishly pushed away when I got scared. The one I wanted to leave before he could leave *me.*

That's why I ran, isn't it?

I ran away from him because I couldn't process all of those big feelings inside of me.

The man who has protected me, taken care of me, and selflessly sacrificed so many things to simply be with *me.*

The only way I can fix this is by being honest and not running from my feelings like a coward, no matter how impossibly big they feel.

I know that now, because the only other option is to lose him, and that's really not even an option, not really. I want to be with him because I do love him. I know that now. Hell, I knew it when he told me he loved me; I was just too overwhelmed to accept it. What I know right now is that I want him. And I have to fix what I broke to make that happen.

Turning the corner to the hallway that leads to my dad's office, I'm so lost in thought that I'm not paying attention to where I'm going, suddenly running into someone hard, losing my balance.

A hand flies to my elbow to steady me, and of course...

"Hudson," I breathe, my gaze wide as I take in the wall of a man in front of me. He looks as distraught as I feel. His eyes are tired, and the stubble on his face is slightly longer than I'm used to seeing. God, I hate seeing him like this... I hate the exhausted look in his eyes.

"Bubblegum."

The nickname falls easily from his lips, and it makes me smile, even with the world on fire around us. It gives me hope that maybe I can actually fix this.

"W-what are you doing here?"

His lips tug up into a sad smile, one that hits me directly in the middle of my already aching chest. "Had to see Coach. Try and put out a few fires."

I nod, biting my lip, trying to keep the tears at bay. "Hudson... I-I'm so sorry. I'm so incredibly embarrassed and more sorry than you'll ever know that my behavior caused this whole thing. I'm going to my dad right now to talk to him, to tell him the truth and fix this. Fix all of it."

I am obviously doing a shit job at keeping my emotions under control because I feel the hot tears sliding down my face, and I sniffle, tearing my gaze from his as I blink them away.

"Hey, hey, Bubblegum... don't cry. Don't do that, baby," he whispers, stepping forward and bringing his hands to my jaw. He frames it in his hands, using his thumb to swipe away the tears wetting my cheeks. "Don't you dare fucking apologize. I would do it again in a heartbeat, even knowing the outcome."

"But-t hockey. It's your job—it's everything to you. I ruined *everything*. The things they're saying about yo-u-u..." I'm stuttering, crying, full-on waterworks now, but I can't help it. I'm devastated that I'm the cause of all of this. Devastated that this perfect man has to deal with the fallout simply because I can't hold my liquor. Because he got caught with me. "They..."

"Don't matter. Because I was protecting the girl I love. And that is the kind of man I want to be. The man I'm fucking proud of. Who can admit he's head over heels in love with his coach's daughter, who's thirteen years younger than him."

"And in college." A teary laugh escapes as his grin widens.

"Who's in college *and* in a sorority. Even though it's

fucking crazy and we're on two opposite ends of our lives... I can't live without her. And I don't want to. Not even going to try."

My heart slams against my chest at his declaration. He makes everything sound so easy. So uncomplicated. If only that were true.

"This is crazy. All of it. It's a mess."

He nods, swiping away another tear, dropping his head closer to mine. His piercing eyes see past the fear in me, past the uncertainty. "It is. But it doesn't change a thing, Bubblegum. Not a fucking thing. I'm still just as crazy about you as I was before last night. Maybe even more now, and I didn't think that was possible. We need to talk about everything. I know we can work through this."

I swallow down the emotion, bringing my hands to his wrists as they frame my face. He unravels the inside of me, drawing every single thing to the surface that has bubbled underneath since the night I met him.

"I need to see my dad first, Hudson. Please, let me try to fix this, and then I want to come to you. I want to figure everything out between us, but I have to talk to him first."

His eyes search mine, and then he nods. "I'll be here, Bubblegum. Whenever you're ready."

"Thank you. For being patient. I have a lot I need to say when we talk, but just know I'm so sorry for hurting you," I whisper, letting go of his hands and taking a small step back so I can think clearly. It's impossible to think of anything but him when his hands are on me, his scent invading me.

"I've waited for you, Caroline, before I even knew that I was. I'll wait as long as you need."

With that, he leans forward and presses his lips to my forehead in the most tender, sweet kiss I've ever experienced, and my eyes sting as he turns and walks away down the hall until he's out of view.

I suck in a breath and dry my eyes the best I can since the tears seem to keep falling and walk to my dad's door, knocking lightly.

A few moments later, it swings open, and he's on the other side of the door, looking so very tired. The lines are prominent around his eyes, and it looks like he's aged five years overnight. I hate that I'm part of the reason that this is happening, not just to Hudson but to my dad too.

"Care Bear," he whispers, and that's all that it takes for a sob to escape my lips. He steps forward, dragging me into his arms, crushing them around me as I cry into his chest. Heavy, heart-wrenching sobs that I couldn't stifle even if I tried. There are too many emotions coursing inside of me to contain any longer.

"Don't cry, Caroline. God, baby girl, don't cry. Please, I can't stand to see you cry," he says with his lips pressed against my hair. "Talk to me. Tell me what's going on."

"You can't have Hudson traded, Dad. I need you to listen to me, okay? Please." I pull back and untangle myself from his embrace before walking further into his office and pacing nervously. "He didn't do anything wrong. All the stuff the media is saying, I'm sure you've seen it, but you can't listen to it. That girl... It's me in that picture. I'm the one he picked up last night."

I wait for him to explode, but he just nods, his eyes softening. "I know."

I freeze. "What—what do you mean you know?"

"He told me everything. About the two of you. He told me the truth—that he was protecting you. That he loves you. Is that true, Care Bear?"

Oh, Hudson.

You big, beautiful, *stupid* man. What have you done? I was so happy to see him I didn't even stop to ask myself why he was here.

Nodding, I sit in the chair across from his desk, dropping my head into my hands and sucking in a deep breath before lifting my head to meet his gaze. "It is. I love him too, Dad, and if you have him traded just because of our relationship, I will never forgive you. All he's done is make me happy from the very first day, and he is a good, kind man."

He shakes his head. "Caroline, baby girl, there has to be consequences. He's been seeing my daughter behind my back for months. My much younger daughter, who I asked him to look out for. A coach has to have trust with his players. I can't just let this go."

I spring from the chair. "Yes, you can! Dad, why would you not want me to be loved by someone like Hudson? Unconditionally, who does everything in their power to make me feel happy and safe, who protects me and makes me feel like the most beautiful person in the world? Why would you punish someone for loving me?"

"Of course I want that for you, Caroline! But baby, he is on my *team*. He is a professional hockey player almost *double* your age. You snuck around, lied to my face. How can I trust him as my player fully knowing that? It's not about punishing him for caring about you—it's about trust. And him being *right* for you. You can't expect me to be okay with this..." he says raggedly, dragging his hand down his face in exasperation.

My jaw clenches, and I set it in determination. I love my dad, as much as I can love a man who's been absent most of my life, and I don't want to let him down or hurt him in any way. But I also know that if he has Hudson traded or does anything to hurt his career... the rift in our already fragile relationship will be unrepairable.

There's no fixing it.

"That's exactly what I expect, Dad." I walk over to his desk and grab his hand as I speak, squeezing it in mine tightly. "I love him. I am *in* love with him. And you may think that I'm too young and immature to know that feeling, but you're wrong. And I deserve to be loved by a man as selfless and amazing as Hudson. Please, don't make me choose. Please don't do that to me."

His mouth opens as if he wants to respond to that but thinks better of it, and then a deep, weary sigh rumbles from his chest. "I would never ask that of you, Care Bear. I just... he's a playboy, and you're my baby girl. You're my little girl, and I don't want to see you get hurt. I only want you to be happy, and I want whatever is best for you."

"*Hudson* makes me happy. *He* is what's best for me, and I know that might not be easy to hear, and I understand. I'm sorry that we've been seeing each other in secret, but we both knew that you'd react this way, and I didn't want him to lose everything he's worked for just to be with me. I can't be that reason. Please don't let this happen. Please don't be the reason my heart breaks... again."

The line between his brow depends as his frown does, his eyes misting over. "I'm sorry, Caroline. I'm sorry that I left you and your mom, and I don't think you'll ever know how much regret I live with that I didn't handle that differently. How it suffocates me every damn day I'm breathing. Leaving you two was the biggest mistake of my life."

His words break something inside of my heart, something that I've been stitching back together for a very long time. The fragile thread bursting open at the seams.

"Dad..." I cry, hot tears blurring my vision.

He shakes his head, squeezing my hand tenderly.

"Please. I should've said this a very long time ago, Caroline. I should've never left, and that's something I'll have to live with. I missed so many moments of your life because I was a fool. I'm fighting for a place in your life now, trying to make a spot for myself, and it's what I deserve. I just need you to know how sorry I am. How I would do anything to turn time around and change it. To stay and never have left you."

I'm crying so hard I can hardly catch my breath. I've waited so long to hear this, to hear him take responsibility for being the first man to break my heart. It doesn't feel good—it doesn't feel anything like I once hoped it would. It won't turn back time and give us those years back.

I cover my mouth to stifle the sob as he continues. "I can't do that, Care Bear. I'd do anything to make that happen, but I can't. All I can do is fight like hell to earn my place in your life. To be the father you deserve for the time that we have left. To cherish every single second I have with you. I just hope that you can forgive me."

I nod. "I do, Dad. I do forgive you."

He squeezes my hand, reaching up to wipe away my tears. "I can't lose you again, baby girl. It would be like ripping my heart straight from my chest, and I can't do it. I love you, more than you will ever know. And if he makes you happy, if he's going to treat you like the precious thing that you are, then I'll just have to get over it. I'm not trying to hurt either of you; I just want to protect you... so be patient with your old man as I figure this out. I'm still processing it all."

Leaping off the desk, I throw my arms around him, holding him tightly to me. "Thank you. For trusting me enough to know what's best for me and for not punishing him. I don't want anything to ever tear us apart again, Dad. I'm sorry I didn't come to you with this—I wasn't sure I could, but I want to build trust together moving forward. All I want is to have you in my life and to be happy."

"That's all I want too, baby girl. I don't want you to ever question my love for you."

"I know, Dad." I sniffle, trying to stop the tears and failing miserably. "I don't. And I need your help. I have to fix this situation with Hudson in the media."

He nods in agreement. "I know. I've had PR on it since he left my office earlier."

Woah.

"So, you knew before I came in here that you weren't going to punish him?"

"I knew that if my baby girl loves him, then he has to be a good guy, and I would believe in her even if I wasn't convinced about him. And I knew you wouldn't want him to be hurt by this. I just needed to have this discussion with you, see how you truly felt about him."

He trusted in me, even when I didn't trust him to make the right decision.

Somehow, it only makes me love him more.

TWENTY-FOUR
HUDSON

The only way I stopped myself from driving to Caroline's sorority house was that I didn't want to draw any attention to the fact that the photo is of her. The last thing I want is for the media to discover that she's the girl in the photo.

Imagine if they knew we'd been seeing each other in secret for months.

They'd camp outside the damn sorority house just to get a shot of her.

I've spent the last couple of hours fixing shit around my house that wasn't even really broken to begin with, puttering around with things to keep my mind busy until I decided to get in the pool and swim laps. It seems to be the only thing that is truly giving me a minute of reprieve, and it's nights like tonight when I'm thankful for it being heated. It's cold as fuck, but the water itself is seventy, making this my favorite part of the house.

My phone died before I even got home from Coach's office from the sheer amount of notifications, and I didn't bother to charge it. The guys know where I'm at, and there's no one else besides my girl that I even want to talk to right now. When she's ready.

Pushing myself, I swim faster, harder, until my muscles burn with exertion. Only when my arms shake and my chest burns do I come up and suck a deep breath, groaning as I prop myself against the side of the pool.

A throat clears, and I whip around, my brow furrowing. What the hell?

Caroline's standing near the edge of the pool, her arms crossed over her chest as she runs her hands up her arms to keep the chill away.

"Hi, Romeo."

I can't stop the smile that spreads on my face, even if I fucking wanted to. The best thing I ever did was fall in love with this woman. And give her the code to my house.

"Bubblegum," I say, eyebrows raised. "Whatcha doin'?"

She pops her shoulder. "Just enjoying the view."

"Uh-huh. I see." Pulling myself from the pool, I make my way over to her, water dripping off me. "Just wanted to watch me swim? Sure that's it?"

Her eyes widen when she realizes exactly what's

about to happen, and she starts to scramble backward, tripping over her own feet to get away from me.

"Don't. You. Dare." She screeches the moment my arms close around her waist, and I haul her against my soaked body, drenching her.

Not that I was going to listen. I pick her up, kicking and laughing, and I jump off the edge of the pool into the deep water, then kick us to the surface.

The moment she sucks in a breath, she squeals, "Oh, I am so getting you back for that."

I smirk, my arms still around her waist, holding her close as I tread water to keep us up.

"Worth it."

Her eyes roll, but the grin on her lips never leaves. Slowly, she loops her arms around my neck, her legs locking around my waist as she holds on while I swim us over to where my feet can touch the concrete bottom.

For the first time in days, I feel completely at peace. I feel so goddamn relieved to have her in my arms again, regardless of what it means for us. She's here... but there is still so much for us to work through.

"You okay, Bubblegum?"

My eyes flit down to the droplets of water that cling to her sweet lips, wanting to lick away those little rivulets.

She nods, her fingers dragging over the buzzed hair at my nape. "I'm more than okay now. I was so afraid earlier. When I realized that I might not get the chance to apologize to you. For pushing you away when I got scared. For running when the only thing I should've done is stay. All of these feelings... they're big, and they're scary, Hudson."

Her voice is a whisper, soft and low, as her blue eyes shine with unshed tears. "I've never been in love before, not until you. And realizing that I had fallen in love with you somewhere along the way was like a shock to my system. It snuck up on me until it consumed me whole. But I *am* in love with you, Hudson Rome. Irrevocably. And even though it took me a little while to realize that... it doesn't make the feeling any less fierce."

"Say it again," I croak, squeezing her to me tighter.

"I love you. You, Hudson. Not the guy that the media portrays. Not the one that your fans think they know or even the man that my dad once thought you were. I love *you*. The man who volunteers with a youth hockey team because he loves seeing his players working together. The man that loves his nieces and nephews, who cares about his family. The man who takes my makeup off when I'm too drunk to see straight. The man that loves sharing his city with me and feeding me all my favorite foods. The man who knows my body even better than I do and the man who puts me first. Every single time. That's the man that I love." She pauses, pressing the softest, sweetest fucking kiss to the corner of my mouth, then another to the center of my lips, before pulling back and looking into my eyes. "That's the man that I want it all with. I'm yours, you know?"

My arms tighten around hers as I slam my lips against her, kissing her with every ounce of longing from the past two days. She moans breathlessly into my mouth, and I swallow it, my tongue sweeping along hers.

Somehow, someway, I tear my lips away and rest my forehead against hers as I tell her breathlessly, "When you walk into a room, you are the only thing that I see. I'm so in love with you, Caroline Evans, I can't see anything but you. My wild, carefree, beautiful girl. It's you."

Hockey has always been the center of my universe.... Until suddenly it wasn't.

It's her.

A teary cry leaves her lips, her entire body melting against me, surrendering just as I have to her. She ducks her head under my chin, nuzzling into my neck.

"I'm so sorry I was so stupid," she says contritely. "I'm sorry that my first instinct was to run when you've been nothing but truthful with me. I'm sorry that I put your career in jeopardy with that stupid party. I'm just sorry for so many things, Hudson, and I'm scared that I'll just keep making the same stupid mistakes."

"Baby, having to pick you up because you got drunk is nothing. You're young—you're going to make fucked-up mistakes because it's what life is. You make mistakes, and you learn from them," I tell her as my hands slide up her back and across her shoulders to frame her face as I ghost my lips along hers. "Let's make them together. You and I."

She nods over and over, like eventually my words will click into place in her head.

"I told my father everything, Hudson. I told him that I loved you and that if he damaged your career in any way that our relationship wouldn't survive the fallout."

"Caroline..." I say, and she shakes her head, placing her finger over my lips to silence me.

"Loving you isn't conditional. It isn't something that I can turn off. It's not something that I can walk away from without breaking my own heart. I could never sit back and watch my dad hurt the man that I love, no matter how good his intentions were. He doesn't know the *real* you, Hudson, and that's a shame because everyone should know the man in here." She places her hand over my heart and rubs her thumb back and forth lovingly. "If he wants to have a place in my life, then he has to make the effort to accept the fact that I'm yours, and you're mine. That's not changing."

"Fuck, I love hearing you say that. Mine."

Rolling her lip between her teeth, she nods. "We talked for a long time today, cleared a lot of things up between us and said things that have needed to be said for a long time, and he promised me that he's not going to punish you in any way. He should be calling this evening. He thinks that you should both make a joint statement together and explain that you're in a relationship with his daughter and that he supports the relationship fully. That last night was an invasion of our personal life, and although it needs no explanation, he's going to explain that you were protecting and taking care of me, just as any boyfriend would do."

I don't bother to hide the shock on my face. I mean, I don't know exactly what I expected from Coach after our talk. I didn't expect him to embrace the fact that I love his daughter, that's for sure, but I walked out of his office fully accepting the fact that he might make my life a living hell from this point on because I refuse to walk away from her. No matter what he inflicted on me.

But this?

Making a statement to essentially clear my name? To have my back?

"Don't look so shocked, Hudson. He was upset about the headline and that we've kept our relationship a secret, of course, but I think he also knows that you're not the same person you used to be. I just... I need you to make an effort to have an amicable relationship with him, not just because he's your coach but because he's my dad. If we want to make this work, however we do that, he's part of it."

"You asking me to be your boyfriend, Bubblegum?" I say lightly, loving the way she tosses her head back and laughs.

She bites her lips, her nose scrunching slightly. "Yes, I am."

"Then, I accept. And I promise to work on things with your dad. Whatever it takes. Your happiness is everything to me."

She nods, leaning forward and melding her lips with mine. At first, it's soft and sweet, and then it burns bright. Her tongue coaxes my lips open, and she sucks on mine, sending a jolt straight to my cock When I pull back, both of us are panting.

As much as I want to take her inside and spend the rest of the night making love to her, I want to finish this discussion first. The way things are headed with that kiss, there's not going to be anything else said but my name as she comes.

"Bubblegum, slow down because I only have so much damn restraint."

A giggle erupts, and she doesn't look the least bit fucking sorry. Little devil.

"I'm worried about when the media gets a hold of your name. They're fucking relentless. They'll camp outside the sorority house just to get a photo of you, follow you at school. I don't want that shit. I want you to be able to enjoy your college life like you planned to."

"I know, but with us writing a press release and only releasing the information we want, it allows us to control the narrative. I think that we give the media enough to call them off, but other than that, we exist in our little bubble as much as we can. We'll figure it out. I know that may sound naive, but it *will* eventually die down, and we focus on keeping our relationship as private as we can. My dad and I also discussed me moving out of the sorority house, possibly into a gated apartment complex with twenty-four-hour security, just so he feels confident that I'm safe."

As much as I hate that she's having to make sacrifices in order to be with me, a part of me is fucking relieved after last night at that frat house and me almost having to commit a goddamn murder. Not to mention how easy it was for me to sneak into her window that night.

"Is that what you want?"

Her shoulder dips slightly. "I don't feel connected to them in the way that I did with my girls in Seattle. I mean, Tatum, of course—we'll always be close. And I'll still be in the sorority; I just won't be *living* there. Lots of girls live off campus."

I nod, seeing the truth in her eyes. "I support whatever you decide, but I want you to be safe, and I want to be the one to keep you safe, Bubblegum."

"You do keep me safe, Hudson. You kept me safe last night, even after our fight, even when you were hurt you put me first."

I press a heated kiss to her lips. "Always. I know asking you to dinner with my family scared you, and I know you might not still be ready even now that we're officially a couple, but I do want you to meet my family and my guys. I want them to know you. I want them to meet the reason I've changed, the reason that I'm happier."

"I wasn't scared to meet them, Hudson. It was just what made me confront my real feelings for you. When you asked, it made me realize that things were actually getting serious and not just a casual hookup like I thought. I thought at first my apprehension was that I didn't want that, but when I thought about it, I realized I was worried for the opposite reason because I *do* want that. I'd love to meet them. All of them."

Fuck yeah.

"Really?"

She nods, her grin widening. "I want to meet the people who love you as much as I do. I want to be part of each other's lives, not just in secret. I want to know what it's like to be yours in front of the entire world."

And that is irrevocably true.

Caroline Evans is *mine*.

Not that there was ever really a question.

Not since I tasted that bubble gum on her lips.

Not since she stole my heart in a darkened broom closet and never gave it back.

Not since the only *play* I would be making is the one where I keep her forever.

Three weeks later

"I CAN'T BELIEVE Christmas is like two weeks away," Caroline says as she adjusts the gifts under the Christmas tree for at least the sixth time. "It snuck on me, and I am totally unprepared."

"Bubblegum, aside from Mariah Carey herself decorating this house, it couldn't possibly look any more festive. And even then, I still think you'd show her up."

That earns me a full-blown smile, one that lights up her entire face and causes my heart to hammer against my chest.

She's so fucking beautiful.

"That is practically the best compliment ever. Thanks, Romeo."

After rearranging the presents once more, she moves on to the mantle above the fireplace and takes everything off, piece by piece, until it's empty. A blank canvas. Then, she stands back and chews on the end of her red-and-green-painted nail as she stares intently at the mantle.

It's so goddamn cute. *She's* so goddamn cute.

And I think a little nervous, which is saying a lot because in the time that I've known Caroline, she's been nothing but confident and sure in whatever situation she's been thrown in.

It would explain all of the rearranging just to rearrange again and the fact that she's been uncharacteristically worrisome about everything looking perfect. Obsessing over every little detail.

I walk over to where she's standing and pull her to me, taking her chin between my fingers, "You nervous about meeting my family, Bubblegum?"

"No, of course not. Why would I be nervous? What's there to be nervous about? There is absolutely nothing to be nervous about." Her words come out in a rush, and when I grin, she blows out a breath. "Yes. I'm so fucking nervous, Hudson, and I don't ever get nervous. It's just... they're the most important people in your life, and I want them to like me. I need everything to be perfect."

"Baby, listen to me. They are going to love you just as much as I love you," I tell her, tipping her chin up so I can brush my lips along hers. She sighs against my mouth. "I promise, they're going to love everything you've done here. You've made my house a damn home in the past two weeks, and that's what matters. Not how many trees are up."

She didn't hesitate when I asked her to take my card and decorate for the holidays after we decided that I'd host everyone here during the two days we have off. I'm so fucking excited for her to meet my parents, my sister, and my guys.

So far, we've fallen into a routine that's just... us. It's not easy trying to juggle both of our schedules and still have time for each other, but the time we do have, we take full advantage of.

"Okay. You're right. I'm just freaking out."

"Don't, Bubblegum. Stop worrying about the house, and go change into that dress that I peeled off of you earlier." I smirk, turning her toward the stairs and tapping her ass with my palm. "Go on. I'll put this up."

"Fine. Only because it's an act of God to get myself into that dress."

She's right, and if she hadn't threatened to not suck my dick for a week, I would've torn it right off her when I pressed her against the wall in my bedroom earlier and fucked her, fast and hard.

Disappearing up the stairs, she leaves me alone with the contents of the mantle, which I quickly put back as best as I can, trying to remember how she had it the last time she rearranged things.

Everything else is ready. I had the party catered, so the food is out and ready to go. There's eggnog, drinks for the kids, and the fire pit is already lit.

Pulling out my phone, I pull up Coach's contact and copy the link from my notes app that I saved earlier this morning.

Hudson: This one seems promising. Gated. Heated pool. Security at each entrance. Take a look.

A few minutes later, he responds.

Coach: Not a bad choice. Maybe we can meet with management after the holidays for a tour.

Hudson: Sure. Just so you know though... I'm going to ask her if she wants to move in here. Not sure she'll say yes, but she'll have the option.

Coach: Just when I was starting to dislike you less... We'll discuss it when I get there later.

I smirk, pocketing my phone into my slacks when the doorbell rings.

... then rings *again* before I can even get to the foyer.

"I'm coming! Shit," I mutter.

When I swing the door open, my jaw drops in complete fucking shock. The kind of shock where you blink wordlessly as you try and snap out of your stupor.

"Hudson! You handsome-ass motherfucker," Graham grunts, pulling me into his arms for a hug as he claps me on the back.

Holy shit.

Graham motherfucking Adams. Our long-distance best friend who used to be our teammate. Well, until he fell in love with Reed's younger sister and moved away to Tennessee.

Fuck, it's good to see him.

"What the hell are you doing here?"

Graham chuckles as he pulls back, throwing his arm over Emery, his wife. "Surprise. We've been planning it for a while. Missed home, missed you guys. Knew it was time to come home."

Maybe it's the holidays, or maybe I'm just a gigantic pussy, but I feel a little sting behind my eyes. Fuck. Blinking it away, I clear my throat, then lean forward and kiss Em's cheek. She's holding their newborn son, Mark.

"Hi, Em."

"Hi, Huds."

I squat down in front of his baby girls. They've gotten so big and so beautiful. They look like both of their parents, but damn, I see their uncle Reed in them too, which I know makes him happy as hell. They've got pretty red dresses on with little reindeer on the front and matching headbands.

"Hi, sweet girls. I know you probably don't remember me, but I'm your uncle Hudson."

Charlotte grins cheekily, never hesitating as she launches forward and throws her tiny little arms around my neck, squeezing tightly. My arms circle around her, holding her to me. Quinn looks a little more reserved, stepping closer to Graham and wrapping her arm around his leg as she peeks from behind him.

"I'm so glad that you're here. All of you." I scoop Charlotte up and put her on my hip as I hold the door open. "Let's get inside. It's freezing out here."

We step across the threshold, and Graham looks around the foyer as we walk into the living room. He shakes his head before nudging my shoulder. "The house is amazing, brother. Definitely more space than that old apartment, huh?"

"Yeah, for sure."

"It's beautiful in here. You did this?" Emery asks skeptically. She's rocking the tiny bundle in her arms as she glances around the room.

I chuckle, shaking my head. "Of course not, Em. That's all on my girl."

On cue, she walks down the stairs, and as always, it steals the breath from my lungs. The glittering black dress is fitted to her body like a glove, accentuating her delectable curves, her shapely legs clad with a pair of black heels that wrap up her ankle. Her honey-colored hair glows in the chandelier light as it falls in curls around her.

So fucking beautiful that she never fails to make my heart race.

"And this is her," I say as she makes it to the bottom of the stairs, a bright smile on her red-painted lips.

I set little Charlotte back on her feet and step towards my girl, placing a kiss on her forehead. "Caroline, this is Graham and his wife, Emery."

"Hi, gorgeous," Graham says, bypassing her extended hand and pulling her into his arms. If he wasn't my brother and I didn't know he was obsessed with his wife, he'd currently be less two limbs.

"Hi, Caroline!" Emery says, offering her a kind smile, which Bubblegum returns before her gaze travels to the baby in Emery's arms.

"Oh my gosh, look at this handsome little man," she coos, stepping forward to grip his little sock-covered foot between her fingers. "God, I love babies. He's so sweet and tiny."

Graham makes a noise in the back of his throat, and when I glance at him, he's raising his eyebrows suggestively. I don't even need him to say it out loud—I already know exactly what that motherfucker is thinking.

Christ.

Emery rolls her eyes when he nudges me, obviously used to his ridiculousness, and directs Caroline's attention to the girls. The doorbell rings again just as Em is introducing them, and before I can even open the door, it swings open and Chaney strides in, a huge box in his arms.

"Party's here!" He grins, lifting the box.

Right after he walks through the entryway, Reed, Asher, and Briggs, along with their families, follow closely behind.

I never realized how many of us there were until we're all inside my house, filling my living room, and I start making the rounds, saying hello to everyone and introducing them formally to my girl.

The kids run off toward the table that Caroline set up with gingerbread houses for them to make, and I watch as she excuses herself to go over and help them get set up.

"Dude, where's your sister? I'm dying to meet her," Chaney asks when he walks up with a glass of eggnog.

I narrow my gaze. "Don't make me kill you during Christmas. They're on the way, and you better be on your very best behavior."

He raises his hands in surrender with a shit-eating smirk on his face. "I am, I am."

The guys walk over together, and fuck, it feels so fucking good to have us all here together in one place again. It's been a long time since we could make that happen, and it does something funny to my chest.

Our families are all here, laughing and having fun while we stand together, watching it unfold.

"I'm so fucking happy we're all here together," I say. "Especially you, Graham. Missed you, brother."

"Miss you guys more than you know. Em and I are going to try and make it to a game soon. Things have just been crazy with Mark being born and the girls growing."

Reed groans. "My nieces are getting so big."

"They sure are, and they are handfuls too," Graham says, gazing at his girls with an expression full of love and adoration.

Evan and Olive are lying in front of the Christmas tree, watching the toy train circle it, and Briggs smiles. "I bet you a hundred dollars the second we leave here she's begging us for a train."

"For sure," I agree. "And tomorrow, she'll have one because you can't tell that baby no."

"Yep. Anything for my Olive Juice."

Graham shakes his head. "Yeah, just wait until you've got babies to say no to. It's fucking impossible."

Asher agrees. "Dude. I'm pretty sure if Alex asked me to take him skydiving off the coast of Ireland, I'd book the next flight out. Especially because he's just such a good fucking kid, it makes it even harder to say no. Auden tells me all the time that I have to be strong."

"Same. Holland tells me all the time that I'm a pushover when it comes to our kids, but I don't care. I live to spoil them." Reed chuckles.

Emery walks over, Mark fast asleep in her arms, and asks if one of us will hold him so she can get a drink.

"Chaney has been dying to hold him all night, Em," I tease.

She turns to Chaney, whose face has completely gone ashen. "What? No."

"Take the baby, Chaney," I tell him. "Right now."

He's shaking his head adamantly as Briggs takes the eggnog from his hand, and Emery places Mark gently into Chaney's arms.

I'm fucking dying. The kid looks like he's about to shit his pants, his arms stiff like a fucking statue.

"See, Chaney? Not so bad. You look like a natural," Graham tells him, clearly picking up on the fact that we're fucking with him.

"No, take this thing out of my arms. Oh god, it just farted. I just got farted on by a fucking tiny child. Take it." He turns toward Briggs, who steps back and holds up his hands, as does everyone else he tries to hand the baby off to.

Finally, Em walks back over and takes him from Chaney, and his relief is palpable.

"I swear to god, I am never having kids. Never," he says. "I need a fucking drink."

Once he's gone, Graham smirks. "You gonna tell him, or should I?"

"Nah, he'll find out on his own."

We all laugh, sharing a secret of our own since every single guy in this group has had their world flipped upside down by one of the women in this room, and generally, babies come shortly after.

My gaze drifts to Caroline as she laughs with the girls on the couch in front of the fire, Quinn perched on her lap, and despite Quinn's reservation when she first arrived, she's burrowed into Caroline's neck, twirling a piece of my girl's blonde hair around her finger affectionately.

Fuck, she's going to be the best mom. It might be a while from now, much later down the road for us, but I can't wait for that moment. I can't wait to have this girl by my side forever. To share all of these moments with her that my friends have had with their families.

"I know that look," Reed says, "You deserve that happiness, Hudson. I'm glad you found your purpose in her."

He's right. I did find my reason in her. I was lost, drifting along, unsure of my place, never truly feeling like I was at home anywhere. Until her.

Until I realized that Caroline Evans *is* home.

And she will always be the best *play* I ever made.

EPILOGUE

Caroline
9 months later

"I'm not ready for you to leave again," I mumble against Hudson's chest, burrowing further into the warmth of his body. It's starting to get chilly in Chicago at night, so he's got the fire pit set up in front of us and a projector screen in the back yard so we can watch a movie under the glow of the stars.

It's romantic, and simple, and everything I've come to love about this man.

"I know, Bubblegum, but I'll only be gone for a few days, and it'll give you time to get settled in." I feel his lips press against my hair and his arms tighten around me.

After nearly nine months of renting my apartment near campus, I've finally moved out and officially moved in with Hudson.

We took things slow, at first. We didn't let anyone set the pace for us. We were a new couple, exploring what it meant to be together, and we didn't want to rush anything. Plus, after everything happened with the media, my dad felt more comfortable with me in a gated apartment complex with around the clock security so I stayed there until now.

It definitely takes getting used to... being with a man who's constantly in the public eye, but honestly? We keep our relationship as private as we can, and we're happy.

"I know, I just hate sleeping alone. You know how cold my feet get."

I'm teasing him, and I feel his chest rumble with laughter beneath me, causing me to pull back and gaze up at him. The wide smile on his face only makes him that much more devastatingly handsome. Sometimes I feel like I have to pinch myself that this man is all mine.

What is life?

I came to Chicago to go to school, and to repair my relationship with Dad, and somehow I fell in love with the most perfect man on the planet.

Maybe it was luck... but I think it was fate. I was always meant to be Hudson Rome's, and he was meant to be mine. The universe just had a funny way of making that happen.

"That's all I am to you, Bubblegum, a personal heater. You love to stick those cold feet under my thighs at night, and it scares the shit out of me."

I grin, "Well, I think you have many more talents than just being my personal furnace. Like that thing you do with your tongue in my p-"

"Hey Hudson? Caroline?" Wren says, causing me to scramble into an upright position, fixing my cardigan like I've just been caught in bed with my boyfriend by my mother.

"Oh! Yes, hi, uh... yeah..." I stutter.

Hudson just laughs, his entire body shaking, "What's up, kid?"

"Is it cool if I take a quick shower?"

"Wren, you don't have to ask to take a shower. You stink, take a shower."

Wren shifts from one foot to another, gaze casted downward then drags his eyes back to Hudson, a small smile tugging at his lips, "Thanks, Hudson. Go back to your *kissing*."

Ugh.

Once he disappears back inside the house, I flop back down onto the lounger next to Hudson with an exasperated sigh. He reaches for my hand and laces our fingers together.

"Still getting used to him being here," I say. "I feel like I just got caught with my pants down."

"I mean... once he goes to bed I will definitely have your pants down, but for now you're safe." He laughs, "We just have to be a little more careful about PDA when he's around, that's all."

I nod.

It's not only me who moved in with Hudson. Wren has officially moved in too. And to be honest? This is exactly where he should be. Here with *us*. It's only been a couple of weeks, so we're still getting used to having a teenager in the house with us. But, we're figuring it out.

I still don't even know everything that transpired with Wren's family. I just know that Wren's stepfather was no longer fit to be his parent and being the kind hearted, big teddy bear that Hudson is... he showed up for Wren. Just like he always does for those that he loves.

And now Wren is one step closer to being officially a Rome.

When he appeared on Hudson's doorstep in the middle of the night late this summer, he wordlessly opened the door and brought Wren inside and spent two hours in the living room talking with him. Making sure that he was safe. My goalie, always the protector.

The rest is history.

"How's your dad taking you moving in? He texted me twice today to make sure you were okay." Hudson asks.

A smile touches my lips as I think of how my relationship with my Dad has progressed in the last year. We're doing much better. I've forgiven him, and he's forgiven himself which is something we both needed to happen. And... he's trying to stop hovering. He's making an effort, and it means everything to have him becoming one of my best friends.

"Go figures. The two of you text more than we do these days."

Hudson smirks, popping his shoulder, "What can I say? We've got something incredible in common, so there's always something to talk about."

He and my father are on good terms. I'd venture to even say maybe they've built a friendship? At first... it was rocky. It was not easy as we tried to navigate all of these unchartered waters together. But, they both put in the time to get to know each other in a new light and never gave up while trying to let go of the past, because they knew how important it was to me that they get along.

So they made the effort and have built trust. And now? It feels like we're all part of a family, and it makes me happier than I've ever been.

Loving Hudson makes me happier than I ever dreamed I could be.

"When you get home, I was thinking that we could take Wren to pick out new paint for his room? I really want him to have a space where he feels at home, that's his. This is a new place for him, and I just want him to be comfortable," I tell Hudson, whose arms tighten around me.

He gazes down at me, his finger tipping my chin up, "I love you, Bubblegum. I love your kind, selfless heart, and I can't fucking wait to marry you and make you my wife."

I giggle, "Well, you'd have to *ask me* to marry you in order to actually marry me, Romeo."

"I know." He smirks. "And as soon as you graduate, and I whisk you away to wherever your pretty little heart desires? Then I'll ask you to marry me, and it'll be the proposal of a lifetime."

That was something we agreed on when we started talking about me moving in. That I'd finish school, get my degree, and be on the path to my career dreams before we considered marriage.

"I'm going to be the hottest wife," I quip, raising my eyebrows and tossing him a sultry grin. "I can't wait to marry you one day, Hudson Rome. You make me fall more in love with you every single day."

His gaze softens, and he leans forward to capture my lips in a sweet, tender kiss that has my pink painted toes curling against his sweatpant clad legs. "Then you know exactly the way I feel about you, Bubblegum. You are the best thing that's ever happened to me. My purpose. You and Wren? You're my family, and I'll never stop loving and protecting you."

My heart tugs.

This man.

This perfect man who stole my heart from the very first night and never gave it back.

The one who makes me feel beautiful, even on my worst days. The one who is patient and gentle when I need him to be. And the man who doesn't hold back or treat me like I'm breakable when I need *more*.

It turns out that *more* with Hudson Rome is everything I never knew I needed, and when I stopped running and allowed him to love me?

I found a once in a lifetime kind of love that will never fade. All because I finally listened to my heart.

"You're shivering baby, let's go inside. I think you need a long.... hot.... bath," he murmurs into my hair, pulling my earlobe between his teeth causing me to shiver for a *very* different reason.

"Mmm.... say less, Romeo. Say less."

He used to be the Playboy Playmaker, but now?

He's *my* Romeo.

What's next in your Maren Era?
<u>Coming soon:</u>

INTERNATIONAL BESTSELLING AUTHOR
MAREN MOORE

A billionaire, fake dating, forced proximity romance that brings even **MORE** spice.
Get your copy here.

ALSO BY MAREN MOORE

<u>Totally Pucked</u>
Change on the Fly
Sincerely, The Puck Bunny
The Scorecard
The Final Score
The Penalty Shot
Playboy Playmaker

<u>Standalone</u>
The Enemy Trap
The Newspaper Nanny
The Mistletoe Bet
The Ex Equation ***(coming soon)***

COMPLETE SERIES

The Totally Pucked series is a <u>COMPLETE</u> series, and you can start back at the beginning with Reed & Holland's story.

A best friend's brother single dad romance.

Flip the page to read the first chapter!

CHAPTER ONE

REED

There are a lot of perks to being a professional hockey player. Hell, an athlete in general. Besides the money, the fame, the endorsements. The free shit that sports companies throw at you.

And one of those perks is currently perched on my lap, trailing her hot pink manicured finger up my chest.

Her name is Elizabeth. And honestly, I'm surprised I even remember her name because our entire interaction at Liam and Juliet's wedding lasted about fifteen minutes in a cramped bathroom stall and there was definitely no talking done. Or any talking during any of the times after that.

You see, I'm the kind of guy that enjoys the finer things in life...without all of the complications that people seem to add. Why make anything hard when it's already sweet?

I'm twenty-eight and living my dream, playing hockey for one of the best teams in the country. I've got the most beautiful women at my fingertips, fans who adore me, and then I have my ma and my sister Emery. Nothing to hold me back and *no one* to answer to. And that's exactly how I want it.

Seriously, life is *good.*

"Has anyone told you tonight that you are the most beautiful girl in the entire room?" I say to the busty blonde in my lap. Her plump, bright red lips stretch into a wide, confident grin. It's not a lie, she is gorgeous. It's just part of the game. You say what they want to hear, and everyone's happy.

"That's because I'm the *only* girl in the room, Reed Davidson." She giggles before tossing her long, sleek hair over her tan shoulder that peeks out from her sleeveless dress.

I grin cheekily, revealing the dimple that always seals the deal. Just as I'm leaning in, Briggs, my best friend, walks up and flops down onto the couch next to us. I shoot him a look that says "get the fuck out of here, cock-blocker," but Briggs being Briggs, doesn't pick up on the signal.

"Tonight sucks," he mutters. He's nursing a still full beer, and moping around the bar like he's lost his puppy dog.

Sighing heavily, I nudge blondie from my lap and

thankfully, she takes the hint and scampers off back toward her group of friends, leaving me alone with Briggs.

"Alright, what's up? What are you cryin' in your beer about?"

His jaw clenches at my jab, but he just shakes his head, staring off into the distance. Best forward in the NHL or not, the guy is dramatic and broody as shit. I've just learned to live with it, and fuck with him any chance I get.

"Briggs."

"Just some shit."

Another blasé answer. A Briggs's specialty.

I pull my phone from my pocket and swipe away the unopened texts from puck bunnies who text me weekly for a hookup, and instead, I go straight to my other best friend, Liam's text and open it. He's sent a photo of him, Juliet and the girls on the beach. The girls are posing next to a sandcastle as big as they are, and it brings a genuine smile to my face. Liam and I have been best friends for as long as I can remember. We played hockey together, until he became the coach of the Avalanche last year. Now that he's married to Juliet, he's coaching high school hockey and I miss seeing him and the girls as much as I used to.

They've been in the Bahamas for over a week, while I'm stuck here babysitting Briggs. I can't wait for the girls to get home to tell me all about their vacation.

I love those two sassy girls. Being their uncle Reed is

one of the best things in my life. But me as a dad? The last thing I could ever see myself as is a father *or* a husband, or anything even close. As much as I love Ari and Ken... I love bringing them back to Liam at the end of the night, so I can go out with the boys, catch a game, enjoy the single unattached life.

I'm a perpetual bachelor, and that's *exactly* how I plan to stay.

Which is why Broody Briggs, myself, Asher, Hudson and Graham are at a bar on a Tuesday night... because, why not? We're all single, hot professional hockey players with no one to go home to, so why not spend it out on the town with a few beers? We all play together for the Chicago Avalanche, and it's the best job on the damn planet.

When people say, "do what you love and you'll never work a day in your life," it's true. Sometimes it's hard to believe that I get to wake up and play hockey for a living, but at the same time, I busted my ass to be here. I worked from sun up to sun down to be the player I am today.

To celebrate another great practice, we decided to come out tonight for a night of bunnies and booze. Except, as of late, things have been... less exciting, since Briggs is walking the straight and narrow or he's off the team. He's been in more fights the past six months than I have in my entire hockey career.

So, to make sure that he stays out of trouble, that he

doesn't find himself in front of a pap's camera, or worse, stuck in a jail cell for another night, I'm stuck babysitting until further notice.

Hockey player or hockey-player nanny? That is the real question.

The rest of the night passes uneventfully, thanks to Briggs's sour mood. Asher, Hudson and Graham each found a puck bunny for the night and dipped out before midnight, leaving me and Briggs alone, so I decide to cut out as well.

"I'm headed out, you want a ride?" I ask Briggs, who's rapid-fire typing on his phone.

He doesn't answer me, so I punch him in the shoulder to get his attention.

"Fuck, what was that for?"

"Dude, you're in a *bar* and have been glued to your phone all night. I'm out, you need a ride?"

He shakes his head no. "I'll call an Uber later."

"Stay out of shit, dude, seriously. I'm not bailing you out of jail, and please, for God's sake, wrap it up. We don't need miniature versions of you skating around." I grin, teasing him.

The dick nods, barely acknowledging me, eyes still focused on his phone. Asshole. I down the rest of my beer and leave the bottle on the table, with a few bills I pull from my wallet, and then make my way out of the bar. Thankfully, we frequent this place often, and the owner lets us use the back door, so we can avoid fans and the media. As much as I love having my picture taken, I'm not a fan of the paps.

I open the back door of the building and step outside into the cool night air, inhaling a deep breath before I begin walking across the pavement to find my truck in the sea of vehicles. Just as I'm about to unlock it, my phone rings in my pocket. I fish it out and see it's Holland, my sister's best friend.

Weird. Why would she be calling me after midnight?

I swipe and answer, "You know that they say any calls after ten are booty calls, right?"

"Reed?" She all but yells into the phone. The music in the background is so damn loud I can hardly hear her.

"Holland? What's up? You realize it's after midnight?"

I unlock my truck and jump inside, starting the engine.

"Uh, well, something happened." Her words are muffled. The connection sounds like shit, and I can barely hear what she's saying. "Can you come get us, please? We're at Sorority Row."

I've known Holland since we were kids and never once has she asked me to pick her or Emery up anywhere, since they generally Uber everywhere. It makes me worried that something happened.

"Are you and Emery safe?"

"Yes. Emery just... had a *tiny* bit too much tonight," she mutters.

"I'll be there in ten. Where are you?"

"Upstairs bathroom." A second later, I hear the sound of heaving. Great, Emery's drunk as shit. I make a mental note to grab a bucket at the sorority house.

I slam my truck into drive and pull out of the parking lot opposite the club. Thank fuck I'm downtown, and not at home, because this drive would've taken twice as long. Sorority Row is only ten minutes from the bar.

My tires ramp up the curb when I come to a stop then park, not bothering to even shut the truck off before I hop out and stalk up the steps of the house. By the looks of it, there's a massive party happening, and it makes my blood boil. I hate my sister going here. I know this is where entitled, rich douchebags party, and I want Emery nowhere near them. Especially since I can't have eyes on her.

I'm a big brother, sue me. I've always protected her and it's not any different now that she's an adult.

Once I'm inside the house, there's people everywhere dressed in togas and skimpy lingerie. I've spent many nights here, pre-NHL days, and I know exactly what tonight's about. It's rush week. The craziest week of the entire year, where everyone is doing whatever they can to be selected to pledge. There's fighting, hazing, a bunch of shit they shouldn't be doing. Meaning, my little sister shouldn't fucking be here.

I push through a crowd of people, trying to make my way to the stairwell.

A guy, wearing a toga, steps in front of me as I'm about to climb the stairs, and I run smack into him.

Damnit.

"Holy shit! You're Reed Davidson, can I have a photo, man?"

"Sorry, dude, I'm looking for someone." I sidestep him then take the stairs two at a time and make my way down the hallway until I find the bathroom. When I swing the last door to the right open, I find my sister sitting on the edge of the bathtub, mascara streaking down her cheeks and a drunken grin.

"Oh, it's my brother, lovely," she slurs. "What the hell are you doing here?"

She drops her head in her hands and groans obnoxiously loud. "He always ruins my buzz."

Well damn, I'm hurt. Sorry I have to be the semi-responsible one of the two of us.

"Went a lil' hard tonight, did ya, Em?" I tease.

My eyes drift to Holland, who's leaning against the vanity wearing a worried expression. I get it. Em's shit-faced and puking everywhere, but it's nothing some painkillers and water can't cure.

Em looks up at me and grins. "Well, someone has to have fun for the both of us. You're kinda a stick in the mud now."

"Nah, baby sis, I just don't like getting trashed and then puking in the sorority girls' toilet."

She flips me the middle finger with her black manicured nail, but laughs, which quickly turns into a moan. "Shit, my head. There's two of you. Why are there two of you? I can barely handle one."

Holland throws her head back and laughs, and I narrow my eyes at her then Emery.

"You know, for being your knight in shining armor, you two sure are mouthy."

Holland rolls her eyes and looks like she's going to say something, but Emery speaks up instead. "My jerk of a frat douchebag booooooyfriend broke up with me so we took looooots of shots. Lots and lots of shots. I lost count."

"Thank fuck, I thought I was gonna have to beat the shit out of the guy to get rid of him."

"Shut up. He was nice... and smart."

I laugh. "Yeah, just your type."

I'm sure Em gets sick of my teasing, but it's what we do. We talk shit to each other like it's our religion. If Emery wasn't talking shit to me on the daily, I'd think something was wrong.

"So, you want me to help you up or do you plan on sleeping here tonight?"

"I'm becoming one with the floor." She groans.

I reach down and lift her off her feet, and she stands

shakily on her heels. I toss my arm over her shoulder to steady her.

"Please do not puke in my truck or I'm leaving you on the side of the road."

"Ha ha, very funny."

I stop dead and look at her. "I'm serious."

Even though I'm not. I chuckle and take the damp rag that Holland is holding out for me then wipe Em's face. Em's got her eyes closed and she's looking a bit green, so I do her the favor of wiping some of the smeared makeup and dried throw up off, before handing it back to Holland.

Growing up, I'd been the one Em called when she needed someone. We didn't have a dad, so she had me. I changed her tires in high school and beat the shit out of the guy that called her a slut after she wouldn't sleep with him.

I've always done whatever I could to protect her, that's what I'm here for. When we were kids, she'd follow me around and do everything that I did. She had a stick in her hand at five years old and could skate circles around most of my friends, even though we were eight and twice as big as her. My entire life she's been my shadow and I guess there could be a worse best friend than your baby sister.

We walk out of the sorority house, down the concrete driveway and when we get to my truck, I pick Emery up and put her in the passenger seat.

She moans and groans the entire time, like she's losing a damn limb.

"Sheesh, you're dramatic."

"Runs in the family, I guess."

I scoff. "That is about enough out of you tonight." I grab the bucket Holland thought to grab and put it in Em's lap then shut the door, silencing her protest.

When I'm done, I turn to Holland. Her deep blue eyes are filled with amusement at my expense, not Emery's. She loves our banter.

Her arms are wrapped around her torso, hugging herself. For Christ's sake, I didn't even realize she had this tiny top on; she's got to be freezing. For some reason, at this moment, it dawns on me that I've never really... noticed Holland as anything other than my little sister's best friend, until right now. Maybe it's because she's dressed in a crop top that shows more cleavage than I've ever seen her with or because the skirt she's wearing makes me want to cover her up so no one can see how short it is. Or it could be the way that her legs look paired with those heels. Even though they've gotta be five-inches tall, she's still at least half a foot, if not shorter, than me. Her long, blonde hair falls past her chest to her waist.

Fuck, she's *gorgeous.*

That's the last thing I should be thinking about, yet here we are. I've watched her grow from a boy-band crazed teenager into... this beautiful *woman.*

A woman who is so off-limits, it's not even funny.

What the hell are you thinking, Davidson?

Get your shit together.

I clear my throat. "You cool with crashing at my place tonight? I'm sure Ma wouldn't appreciate me dropping off the brat at her house tonight in her drunken state."

Holland nods. "Yeah, I can go get my car tomorrow. Uh, could you possibly help me into the truck?" She looks down at her skirt, nervously. "This skirt and these shoes..."

Yeah, I can't imagine she'd be able to get in there without flashing me and the world what's underneath it. Not like I'd complain right now...

What? I'm a guy.

"Yeah, of course." I place my hands on her waist, ignoring the feel of her silky skin beneath my touch, and hoist her into the back seat of the truck. Definitely not taking a glimpse at her ass as she did so.

Nope. Absolutely not. I wouldn't. Scout's honor.

"Fuck," I mutter to myself. This is bad. Obviously I should've picked a bunny and gone home with her, since I'm suddenly lusting after my little sister's best friend.

It's probably just an off night, and definitely a fluke.

Definitely.

Em falls asleep before I even pull away from the curb. She's slumped awkwardly against the window, drool pooling in the corner of her mouth. I should snap a picture, so I can torture her with it later.

I grin at the thought.

The entire drive back to my house, I force myself to focus on the road, and not drag my eyes to the rearview mirror where Holland's perched in the back seat, directly in my line of vision.

I only stole a few glances, and I didn't think she noticed until our eyes connected in the mirror and something... different passes through our gaze.

Fuck, what is happening?

Tearing my gaze from hers, I fumble with the radio and turn it up to distract myself for the remainder of the drive. Once I pull into the driveway and come to a stop, Emery flies forward and her eyes pop open.

"What happened? What did I miss?"

Holland laughs her ass off at Emery's sudden outburst, and then Em's slumping back against the seat and letting out a soft snore.

"I'm not claiming her," I mutter as I hop out of the truck, then open Holland's door. She places her hand in mine and I help her out before going around to grab Em. It's a whole damn production to get her into the house and up the stairs, but thank fuck, Holland takes over once we make it to the guest room.

They disappear through the door, and I head to my room and take a lightning-fast shower and throw on a pair of grey sweats and a faded black tee before walking back out to the hallway. Holland's leaning against the wall next to the door, scrolling on her phone. She's shed the heels and is standing barefoot now.

"Hey, uh, do you need something to sleep in? I have a shirt and some boxers I can give you?"

She jumps, clearly startled. "Holy crap, I didn't even hear you come up. Yes, that would be great."

I nod, and go back to my room, grabbing her an old hockey shirt and a pair of boxers. This is the first time since probably high school that I've slept in the same house as Holland, and it definitely feels nothing like it did back then.

Walking back out to the hallway, I hand her the clothes, and she smiles shyly before taking them from me.

"Shower's over there. If you need something, just let me know."

"Thanks, Reed. I mean for letting us stay here, but also thanks for coming to get us."

I shrug. "It's nothing. I'd rather pick you two up then have you take an Uber home when Em can hardly hold her head up. I appreciate that you thought enough to call me. Night, Holland."

"Goodnight."

I walk back toward my room and I hear the guest bathroom door shut behind me and the water turn on. And now what am I definitely not going to do? Think about her naked on the other side of that door.

That's what I tell myself for the next two hours as I

toss and turn. From one side to the other, sleep evading me. I put my pillow over my head and groan. Finally, I just give up.

Fuck it. When you can't sleep... the remedy is always cereal.

Don't tell my coach that, and definitely not the trainer, but sugar cures everything. Especially in high doses of Captain Crunch.

My secret though.

I toss the blanket aside and crack my door open quietly, careful not to wake Em and Holl, and tiptoe down the hallway into the kitchen. I grab a bowl, the box of cereal from the pantry and open the fridge to get the milk.

"Reed?" A whispered voice comes from behind me, scaring the fuck out of me so badly that I send the milk flying across the island, where it lands with a wet squelch, puddling around the now-busted carton.

Goddamnit.

Holland's staring at me with wide eyes. Her hair is down and messy, obviously disheveled from sleep.

"Holy fuck, Holland, you scared the shit out of me!" I grunt. My heart's still racing in my chest.

Damn Reed, you're turning into a pussy.

She starts laughing, quietly at first, placing her hand over her mouth when she sees the milk spilled on the floor.

"I'm so... sor-ry," she says through her laugh. I walk across the room to where both she and the milk are, grabbing the towel from the counter before bending down to clean it up.

Then her laugh is gone, replaced by a sharp hiss, and when I look up and see her thick thighs staring back at me, I realize what she's wearing...

Nothing but my t-shirt and fuck, nothing has ever looked so good. The dark shirt hits her mid-thigh, covering all of the good stuff, still leaving enough covered for my imagination to do the rest.

I clear my throat and stand abruptly, not wanting to make her uncomfortable, and she steps back.

"Shit, I'm sorry, Holland, I didn't realize."

"No, it's okay. I'm sorry."

We both speak at the same time.

"Uh, sometimes when I can't sleep... I eat a bowl of-"

Before I can finish, she says, "Cereal?"

I grin. "You remember?"

She nods then smiles slightly. "You would wake up all the time just to eat Captain Crunch. At some point, Em started to call you 'Captain' behind your back."

"She would. I guess the tradition kind of carried over to adulthood. Not nearly as fun, though, as when I was sneaking around to eat it in the middle of the night."

My hopes of cereal are gone since the only milk I had is in a puddle on the floor, but suddenly, I'm not sorry that it happened.

"So, looks like no Captain Crunch tonight, but I've

got... Pop-Tarts," I offer. For a professional athlete, I probably shouldn't have this much sugar in my kitchen, but I keep my body in the best condition I can, so it generally doesn't become an issue.

I get us both a Pop-Tart from the pantry then put the box back inside. She's sitting at the bar now with her chin in her hand. Not a lick of makeup on, and damn, she's beautiful. And for the second time tonight, even though I know I shouldn't, I realize just how much of a woman she's become.

Somehow, I never noticed it. I never let myself notice it. I probably shouldn't now, but I do.

And that's how the rest of the night is spent, talking about nothing with Holland, eating a Pop-Tart, and for the very first time, I realize that I might be in some seriously deep shit.

Want to find out what happens next?
Change on the Fly is FREE with KU.
Click here.

ABOUT MAREN

ABOUT THE AUTHOR

Top 20 Amazon Bestselling author, Maren Moore writes romantic sports comedies with alpha daddies. Her heroines are best friend material, and you can always expect a HEA with lots of spice. When she isn't in front of her computer writing you can find her curled up with her kindle, binge watching Netflix, or chasing after her little ones.

Be sure to sign up for her newsletter to receive book news FIRST, including exclusive excerpts, giveaways and sales!

Sign up here.

ACKNOWLEDGMENTS

**I can't believe it's over.
The end of an era.
One that I will never forget.
And there are so many people to thank for
getting me here, for pushing me even when it
felt impossible to end this series and give these
characters the ending they deserved.**

Katie Friend: Thank you for keeping me organized, on task, and for being the best momager. I couldn't do it without you, and I will never be able to adequately put into words how thankful I am to have you. I appreciate all of the sacrifices you make to make things happen for me. I love you forever.

To Mj, Trilina and Kat: My best friends. I wouldn't have finished this without you, and that's a fact. Thank you for all our late night zoom calls, the tears, the laughs, all of it. I love you so much.

Cat with TRC designs: Thank you for brining my

visions to life, and creating the most perfect covers for the entire series. Love you Cinny!

Sandy: Thank you for taking the mess that this first draft was and helping me to turn it into something beautiful. So excited to be working with you!

Caroline: My muse. Hehe! Thank you for proofing this baby, and getting it final ready. I adore you, and am so thankful the book world brought us together.

Mia: My darling, the real love of my life (don't tell my husband) You are invaluable to me, and I will love you forever. Everyone needs a Mia, just not mine.

Sarah: I love you more than you love Taylor Swift, and that says it all.

Kristen: Thank you for being my biggest hype girl. You are the friend everyone wishes they had in their corner. I love you, endlessly.

All my author friends: Mary, Laura, Willow, Kandi, Elsie, Marni: I couldn't have finished without your unwavering support and encouragement. You guys have been my cheerleaders for months while I struggled, and it pushed me to the finish line. Not only that, but your advice and willingness to help in this community is invaluable. You girls are truly the best, and I adore you all so much.

Jenn: I love you, and am so proud of everything you've accomplished. In the midst of being a bad ass debut author, you took so many photos for me and I appreciate you so much. Here's to your success babe.

And to every reader who has picked this series up in the last year and a half.
Thank you for taking a chance on me, and these guys.
I hope that I was able to give them the kind of ending that they deserve, and I hope that you'll always have a special place in your heart for them, just like I do.
It's because of you that I get to live out my dreams and write these crazy stories, and I will never stop trying to express how grateful I am for that.
This book was for you.
I love you all.